PRAXIS

ELEMENTARY EDUCATION
0011, 0012, 5011, 5015

By: Sharon Wynne, M.S.

XAMonline, INC.
Boston

To obtain permission(s) to use the material from this work for any purpose including workshops or seminars, please submit a written request to:

XAMonline, Inc.
25 First Street, Suite 106
Cambridge, MA 02141
Toll Free 1-800-509-4128
Email: info@xamonline.com
Web: www.xamonline.com
Fax: 1-617-583-5552

Library of Congress Cataloging-in-Publication Data

Wynne, Sharon A.
    PRAXIS Elementary Education 0011, 0012, 5011, 5015 / Sharon A. Wynne. 1st ed
    ISBN 978-1-60787-312-9
    1. Elementary Education 0011, 0012, 5011, 5015
    2. Study Guides
    3. PRAXIS
    4. Teachers' Certification & Licensure
    5. Careers

Disclaimer:

The opinions expressed in this publication are the sole works of XAMonline and were created independently from the National Education Association, Educational Testing Service, or any State Department of Education, National Evaluation Systems or other testing affiliates.

Between the time of publication and printing, state specific standards as well as testing formats and Web site information may change and therefore would not be included in part or in whole within this product. Sample test questions are developed by XAMonline and reflect content similar to that on real tests; however, they are not former test questions. XAMonline assembles content that aligns with state standards but makes no claims nor guarantees teacher candidates a passing score. Numerical scores are determined by testing companies such as NES or ETS and then are compared with individual state standards. A passing score varies from state to state.

Printed in the United States of America   œ-1

PRAXIS Elementary Education 0011, 0012, 5011, 5015
ISBN: 978-1-60787-312-9

Table of Contents

DOMAIN III
SCIENCE

COMPETENCY 7
SCIENCE CURRICULUM

COMPETENCY 8
SCIENCE INSTRUCTION

COMPETENCY 9
SCIENCE ASSESSMENT

DOMAIN IV
SOCIAL STUDIES

COMPETENCY 10
SOCIAL STUDIES CURRICULUM

DOMAIN VI
GENERAL INFORMATION ABOUT CURRICULUM, INSTRUCTION, AND ASSESSMENT

PRAXIS
ELEMENTARY EDUCATION 0011, 0012, 5011, 5015

X

SECTION 1
ABOUT XAMONLINE

XAMonline—A Specialty Teacher Certification Company

Created in 1996, XAMonline was the first company to publish study guides for state-specific teacher certification examinations. Founder Sharon Wynne found it frustrating that materials were not available for teacher certification preparation and decided to create the first single, state-specific guide. XAMonline has grown into a company of over 1,800 contributors and writers and offers over 300 titles for the entire PRAXIS series and every state examination. No matter what state you plan on teaching in, XAMonline has a unique teacher certification study guide just for you.

XAMonline—Value and Innovation

We are committed to providing value and innovation. Our print-on-demand technology allows us to be the first in the market to reflect changes in test standards and user feedback as they occur. Our guides are written by experienced teachers who are experts in their fields. And our content reflects the highest standards of quality. Comprehensive practice tests with varied levels of rigor means that your study experience will closely match the actual in-test experience.

To date, XAMonline has helped nearly 600,000 teachers pass their certification or licensing exams. Our commitment to preparation exceeds simply providing the proper material for study—it extends to helping teachers **gain mastery** of the subject matter, giving them the **tools** to become the most effective classroom leaders possible, and ushering today's students toward a **successful future**.

SECTION 2
ABOUT THIS STUDY GUIDE

Purpose of This Guide

Is there a little voice inside of you saying, "Am I ready?" Our goal is to replace that little voice and remove all doubt with a new voice that says, "I AM READY. **Bring it on!**" by offering the highest quality of teacher certification study guides.

Organization of Content

You will see that while every test may start with overlapping general topics, each is very unique in the skills they wish to test. Only XAMonline presents custom content that analyzes deeper than a title, a subarea, or an objective. Only XAMonline presents content and sample test assessments along with **focus statements**, the deepest-level rationale and interpretation of the skills that are unique to the exam.

Title and field number of test

Each exam has its own name and number. XAMonline's guides are written to give you the content you need to know for the specific exam you are taking. You can be confident when you buy our guide that it contains the information you need to study for the specific test you are taking.

Subareas

These are the major content categories found on the exam. XAMonline's guides are written to cover all of the subareas found in the test frameworks developed for the exam.

Objectives

These are standards that are unique to the exam and represent the main subcategories of the subareas/content categories. XAMonline's guides are written to address every specific objective required to pass the exam.

Focus statements

These are examples and interpretations of the objectives. You find them in parenthesis directly following the objective. They provide detailed examples of the range, type, and level of content that appear on the test questions. **Only XAMonline's guides drill down to this level.**

How Do We Compare with Our Competitors?

XAMonline—drills down to the focus statement level.
CliffsNotes and REA—organized at the objective level
Kaplan—provides only links to content
MoMedia—content not specific to the state test

Each subarea is divided into manageable sections that cover the specific skill areas. Explanations are easy to understand and thorough. You'll find that every test answer contains a rejoinder so if you need a refresher or further review after taking the test, you'll know exactly to which section you must return.

How to Use This Book

Our informal polls show that most people begin studying up to eight weeks prior to the test date, so start early. Then ask yourself some questions: How much do you really know? Are you coming to the test straight from your teacher-education program or are you having to review subjects you haven't considered in ten years? Either way, take a **diagnostic or assessment test** first. Also, spend time on sample tests so that you become accustomed to the way the actual test will appear.

This guide comes with an online diagnostic test of 30 questions found online at *www.XAMonline.com*. It is a little boot camp to get you up for the task and reveal things about your compendium of knowledge in general. Although this guide is structured to follow the order of the test, you are not required to study in that order. By finding a time-management and study plan that fits your life you will be more effective. The results of your diagnostic or self-assessment test can be a guide for how to manage your time and point you toward an area that needs more attention.

After taking the diagnostic exam, fill out the **Personalized Study Plan** page at the beginning of each chapter. Review the competencies and skills covered in that chapter and check the boxes that apply to your study needs. If there are sections you already know you can skip, check the "skip it" box. Taking this step will give you a study plan for each chapter.

Week	Activity
8 weeks prior to test	Take a diagnostic test found at www.XAMonline.com
7 weeks prior to test	Build your Personalized Study Plan for each chapter. Check the "skip it" box for sections you feel you are already strong in. ✗ SKIP IT ☐
6-3 weeks prior to test	For each of these four weeks, choose a content area to study. You don't have to go in the order of the book. It may be that you start with the content that needs the most review. Alternately, you may want to ease yourself into plan by starting with the most familiar material.
2 weeks prior to test	Take the sample test, score it, and create a review plan for the final week before the test.
1 week prior to test	Following your plan (which will likely be aligned with the areas that need the most review) go back and study the sections that align with the questions you may have gotten wrong. Then go back and study the sections related to the questions you answered correctly. If need be, create flashcards and drill yourself on any area that makes you anxious.

SECTION 3
ABOUT THE PRAXIS EXAMS

What Is PRAXIS?

PRAXIS II tests measure the knowledge of specific content areas in K-12 education. The test is a way of insuring that educators are prepared to not only teach in a particular subject area, but also have the necessary teaching skills to be effective. The Educational Testing Service administers the test in most states and has worked with the states to develop the material so that it is appropriate for state standards.

PRAXIS Points

1. The PRAXIS Series comprises more than 140 different tests in over seventy different subject areas.

2. Over 90% of the PRAXIS tests measure subject area knowledge.

3. The purpose of the test is to measure whether the teacher candidate possesses a sufficient level of knowledge and skills to perform job duties effectively and responsibly.

4. Your state sets the acceptable passing score.

5. Any candidate, whether from a traditional teaching-preparation path or an alternative route, can seek to enter the teaching profession by taking a PRAXIS test.

6. PRAXIS tests are updated regularly to ensure current content.

Often **your own state's requirements** determine whether or not you should take any particular test. The most reliable source of information regarding this is either your state's Department of Education or the Educational Testing Service. Either resource should also have a complete list of testing centers and dates. Test dates vary by subject area and not all test dates necessarily include your particular test, so be sure to check carefully.

If you are in a teacher-education program, check with the Education Department or the Certification Officer for specific information for testing and testing timelines. The Certification Office should have most of the information you need.

If you choose an alternative route to certification you can either rely on our Web site at *www.XAMonline.com* or on the resources provided by an alternative certification program. Many states now have specific agencies devoted to alternative certification and there are some national organizations as well:

National Center for Education Information
http://www.ncei.com/Alt-Teacher-Cert.htm

National Associate for Alternative Certification
http://www.alt-teachercert.org/index.asp

Interpreting Test Results

Contrary to what you may have heard, the results of a PRAXIS test are not based on time. More accurately, you will be scored on the raw number of points you earn in relation to the raw number of points available. Each question is worth one raw point. It is likely to your benefit to complete as many questions in the time allotted, but it will not necessarily work to your advantage if you hurry through the test.

Follow the guidelines provided by ETS for interpreting your score. The web site offers a sample test score sheet and clearly explains how the scores are scaled and what to expect if you have an essay portion on your test.

Scores are usually available by phone within a month of the test date and scores will be sent to your chosen institution(s) within six weeks. Additionally, ETS now makes online, downloadable reports available for 45 days from the reporting date.

It is **critical** that you be aware of your own state's passing score. Your raw score may qualify you to teach in some states, but not all. ETS administers the test and assigns a score, but the states make their own interpretations and, in some cases, consider combined scores if you are testing in more than one area.

What's on the Test?

PRAXIS tests vary from subject to subject and sometimes even within subject areas. For PRAXIS Elementary Education 0011/5011, the test can either be taken as a paper and pencil test (0011) or as a computer-delivered test (5011). The test lasts for 2 hours and consists of approximately 110 multiple-choice questions, regardless of which testing method is used.

For PRAXIS Elementary Education 0012, the test lasts for 2 hours and consists of 4 essays given as four 30-minute problems requiring an extended response.

For states the require the combination Praxis Elementary Education 0011, 0012, the new test code is 5015. The 5015 test is computer-delivered, lasts 2 hours, and consists of 90 multiple-choice questions and 4 constructed-response essays.

The breakdown of the questions is as follows:

Category	Approximate Number of Questions	Approximate Percentage of the test
0011/5011: Curriculum, Instruction, and Assessment		
I: Reading/Language Arts Curriculum, Instruction, and Assessment	38	35%
II: Mathematics Curriculum, Instruction, and Assessment	22	20%
III: Science Curriculum, Instruction, and Assessment	11	10%
IV: Social Studies Curriculum, Instruction, and Assessment	11	10%
V. Arts and Physical Education Curriculum, Instruction, and Assessment	11	10%
VI: General Information about Curriculum, Instruction, and Assessment	17	15%
0012: Content Area Exercises		
I: Reading/Language Arts	1	25%
II: Mathematics	1	25%
III: Science or Social Studies	1	25%
IV: Interdisciplinary Instruction	1	25%
0011, 0012 (new 5015):		
Instructional Practice and Applications		
I: Reading/Language Arts	40	35%
II: Mathematics	24	21%

III: Science	13	12%
IV: Social Studies	13	12%
V: Applications (Constructed Response)	4	20%

This chart can be used to build a study plan. Thirty-five percent may seem like a lot of time to spend on Reading/Language Arts Curriculum, Instruction, and Assessment, but when you consider that amounts to about 1 out of 3 multiple choice questions, it might change your perspective.

Question Types

You're probably thinking, enough already, I want to study! Indulge us a little longer while we explain that there is actually more than one type of multiple-choice question. You can thank us later after you realize how well prepared you are for your exam.

1. Complete the Statement. The name says it all. In this question type you'll be asked to choose the correct completion of a given statement. For example:

> **The Dolch Basic Sight Words consist of a relatively short list of words that children should be able to:**
>
> A. Sound out
>
> B. Know the meaning of
>
> C. Recognize on sight
>
> D. Use in a sentence

The correct answer is C. In order to check your answer, test out the statement by adding the choices to the end of it.

2. **Which of the Following.** One way to test your answer choice for this type of question is to replace the phrase "which of the following" with your selection. Use this example:

> **Which of the following words is one of the twelve most frequently used in children's reading texts:**
>
> A. There
>
> B. This
>
> C. The
>
> D. An

Don't look! Test your answer. _____ is one of the twelve most frequently used in children's reading texts. Did you guess C? Then you guessed correctly.

3. **Roman Numeral Choices.** This question type is used when there is more than one possible correct answer. For example:

> **Which of the following two arguments accurately supports the use of cooperative learning as an effective method of instruction?**
>
> I.   Cooperative learning groups facilitate healthy competition between individuals in the group.
>
> II. Cooperative learning groups allow academic achievers to carry or cover for academic underachievers.
>
> III. Cooperative learning groups make each student in the group accountable for the success of the group.
>
> IV. Cooperative learning groups make it possible for students to reward other group members for achieving.
>
> A. I and II
>
> B. II and III
>
> C. I and III
>
> D. III and IV

Notice that the question states there are **two** possible answers. It's best to read all the possibilities first before looking at the answer choices. In this case, the correct answer is D.

4. Negative Questions. This type of question contains words such as "not," "least," and "except." Each correct answer will be the statement that does **not** fit the situation described in the question. Such as:

> **Multicultural education is not**
>
> A. An idea or concept
>
> B. A "tack-on" to the school curriculum
>
> C. An educational reform movement
>
> D. A process

Think to yourself that the statement could be anything but the correct answer. This question form is more open to interpretation than other types, so read carefully and don't forget that you're answering a negative statement.

5. Questions that Include Graphs, Tables, or Reading Passages. As always, read the question carefully. It likely asks for a very specific answer and not a broad interpretation of the visual. Here is a simple (though not statistically accurate) example of a graph question:

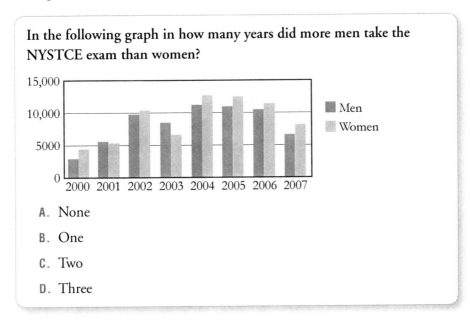

> **In the following graph in how many years did more men take the NYSTCE exam than women?**
>
> A. None
>
> B. One
>
> C. Two
>
> D. Three

It may help you to simply circle the two years that answer the question. Make sure you've read the question thoroughly and once you've made your determination, double check your work. The correct answer is C.

SECTION 4
HELPFUL HINTS

Study Tips

1. **You are what you eat.** Certain foods aid the learning process by releasing natural memory enhancers called CCKs (cholecystokinin) composed of tryptophan, choline, and phenylalanine. All of these chemicals enhance the neurotransmitters associated with memory and certain foods release memory enhancing chemicals. A light meal or snacks of one of the following foods fall into this category:

   - Milk
   - Rice
   - Eggs
   - Fish
   - Nuts and seeds
   - Oats
   - Turkey

   The better the connections, the more you comprehend!

2. **See the forest for the trees.** In other words, get the concept before you look at the details. One way to do this is to take notes as you read, paraphrasing or summarizing in your own words. Putting the concept in terms that are comfortable and familiar may increase retention.

3. **Question authority.** Ask why, why, why? Pull apart written material paragraph by paragraph and don't forget the captions under the illustrations. For example, if a heading reads *Stream Erosion* put it in the form of a question (Why do streams erode? What is stream erosion?) then find the answer within the material. If you train your mind to think in this manner you will learn more and prepare yourself for answering test questions.

4. **Play mind games.** Using your brain for reading or puzzles keeps it flexible. Even with a limited amount of time your brain can take in data (much like a computer) and store it for later use. In ten minutes you can: read two paragraphs (at least), quiz yourself with flash cards, or review notes. Even if you don't fully understand something on the first pass, your mind stores it for recall, which is why frequent reading or review increases chances of retention and comprehension.

5. **Place yourself in exile and set the mood.** Set aside a particular place and time to study that best suits your personal needs and biorhythms. If you're a night person, burn the midnight oil. If you're a morning person set yourself up with some coffee and get to it. Make your study time and place as free from distraction as possible and surround yourself with what you need,

be it silence or music. Studies have shown that music can aid in concentration, absorption, and retrieval of information. Not all music, though. Classical music is said to work best

6. Get pointed in the right direction. Use arrows to point to important passages or pieces of information. It's easier to read than a page full of yellow highlights. Highlighting can be used sparingly, but add an arrow to the margin to call attention to it.

7. Check your budget. You should at least review all the content material before your test, but allocate the most amount of time to the areas that need the most refreshing. It sounds obvious, but it's easy to forget. You can use the study rubric above to balance your study budget.

The proctor will write the start time where it can be seen and then, later, provide the time remaining, typically fifteen minutes before the end of the test.

8. The pen is mightier than the sword. Learn to take great notes. A by-product of our modern culture is that we have grown accustomed to getting our information in short doses. We've subconsciously trained ourselves to assimilate information into neat little packages. Messy notes fragment the flow of information. Your notes can be much clearer with proper formatting. **The Cornell Method** is one such format. This method was popularized in *How to Study in College*, Ninth Edition, by Walter Pauk. You can benefit from the method without purchasing an additional book by simply looking up the method online. Below is a sample of how *The Cornell Method* can be adapted for use with this guide.

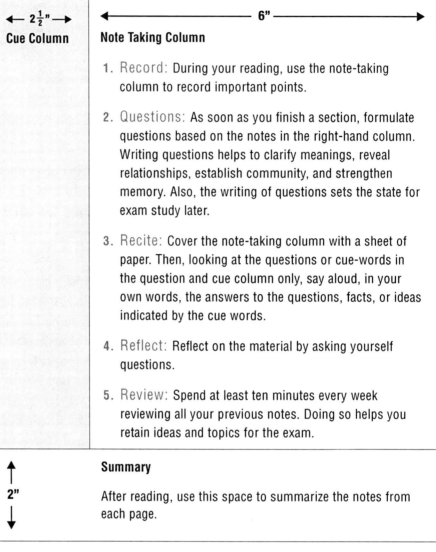

← 2½" → **Cue Column**	← 6" → **Note Taking Column**
	1. Record: During your reading, use the note-taking column to record important points.
	2. Questions: As soon as you finish a section, formulate questions based on the notes in the right-hand column. Writing questions helps to clarify meanings, reveal relationships, establish community, and strengthen memory. Also, the writing of questions sets the state for exam study later.
	3. Recite: Cover the note-taking column with a sheet of paper. Then, looking at the questions or cue-words in the question and cue column only, say aloud, in your own words, the answers to the questions, facts, or ideas indicated by the cue words.
	4. Reflect: Reflect on the material by asking yourself questions.
	5. Review: Spend at least ten minutes every week reviewing all your previous notes. Doing so helps you retain ideas and topics for the exam.
↑ 2" ↓	**Summary** After reading, use this space to summarize the notes from each page.

Adapted from How to Study in College, Ninth Edition, by Walter Pauk, ©2008 Wadsworth

Testing Tips

1. **Get smart, play dumb.** Sometimes a question is just a question. No one is out to trick you, so don't assume that the test writer is looking for something other than what was asked. Stick to the question as written and don't overanalyze.

2. **Do a double take.** Read test questions and answer choices at least twice because it's easy to miss something, to transpose a word or some letters. If you have no idea what the correct answer is, skip it and come back later if there's time. If you're still clueless, it's okay to guess. Remember, you're scored on the number of questions you answer correctly and you're not penalized for wrong answers. The worst case scenario is that you miss a point from a good guess.

3. **Turn it on its ear.** The syntax of a question can often provide a clue, so make things interesting and turn the question into a statement to see if it changes the meaning or relates better (or worse) to the answer choices.

4. **Get out your magnifying glass.** Look for hidden clues in the questions because it's difficult to write a multiple-choice question without giving away part of the answer in the options presented. In most questions you can readily eliminate one or two potential answers, increasing your chances of answering correctly to 50/50, which will help out if you've skipped a question and gone back to it (see tip #2).

5. **Call it intuition.** Often your first instinct is correct. If you've been studying the content you've likely absorbed something and have subconsciously retained the knowledge. On questions you're not sure about trust your instincts because a first impression is usually correct.

6. **Graffiti.** Sometimes it's a good idea to mark your answers directly on the test booklet and go back to fill in the optical scan sheet later. You don't get extra points for perfectly blackened ovals. If you choose to manage your test this way, be sure not to mismark your answers when you transcribe to the scan sheet.

7. **Become a clock-watcher.** You have a set amount of time to answer the questions. Don't get bogged down laboring over a question you're not sure about when there are ten others you could answer more readily. If you choose to follow the advice of tip #6, be sure you leave time near the end to go back and fill in the scan sheet.

Do the Drill

No matter how prepared you feel it's sometimes a good idea to apply Murphy's Law. So the following tips might seem silly, mundane, or obvious, but we're including them anyway.

1. **Remember, you are what you eat, so bring a snack.** Choose from the list of energizing foods that appear earlier in the introduction.

2. **You're not too sexy for your test.** Wear comfortable clothes. You'll be distracted if your belt is too tight or if you're too cold or too hot.

3. **Lie to yourself.** Even if you think you're a prompt person, pretend you're not and leave plenty of time to get to the testing center. Map it out ahead of time and do a dry run if you have to. There's no need to add road rage to your list of anxieties.

4. **Bring sharp number 2 pencils.** It may seem impossible to forget this need from your school days, but you might. And make sure the erasers are intact, too.

5. **No ticket, no test.** Bring your admission ticket as well as **two** forms of identification, including one with a picture and signature. You will not be admitted to the test without these things.

6. **You can't take it with you.** Leave any study aids, dictionaries, note-books, computers, and the like at home. Certain tests **do** allow a scientific or four-function calculator, so check ahead of time to see if your test does.

7. **Prepare for the desert.** Any time spent on a bathroom break **cannot** be made up later, so use your judgment on the amount you eat or drink.

8. **Quiet, Please!** Keeping your own time is a good idea, but not with a timepiece that has a loud ticker. If you use a watch, take it off and place it nearby but not so that it distracts you. And **silence your cell phone**.

To the best of our ability, we have compiled the content you need to know in this book and in the accompanying online resources. The rest is up to you. You can use the study and testing tips or you can follow your own methods. Either way, you can be confident that there aren't any missing pieces of information and there shouldn't be any surprises in the content on the test.

If you have questions about test fees, registration, electronic testing, or other content verification issues please visit *www.ets.org*.

Good luck!

Sharon Wynne
Founder, XAMonline

DOMAIN I
READING AND LANGUAGE ARTS

PERSONALIZED STUDY PLAN

COMPETENCY 1
READING AND LANGUAGE ARTS CURRICULUM

SKILL 1.1 Phonemic awareness

PHONEMIC AWARENESS is the acknowledgement of sounds and words, for example, a child's realization that some words rhyme. Onset and rhyme, for example, are skills that might help students learn that the sound of the first letter "b" in the word "bad" can be changed with the sound "d" to make it "dad." The key in phonemic awareness is that when you teach it to children, it can be taught with the students' eyes closed. In other words, it's all about sounds, not about ascribing written letters to sounds.

To be phonemically aware, means that the reader and listener can recognize and manipulate specific sounds in spoken words. Phonemic awareness deals with sounds in words that are spoken. The majority of phonemic awareness tasks, activities, and exercises are oral.

Teaching Phonemic Awareness

Since the ability to distinguish between individual sounds, or phonemes, within words is a prerequisite to association of sounds with letters and manipulating sounds to blend words—a fancy way of saying "reading"—the teaching of phonemic awareness is crucial to emergent literacy (early childhood K-2 reading instruction). Children need a strong background in phonemic awareness in order for phonics instruction (sound –spelling relationship-printed materials) to be effective.

> **PHONEMIC AWARENESS:** the acknowledgement of sounds and words, for example, a child's realization that some words rhyme

> *The key in phonemic awareness is that when you teach it to children, it can be taught with the students' eyes closed. In other words, it's all about sounds, not about ascribing written letters to sounds.*

Sample Test Questions and Rationale

For sample test questions and rationales requiring a reading passage, see page 87.

SKILL Phonics
1.2

> **PHONICS**: the connection between the sounds and letters on a page

As opposed to phonemic awareness, the study of **PHONICS** must be done with the eyes open. It is the connection between the sounds and letters on a page. In other words, students learning phonics might see the word "bad" and sound each letter out slowly until they recognize that they just said the word.

Phonological Awareness

> **PHONOLOGICAL AWARENESS**: the ability of the reader to recognize the sounds of spoken language

PHONOLOGICAL AWARENESS means the ability of the reader to recognize the sounds of spoken language. This recognition includes how these sounds can be blended together, segmented (divided up), and manipulated (switched around). This type of awareness then leads to phonics, which is a method for teaching children to read. It helps them to "sound out words."

> *Development of phonological skills may begin during the pre-K years. Indeed, by the age of five, a child who has been exposed to rhyme can typically recognize another rhyme.*

Development of phonological skills may begin during the pre-K years. Indeed, by the age of five, a child who has been exposed to rhyme can typically recognize another rhyme. Such a child can demonstrate phonological awareness by filling in the missing rhyming word in a familiar rhyme or rhymed picture book. It isn't unheard of for children to surprise their parents by filling in missing rhymes in a familiar nursery rhyme book at the age of four or even earlier.

Children are taught phonological awareness when they are taught the sounds made by the letters, the sounds made by various combinations of letters, and the ability to recognize individual sounds in words.

Skills and Strategies with Phonological Awareness

Phonological awareness skills include:

- Rhyming and syllabification

- Blending sounds into words (such as pic-tur-bo-k)

- Identifying the beginning or starting sounds of words and the ending or closing sounds of words

- Breaking words down into sounds (also called "segmenting" words)

- Recognizing small words contained in bigger words by removing starting sounds (hear to ear)

Phonics also involves the spelling of words. Effective spelling strategies should emphasize these principles:

- Knowledge of patterns, sounds, letter-sound association, and syllables

- Memorizing sight words

- Writing those words correctly many times

- Writing the words in personal writing

SKILL 1.3 Fluency

When students work on fluency, they practice reading connected pieces of text. In other words, instead of looking at a word as just a word, they might read a sentence straight through. The point of this is that in order for the student to comprehend what she is reading, she would need to be able to "fluently" piece words in a sentence together quickly. If a student is NOT fluent in reading, he or she would sound each letter or word out slowly and pay more attention to the phonics of each word. A fluent reader, on the other hand, might read a sentence out loud using appropriate intonations.

Challenges to Fluency

Fluency in reading is dependent on automatic word identification, which assists the student in achieving comprehension of the material. Even slight difficulties in word identification can significantly increase the time it takes a student to read material, may require rereading parts or passages of the material and reduces the level of comprehension expected. If the student experiences reading as a constant struggle or an arduous chore then he or she will avoid reading whenever possible and consider it a negative experience when necessary. Obviously, the ability to read for comprehension, and learning in general, will suffer if all aspects of reading fluency are not presented to the student as acquirable skills which will be readily accomplished with the appropriate effort.

AUTOMATIC READING (or automaticity) involves the development of strong orthographic representations, which allows fast and accurate identification of whole words made up of specific letter patterns. Most young students move easily from the use of alphabetic strategies to the use of orthographic representations, which can be accessed automatically. Initially word identification is based on the application of phonic word–accessibility strategies (letter-sound associations). These strategies are in turn based on the development of phonemic awareness, which is necessary to learn how to relate speech to print.

Fluency in reading is dependent on automatic word identification, which assists the student in achieving comprehension of the material.

AUTOMATIC READING: (or automaticity) involves the development of strong orthographic representations, which allows fast and accurate identification of whole words made up of specific letter patterns

PROSODY: concerns versification of text and involves such matters as which syllable of a word is accented

PROSODY concerns versification of text and involves such matters as which syllable of a word is accented. As regards fluency, it is that aspect which translates reading into the same experience as listening, within the reader's mind. It involves intonation and rhythm through such devices as syllable accent and punctuation.

The student's development of the elements necessary to automaticity continually moves through stages. Another important stage involves the automatic recognition of single graphemes as a critical first step to the development of the letter patterns that make up words or word parts. English orthography is made up of four basic word types:

1. Regular, for reading and spelling (e.g., cat, print)

2. Regular, for reading but not for spelling (e.g., float, brain—could be spelled "flote" or "brane," respectively)

3. Rule based (e.g., canning—doubling rule; faking—drop e rule)

4. Irregular (e.g., beauty)

Students must be taught to recognize all four types of words automatically in order to be effective readers. Repeated practice in pattern recognition is often necessary.

Students must be taught to recognize all four types of words automatically in order to be effective readers. Repeated practice in pattern recognition is often necessary. True automaticity should be linked with prosody and anticipation to acquire full fluency. Such things as which syllable is accented and how word structure can be predictive are necessary to true automaticity and essential to complete fluency.

A student whose reading rate is slow, or halting and inconsistent, is exhibiting a lack of reading fluency. Some students develop accurate word pronunciation skills but read at a slow rate. They have not moved to the phase where decoding is automatic, and their limited fluency may affect performance in the following ways:

• They read less text than peers and have less time to remember, review, or comprehend the text

• They expend more cognitive energy than peers trying to identify individual words

• They may be less able to retain text in their memories and less likely to integrate those segments with other parts of the text

Reading fluency and comprehension involve three cueing methods: orthographic awareness, semantic cueing and syntactic cueing.

Cueing Methods

Reading fluency and comprehension involve three cueing methods: orthographic awareness, semantic cueing and syntactic cueing. Also, sight words and high frequency word skills contribute to reading fluency. Teachers need to be aware of how to assess and teach those skills to enhance reading fluency.

ORTHOGRAPHIC AWARENESS is the ability to perceive and recall letter strings and word forms, as well as the retrieval of letters and words. Sight word vocabulary for both reading and spelling depends on this skill.

A weakness in orthographic awareness results in slow reading rates and problems with spelling. This, in turn, affects reading comprehension and writing fluency.

SYNTACTIC CUEING involves evaluating a word for its part of speech and its place in the sentence. For example, the reader determines if it is a noun, verb, adjective, etc. If it is an adjective, the reader determines which word it modifies. If it is a pronoun, the reader must decide which noun it takes the place of. Syntactic cueing directly affects reading comprehension.

SEMANTIC CUEING requires determining the meaning of the word, phrase or sentence. It involves determining what the passage is about.

> **ORTHOGRAPHIC AWARENESS:** the ability to perceive and recall letter strings and word forms, as well as the retrieval of letters and words

> **SYNTACTIC CUEING:** involves evaluating a word for its part of speech and its place in the sentence

> **SEMANTIC CUEING:** requires determining the meaning of the word, phrase or sentence

---

Sample Test Question and Rationale

(Average)

1. When students understand how sentences are built and the words needed for the sentences to "sound" right, they have developed a sense of:

   A. Morphology

   B. Syntax

   C. Semantics

   D. Fluency

Answer: B. Syntax

Syntax refers to the rules or patterned relationships that correctly create phrases and sentences from words. When readers develop an understanding of syntax, they begin to understand the structure of how sentences are built.

> *Learn more about these cueing systems:*
>
> http://www.sedl.org/reading/topics/cueing.html

> **ROOT WORD:** the primary base of a word

> **PREFIX:** the affix (a morpheme that attaches to a base word) that is placed at the start of a root word, but can't make a word on its own

> **SUFFIX:** follows the root word to which it attaches and appears at the end of the word

---

SKILL Vocabulary
1.4

How Words Are Built

Knowledge of how words are built can help students with basic and more advanced decoding. A ROOT WORD is the primary base of a word. A PREFIX is the affix (a morpheme that attaches to a base word) that is placed at the start of a root word, but can't make a word on its own. Examples of prefixes include re-, pre-, and un-. A SUFFIX follows the root word to which it attaches and appears at the end of the word. Examples of suffixes include –s, -es, -ed, -ly, and –tion. In the word unlikely, "un" is a prefix, "like" is the root word, and "ly" is a suffix.

High Frequency and Sight Words

High frequency words are the words most often used in the English language. Depending on the list used, these range from 100 to 300 words. It has been estimated that 100 words make up 50 percent of all words used in reading. Other lists, such as Dolch and Fry, use the most frequently encountered words in early childhood reading texts.

Sight words are words that the reader learns to read spontaneously either because of frequency or lack of conformity to orthographic rules. For example, words like 'the', 'what', and 'there' are sight words because they don't conform to rules, and words like 'boy,' 'girl,' and 'book' are sight words because they are seen very frequently in reading texts.

Sample Test Questions and Rationale

(Rigorous)

1. **If you have had a cough for a long time, it is said to be:**

    A. Chronic

    B. Prescriptive

    C. Contagious

    D. Malicious

Answer: A. Chronic

The root *—chrono-* means time. Chronic therefore means "a long time."

(Average)

2. **How does adding the prefix *dis-* to the word *continue*, change its meaning?**

    A. It now means "to continue later"

    B. It now means "to do again"

    C. It now means "to not continue"

    D. It doesn't change the meaning

Answer: C. It now means "to not continue"

The prefix *dis-* means *not*. Therefore, the meaning of the word *discontinue* means to "not continue."

(Rigorous)

3. **Besides teaching scientific methods and information, what might be a good lesson to teach along with a book about photosynthesis?**

    A. The first photograph taken

    B. The root *–photo-* means light

    C. The food chain

    D. The letters /ph/ make the "f" sound

Answer: B. The root *—photo-* means light

Although all lessons would be good to teach along with photosynthesis, the best answer is B. Teaching students Latin and Greek roots when it is connected with meaning and prior knowledge is an effective way to enhance learning.

SKILL 1.5 Comprehension

Beginning readers must learn to recognize the conventions that create meaning and expectations in the text. For beginning readers, these literal skills include deciphering the words, punctuation, and grammar in a text. When readers ascertain comprehension, they create meaning from a text. COMPREHENSION occurs when readers are able to make predictions, select main ideas, and establish significant and supporting details of the story.

A successful program of comprehension instruction should include:

- Large amounts of time for actual text reading

- Teacher-directed instruction in comprehension strategies

- Opportunities for peer and collaborative learning

- Occasions for students to talk to a teacher and one another about their responses to reading

Teachers can improve comprehension skills by providing children with opportunities and guidance in making text selections. Student choice is related to interest and motivation, both of which are related directly to learning. Teachers can:

- Encourage rereading of texts, which research suggests leads to greater fluency and comprehension

- Allow time for students to read in pairs, including students of different abilities, which provides regular opportunities for readers to discuss their reading with the teacher and with one another

- Employ guided practice strategies in which feedback is given back to the students' attempts, gradually giving students more and more responsibility for evaluating their own performances

Bloom's Taxonomy as It Relates to Reading Comprehension

Reading comprehension skills such as generating and answering literal, inferential, and interpretive questions to demonstrate understanding about what is read in complex text are often found in the differing levels of Bloom's Taxonomy. These levels, in ascending order of sophistication, are:

1. Knowledge
2. Comprehension
3. Application

4. Analysis
5. Synthesis
6. Evaluation

> **COMPREHENSION:** occurs when readers are able to make predictions, select main ideas, and establish significant and supporting details of the story

> Teachers can improve comprehension skills by providing children with opportunities and guidance in making text selections.

> Reading comprehension skills such as generating and answering literal, inferential, and interpretive questions to demonstrate understanding about what is read in complex text are often found in the differing levels of Bloom's Taxonomy.

Learn more about Bloom's Taxonomy:

http://faculty.washington.edu/krumme/guides/bloom1.html

These higher cognitive questions are defined as those which ask the student to mentally manipulate bits of information previously learned to support an answer with logically reasoned evidence. Higher cognitive questions are also called open-ended, interpretive, evaluative, and inferential questions. Lower cognitive questions are those that ask the student merely to recall verbatim or literally the material previously read or taught by the teacher.

Sample Test Questions and Rationale

(Rigorous)

1. **What are the two basic types of questions?**

   A. Easy and hard questions

   B. Verbal and written questions

   C. In the book and in the reader's head

   D. Teacher made and student made

   Answer: C. In the book and in the reader's head

   Although all choices are two types of questions, in reading there are questions that can be answered by looking in the book and questions that can be answered with thinking.

(Easy)

2. **Engineers thought it would be difficult to *construct* the Golden Gate Bridge because of the weather conditions and the ocean currents that exist in California.**

   What does the word *construct* mean in the sentence above?

   A. Drive across

   B. Close down

   C. Make longer

   D. Build or create

   Answer: D. Build or create

   Engineers are people that build or create things. They thought it would be hard to do that because the weather and the water currents in San Francisco made the job challenging.

SKILL 1.6 Features and types of literature

The major genres in literature include allegory, ballad, drama, epic, epistle, essay, fable, novel, poem, romance, and the short story. At times, even books written for adults are appropriate for children. These major genres are detailed below.

Allegory: A story in verse or prose with characters that represent virtues and vices. There are two meanings: symbolic and literal. John Bunyan's *The Pilgrim's Progress* is the most renowned of this genre.

Ballad: An *in medias res* story that is told or sung—usually in verse—and accompanied by music. Literary devices found in ballads include the refrain (repeated section) and incremental repetition (anaphora) for effect. Earliest forms were anonymous folk ballads. Later forms include Coleridge's Romantic masterpiece, "The Rime of the Ancient Mariner."

Drama: Plays (comedy, modern, or tragedy) that are typically performed in five acts. Traditionalists and neoclassicists adhere to Aristotle's unities of time, place, and action. Plot development is advanced through dialogue. Literary devices include asides, soliloquies, and the chorus, which represents public opinion. Considered by many to be the greatest of all dramatists/playwrights is William Shakespeare. Other dramaturges include Ibsen, Williams, Miller, Shaw, Stoppard, Racine, Moliére, Sophocles, Aeschylus, Euripides, and Aristophanes.

Epic: A long poem usually of book length that reflects values inherent in the generative society. Epic devices include an invocation to a Muse for inspiration, an overall purpose for writing, universal setting, a protagonist and antagonist who possess supernatural strength and acumen, and interventions of a God or the gods. Comparatively, there are few epics in literature: Homer's *Iliad* and *Odyssey*, Virgil's *Aeneid*, Milton's *Paradise Lost*, Spenser's *The Fairie Queene*, Barrett Browning's *Aurora Leigh*, and Pope's mock-epic, *The Rape of the Lock*.

Epistle: A letter that is not always originally intended for public distribution, but due to the fame of the sender and/or recipient, one that becomes public domain. For example, Paul wrote epistles that were later placed in the Bible.

Essay: Typically, a limited length prose work focusing on a topic and propounding a definite point-of-view and authoritative tone. Great essayists include Carlyle, Lamb, DeQuincy, Emerson, and Montaigne (who is credited with defining this genre).

Fable: A terse tale offering up a moral or exemplum. Chaucer's "The Nun's Priest's Tale" is a fine example of a *bete fabliau* (or beast fable) in which animals speak and act characteristically human, illustrating human foibles.

Legend: A traditional narrative or collection of related narratives, popularly regarded as historically factual but actually a mixture of fact and fiction.

Myth: Stories that are more or less universally shared within a culture to explain its history and traditions.

Novel: The longest form of fictional prose containing a variety of characterizations, settings, local color, and regionalism. Most have complex plots, expanded description, and attention to detail. Some of the great novelists include Austen, the Brontës, Twain, Tolstoy, Hugo, Hardy, Dickens, Hawthorne, Forster, and Flaubert.

Poem: The only requirement for a poem is rhythm. Subgenres include fixed types of literature such as the sonnet, elegy, ode, pastoral, and villanelle. Unfixed types of literature include blank verse and dramatic monologue.

Romance: A highly imaginative tale set in a fantastical realm that deals with the conflicts between heroes, villains, and/or monsters. "The Knight's Tale" from Chaucer's *Canterbury Tales, Sir Gawain and the Green Knight*, and Keats' "The Eve of St. Agnes" are prime representatives.

Short Story: A concise narrative that has less background than a novel, but that typically includes many of the same plot developments and techniques. Some of the most notable short story writers include Hemingway, Faulkner, Twain, Joyce, Jackson, O'Connor, de Maupassant, Saki, Poe, and Pushkin.

Children's Literature

Children's literature is a genre of its own. Although it can share some of the same characteristics of adult literature, it emerged as a distinct and independent form in the second half of the seventeenth century. *The Visible World in Pictures* by John Amos Comenius, a Czech educator, was one of the first printed works in existence as well as the first picture book. After its publication, educators acknowledged that children are different from adults in many respects for the first time.

Modern educators acknowledge that introducing elementary students to a wide range of reading experiences plays an important role in their mental, social, and psychological development. Some of the most common forms of literature written specifically for children include:

Traditional literature

TRADITIONAL LITERATURE opens up a world where right wins out over wrong, where hard work and perseverance are rewarded, and where helpless victims find vindication. These worthwhile values are ones that children identify with even as early as kindergarten.

In traditional literature, children are introduced to fanciful beings, humans with exaggerated powers, talking animals, and heroes that will inspire them. For younger elementary children, these stories in Big Book format are ideal for providing predictable and repetitive elements that are easily grasped.

Folktales/Fairy Tales: Adventures of animals or humans and the supernatural typically characterize these stories. The hero is usually on a quest aided by other-worldly helpers. More often than not, the story focuses on good and evil and reward and punishment. Some examples of folktales and fairy tales include:

> *Modern educators acknowledge that introducing elementary students to a wide range of reading experiences plays an important role in their mental, social, and psychological development.*

> **TRADITIONAL LITERATURE:** works where right wins out over wrong, where hard work and perseverance are rewarded, and where helpless victims find vindication

The Three Bears, Little Red Riding Hood, Snow White, Sleeping Beauty, Puss-in-Boots, Rapunzel, and *Rumpelstiltskin.*

Fables: Animals that act like humans are featured in these stories; the animals usually reveal human foibles or teach a lesson. Example: *Aesop's Fables.*

Myths: These stories about events from the earliest times, such as the origin of the world, are often considered true among various societies.

Legends: These are similar to myths except that they tend to deal with events that happened more recently. Example: Arthurian legends.

Tall Tales: These are purposely exaggerated accounts of individuals with super-human strength. Examples: Paul Bunyan, John Henry, and Pecos Bill.

Modern Fantasy: Many of the themes found in these stories are similar to those in traditional literature. The stories start out based in reality, which makes it easier for the reader to suspend disbelief and enter into worlds of unreality. Little people live in the walls in *The Borrowers*, and time travel is possible in *The Trolley to Yesterday*.

Including some fantasy tales in the curriculum often helps elementary-grade children to develop their imagination. The stories typically appeal to ideals of justice and issues having to do with good and evil; because children tend to identify with the characters, the message is more likely to be retained.

> *Including some fantasy tales in the curriculum often helps elementary-grade children to develop their imagination.*

Science Fiction: Robots, spacecraft, mystery, and civilizations from other ages often appear in these stories. Most presume advances in science on other planets or in a future time. Most children like these stories because of their interest in space and the "what if" aspect of the stories. Examples: *Outer Space and All That Junk* and *A Wrinkle in Time*.

Modern Realistic Fiction: These stories are about real problems that real children face. By finding that their hopes and fears are shared by others, young children can find insight into their own problems. Young readers also tend to experience a broadening of interests as the result of this kind of reading. It is good for them to know that a child can be brave and intelligent and can solve difficult problems.

Historical Fiction: This type of literature provides the opportunity to introduce younger children to history in a beneficial way. *Rifles for Watie* is an example of this kind of story. Presented in a historically accurate setting, it's about a sixteen-year-old boy who serves in the Union army. He experiences great hardships but discovers that his enemy is an admirable human being.

Biography: Reading about inventors, explorers, scientists, political and religious leaders, social reformers, artists, sports figures, doctors, teachers, writers, and war heroes helps children to see that one person can make a difference. They also open new vistas for children to think about when they choose a future occupation.

Informational Books: These are ways to learn more about something that children are interested in or something that they know little about. Encyclopedias are good resources, of course, but a book like *Polar Wildlife* by Kamini Khanduri also shows pictures and facts that will capture the imaginations of young children.

SKILL 1.7 Types and traits of writing

Different Types of Writing

Most nonfiction writing falls into one of four different forms:

1. Narrative

2. Descriptive

3. Expository

4. Persuasive

Persuasive writing

PERSUASIVE WRITING:
a piece of writing, a poem, a play, or a speech whose purpose is to change the minds of the audience members or to get them to do something

PERSUASIVE WRITING is a piece of writing, a poem, a play, or a speech whose purpose is to change the minds of the audience members or to get them to do something. This is achieved in a variety of ways:

1. The credibility of the writer/speaker might lead the listeners/readers to a change of mind or a recommended action.

2. Reasoning is important in persuasive discourse. No one wants to believe that he or she accepts a new viewpoint or goes out and takes action just because he or she likes and trusts the person who recommended it. Logic comes into play in reasoning that is persuasive.

3. The third and most powerful force that leads to acceptance or action is emotional appeal. Even if audience members have been persuaded logically and reasonably that they should believe in a different way, they are unlikely to act on it unless moved emotionally. A person with resources might be convinced that people suffered in New Orleans after Katrina, but he or she will not be likely to do anything about it until he or she feels a deeper emotional connection to the disaster. Sermons are good examples of persuasive discourse.

Expository writing

In contrast to persuasion, the only purpose of exposition is to inform. EXPOSITORY WRITING is not interested in changing anyone's mind or getting anyone to take a certain action. It exists to give information. Some examples include directions to a particular place or the directions for putting together a toy that arrives unassembled. The writer doesn't care whether you do or don't follow the directions. He or she only wants to be sure you have the information in case you do decide to use it.

EXPOSITORY WRITING: a form of writing where the only purpose is to inform

Narrative writing

NARRATION is discourse that is arranged chronologically—something happened, and then something else happened, and then something else happened. It is also called a story. News reports are often narrative in nature, as are records of trips or experiences.

NARRATION: discourse that is arranged chronologically

Descriptive writing

DESCRIPTIVE WRITING has the purpose of making an experience available through one of the five senses—seeing, smelling, hearing, feeling (as with the fingers), and tasting. Descriptive words are used to make it possible for readers to "see" with their own mind's eye, "hear" through their own mind's ear, "smell" through their own mind's nose, "taste" with their own mind's tongue, and "feel" with their own mind's fingers. This is how language moves people. Only by experiencing an event can the emotions become involved. Poets are experts in descriptive language. Descriptive writing is typically used to make sure the point is established emotionally.

DESCRIPTIVE WRITING: making an experience available through one of the five senses—seeing, smelling, hearing, feeling (as with the fingers), and tasting

Understanding Nonfiction

Students often misrepresent the differences between fiction and nonfiction. They mistakenly believe that stories are always examples of fiction. The simple truth is that stories are both fiction and nonfiction. The primary difference is that fiction is imaginary, and nonfiction is generally true (or an opinion). It is harder for students to understand that non-fiction entails an enormous range of material from textbooks to true stories and newspaper articles to speeches. Fiction, on the other hand, is fairly simple—imaginary stories, novels, etc. But it is also important for students to understand that most of fiction throughout history has been based on true events. In other words, authors use their own life experiences to help them to create works of fiction.

Students often misrepresent the differences between fiction and nonfiction. They mistakenly believe that stories are always examples of fiction. The simple truth is that stories are both fiction and nonfiction.

Opinion versus truth

The artistry in telling a story to convey a point is important in understanding nonfiction. Realizing what is truth and what is perspective is important in understanding nonfiction. Often, a nonfiction writer will present an opinion, and that opinion is very different from a truth. Knowing the difference between the two is very crucial.

Comparing fiction and nonfiction

In comparing fiction to nonfiction, students need to learn about the conventions of each. In fiction, students can generally expect to find plot, characters, setting, and themes. In nonfiction, students may find a plot, characters, settings, and themes, but they will also experience interpretations, opinions, theories, research, and other elements.

Overall, students can begin to see patterns that identify fiction from nonfiction. Often, the more fanciful or unrealistic a text or story is, the more likely it is fiction, or contains facts that have been "fictionalized."

Nonfiction comes in a variety of styles. While many students simplify nonfiction as being true (as opposed to fiction, which is make-believe), nonfiction is much deeper than that. The following are various types of nonfiction; students should be exposed to all of these.

TYPES OF NONFICTION	
Informational Texts	These types of books explain concepts or phenomena. An informational text might explain the history of a state or the idea of photosynthesis. These types of text are usually based on research.
Newspaper Articles	These short texts rely completely on factual information and are presented in a very straightforward, sometimes choppy manner. The purpose of these texts is to present information to readers in a quick and efficient manner.
Essays	Usually, essays take an opinion (whether it is about a concept, a work of literature, a person, or an event) and describe how the opinion was arrived at or why the opinion is a good one.
Biographies	These texts explain the lives of individuals. They are usually based on extensive research.
Memoirs	In a way, a memoir is like an autobiography, but memoirs tend to be based on a specific idea, concept, issue, or event in life. For example, most presidents of the United States write memoirs about their time in office.

Table continued on next page

Letters	When letters are read and analyzed in the classroom, students are generally studying the writer's style or the writer's true opinions and feelings about certain events. Often, students will find letters of famous individuals in history reprinted in textbooks.
Journals	Similar to letters, journals present very personal ideas. When available (as most people rarely want their journals published), they give students the opportunity to see peoples' thought processes about various events or issues.

Traits or Elements of Writing

STYLE is the artful adaptation of language to meet various purposes. Authors can modify their word choice, sentence structure, and organization in order to convey certain ideas. For example, an author may write on a topic (such as the environment) in many different styles. In an academic style, the author uses long, complex sentences, advanced vocabulary, and very structured paragraphing. However, in an informal explanation in a popular magazine, the author may use a conversational tone in which simple words and simple sentence structures are utilized.

> **STYLE:** the artful adaptation of language to meet various purposes

TONE is the attitude an author takes toward his or her subject. That tone is exemplified in the language of the text. For example, consider the topic of the environment. One author may dismiss the idea of global warming; the tone may be one of derision against environmentalists. A reader might notice this through the style (such as word choice), the details the author decides to present, and the order in which the details are presented. Another author may be angry about global warming and therefore use harsh words and other tones that indicate anger. Finally, yet another author may not care one bit about the issue of the environment either in a positive or negative light. Let's say this author is a comedian who likes to poke fun at political activists. His or her tone may be humorous; therefore, he or she will adjust the language used accordingly. In this example, all types of tones are about the same subject—they simply reveal, through language, different opinions and attitudes about the subject.

> **TONE:** the attitude an author takes toward his or her subject

Finally, POINT-OF-VIEW is perspective. While most of us think of point-of-view in terms of first or third person in fiction (or even the points-of-view of various characters in stories), point-of-view also helps to explain much of language and the presentation of ideas in nonfiction texts. The above environmentalism example proves this. Three points-of-view are represented, and each creates a different style of language.

> **POINT-OF-VIEW:** the perspective of the text

> *Students need to learn that language and text are changed dramatically by tone, style, and point-of-view.*

Putting it all together

Students need to learn that language and text are changed dramatically by tone, style, and point-of-view. They can practice identifying these concepts in everything they read. Doing so takes little time for each text students read in class, and it goes a long way in helping them to comprehend text at a more advanced level.

Sample Test Questions and Rationale

(Easy)

1. **A student writes an essay that shows the similarities and differences between a book and a movie of the same title. What type of essay is it?**

   A. Classification

   B. Compare and contrast

   C. Cause and effect

   D. Statement support

   Answer: B. Compare and contrast

   The student's essay compares and contrasts the book and the movie of the same title.

(Average)

2. **In Writer's Workshop students are asked to write a personal narrative. How should their writing be organized?**

   A. Statement support

   B. Compare and contrast

   C. Sequence of events

   D. Classification

Answer: C. Sequence of events

A narrative is a retelling of events in order.

(Rigorous)

3. **Ants have three main parts to their bodies. The first part is the head which contains the jaw, eyes, and antennae. The second part of an ant's body is the trunk. The trunk has six legs attached to it. The third part of an ant's body is the rear. I was surprised to learn that the rear contains a poison sac. This is one way the ant defends itself.**

   What type of writing is demonstrated in the passage above?

   A. Descriptive

   B. Narrative

   C. Expository

   D. Persuasive

Answer: C. Expository

The passage was written to inform the reader about the parts of an ant's body therefore, it is expository. Had the author described what they saw when they looked at an ant's body under a microscope, it would be a descriptive passage.

(Average)

4. **What type of writing includes headings, subheadings, and titles?**

   A. Persuasive

   B. Descriptive

   C. Narrative

   D. Informative

Answer: D. Informative

Informative writing is usually nonfiction and nonfiction writing normally has headings, subheadings, and titles.

READING AND LANGUAGE ARTS CURRICULUM

SKILL 1.8 The structure of text

Grammar and Punctuation Conventions for Standard American English

Types of sentences

Sentences are made up of two parts: the subject and the predicate. The SUBJECT is the "do-er" of an action or the element that is being joined. Any adjectives describing this do-er or element are also part of the subject. The PREDICATE is made up of the verb and any other adverbs, adjectives, pronouns, or clauses that describe the action of the sentence.

A SIMPLE SENTENCE contains one independent clause (which contains one subject and one predicate).

In the following examples, the subject is underlined once, and the predicate is underlined twice.

> *The dancer bowed.*
> *Nathan skied down the hill.*

A COMPOUND SENTENCE is made up of two independent clauses that are joined by a conjunction, a correlative conjunction (e.g., either-or, neither-nor), or a semi-colon. Both of these independent clauses are able to stand on their own, but for sentence variety, authors will often combine two independent clauses.

In the following examples, the subjects of each independent clause are underlined once, and the predicates of each independent clause are underlined twice. The conjunction is in bold.

> *Samantha ate the cookie, **and** she drank her milk.*
> *Mark is excellent with computers; he has worked with them for years.*
> *Either Terry runs the project **or** I will not participate.*

A COMPLEX SENTENCE is made up of one independent clause and at least one dependent clause. In the following examples, the subjects of each clause are underlined once, and the predicates are underlined twice. The independent clause is in plain text, and the dependent clause is in italics.

> *When Jody saw how clean the house was, she was happy.*
> *Brian loves taking diving lessons, which he has done for years.*

SUBJECT: the "do-er" of an action or the element that is being joined

PREDICATE: made up of the verb and any other adverbs, adjectives, pronouns, or clauses that describe the action of the sentence

SIMPLE SENTENCE: contains one independent clause (which contains one subject and one predicate)

COMPOUND SENTENCE: made up of two independent clauses that are joined by a conjunction, a correlative conjunction (e.g., either-or, neither-nor), or a semicolon

COMPLEX SENTENCE: made up of one independent clause and at least one dependent clause

Sentence completeness

Avoid fragments and run-on sentences. Recognizing sentence elements necessary to make a complete thought, properly using independent and dependent clauses, and using proper punctuation will correct such errors.

Capitalization

Capitalize all proper names of persons (including specific organizations or agencies of government); places (countries, states, cities, parks, and specific geographical areas); things (political parties, structures, historical and cultural terms, and calendar and time designations); and religious terms (any deity, revered person or group, sacred writings).

> *Percy Bysshe Shelley, Argentina, Mount Rainier National Park, Grand Canyon, League of Nations, the Sears Tower, Birmingham, Lyric Theater, Americans, Midwesterners, Democrats, Renaissance, Boy Scouts of America, Easter, God, Bible, Dead Sea Scrolls, Koran*

Capitalize proper adjectives and titles used with proper names.

> *California gold rush, President John Adams, French fries, Homeric epic, Romanesque architecture, Senator John Glenn*

Note: Some words that represent titles and offices are not capitalized unless used with a proper name.

EXAMPLES OF CAPITALIZATION AND NONCAPITALIZATION	
Capitalized	**Not Capitalized**
Congressman McKay	the congressman from Florida
Commander Alger	commander of the Pacific Fleet
Queen Elizabeth	the queen of England

Capitalize all main words in titles of works of literature, art, and music. (See "Using Italics" in the Punctuation section.)

Punctuation

A basic way to show relationships between ideas in sentences is to use punctuation correctly and effectively. Competency exams will generally test the ability to apply the more advanced skills; thus, a limited number of more frustrating rules are presented here. Rules should be applied according to the American style of English, e.g., placing terminal marks of punctuation almost exclusively within other marks of punctuation.

Quotation marks

The more troublesome punctuation marks involve the use of quotations.

Using terminal punctuation in relation to quotation marks

In a quoted statement that is either declarative or imperative, place the period inside the closing quotation marks.

> *"The airplane crashed on the runway during takeoff."*

If the quotation is followed by other words in the sentence, place a comma inside the closing quotations marks and a period at the end of the sentence.

> *"The airplane crashed on the runway during takeoff," said the announcer.*

In most instances in which a quoted title or expression occurs at the end of a sentence, the period is placed before either the single or double quotation marks.

> *The educator worried, "The middle school readers were unprepared to understand Bryant's poem 'Thanatopsis.'"*
>
> *Early book-length adventure stories like* Don Quixote *and* The Three Musketeers *are known as "picaresque novels."*

There is an instance in which the final quotation mark precedes the period: if the content of the sentence is about a speech or quote, and the understanding of the meaning might be confused by the placement of the period.

> *The first thing out of his mouth was "Hi, I'm home."*
>
> *but*
>
> *The first line of his speech began "I arrived home to an empty house".*

In sentences that are interrogatory or exclamatory, the question mark or exclamation point should be positioned outside the closing quotation marks if the quote itself is a statement or command or a cited title.

> *Who decided to lead us in the recitation of the "Pledge of Allegiance"?*
>
> *Why was Tillie shaking as she began her recitation, "Once upon a midnight dreary..."?*
>
> *I was embarrassed when Mrs. White said, "Your slip is showing"!*

In sentences that are declarative but in which the quotation is a question or an exclamation, place the question mark or exclamation point inside the quotation marks.

> *The hall monitor yelled, "Fire! Fire!"*
>
> *"Fire! Fire!" yelled the hall monitor.*
>
> *Cory shrieked, "Is there a mouse in the room?" (In this instance, the question supersedes the exclamation.)*

Using double quotation marks with other punctuation

Quotations—whether words, phrases, or clauses—should be punctuated according to the rules of the grammatical function they serve in the sentence.

> *The works of Shakespeare, "the bard of Avon," have been contested as originating with other authors.*
>
> *"You'll get my money," the old man warned, "when 'Hell freezes over'."*
>
> *Sheila cited the passage that began "Four score and seven years ago...." (Note the ellipsis followed by an enclosed period.)*
>
> *"Old Ironsides" inspired the preservation of the U.S.S. Constitution.*

Use quotation marks to enclose the titles of shorter works: songs, short poems, short stories, essays, and chapters of books. (See "Using Italics" for rules on punctuating longer titles.)

> *"The Tell-Tale Heart" (short story)*
>
> *"Casey at the Bat" (poem)*
>
> *"America the Beautiful" (song)*

Using commas

Use commas to separate two or more coordinate adjectives modifying the same word and three or more nouns, phrases, or clauses in a list.

> *Maggie's hair was dull, dirty, and lice-ridden.*
>
> *Dickens portrayed the Artful Dodger as skillful pickpocket, loyal follower of Fagin, and defendant of Oliver Twist.*
>
> *Ellen daydreamed about getting out of the rain, taking a shower, and eating a hot dinner.*
>
> *In Elizabethan England, Ben Jonson wrote comedy, Christopher Marlowe wrote tragedies, and William Shakespeare composed both.*

Use commas to separate antithetical or complimentary expressions from the rest of the sentence.

> *The veterinarian, not his assistant, would perform the delicate surgery.*
>
> *The more he knew about her, the less he wished he had known.*
>
> *Randy hopes to, and probably will, get an appointment to the Naval Academy.*

Using semicolons

Use semicolons to separate independent clauses when the second clause is introduced by a transitional adverb. (These clauses may also be written as separate sentences, preferably by placing the adverb within the second sentence.)

> *The Elizabethans modified the rhyme scheme of the sonnet; thus, it was called the English sonnet.*
>
> *or*
>
> *The Elizabethans modified the rhyme scheme of the sonnet. It thus was called the English sonnet.*

Use semicolons to separate items in a series that are long and complex or have internal punctuation.

> *The Italian Renaissance produced masters in the fine arts: Dante Alighieri, author of the* Divine Comedy; *Leonardo da Vinci, painter of* The Last Supper; *and Donatello, sculptor of the* Quattro Coronati, *the Four Saints.*
>
> *The leading scorers in the WNBA were Haizhaw Zheng, averaging 23.9 points per game; Lisa Leslie, 22; and Cynthia Cooper, 19.5.*

Using colons

Place a colon at the beginning of a list of items. (Note its use in the sentence about Renaissance Italians previously.)

> *The teacher directed us to compare Faulkner's three symbolic novels:* Absalom, Absalom; As I Lay Dying; *and* Light in August.

Do *not* use a comma if the list is preceded by a verb.

> *Three of Faulkner's symbolic novels are* Absalom, Absalom; As I Lay Dying; *and* Light in August.

Using dashes

Place dashes (called "em" dashes) to denote sudden breaks in thought.

Some periods in literature—the Romantic Age, for example—spanned different time periods in different countries.

Use dashes instead of commas if commas are already used elsewhere in the sentence for amplification or explanation.

The Fireside Poets included three Brahmans—James Russell Lowell, Henry David Wadsworth, and Oliver Wendell Holmes—and John Greenleaf Whittier.

Using italics

Use italics to punctuate the titles of long works of literature and the names of periodical publications, musical scores, works of art, and motion picture, television, and radio programs. (If italic type is not available, you can instruct students to underline text that should be italicized.)

The Idylls of the King	*Hiawatha*	*The Sound and the Fury*
Mary Poppins	*Newsweek*	*The Nutcracker Suite*

Subject-verb agreement

A verb must agree in number with its subject. The subject must be correctly identified to ensure agreement.

One of the boys was playing too rough.

No one in the class, neither the teacher nor the students, was listening to the message from the intercom.

The candidates, including a grandmother and a teenager, are debating some controversial issues.

If two singular subjects are connected by *and*, the verb must be plural.

A man and his dog were jogging on the beach.

If two singular subjects are connected by *or* or *nor*, a singular verb is required.

Neither Dot nor Joyce has missed a day of school this year.

Either Fran or Paul is missing.

If one singular subject and one plural subject are connected by *or* or *nor*, the verb agrees with the subject nearest to the verb.

> *Neither the <u>coach</u> nor the <u>players</u> were able to sleep on the bus.*

If the subject is a collective noun, its sense of number in the sentence determines the verb: singular if the noun represents a group or unit and plural if the noun represents individuals.

> *The <u>House of Representatives</u> <u>has</u> adjourned for the holidays.*
>
> *The <u>House of Representatives</u> <u>have</u> failed to reach agreement on the subject of adjournment.*

Use of verbs: tense

PRESENT TENSE is used to express that which is currently happening or is always true.

> *Randy is playing the piano.*
>
> *Randy plays the piano like a pro.*

PAST TENSE is used to express action that occurred in a past time.

> *Randy learned to play the piano when he was six years old.*

FUTURE TENSE is used to express action or a condition of future time.

> *Randy will probably earn a music scholarship.*

PRESENT PERFECT TENSE is used to express action or a condition that started in the past and is continued or completed in the present.

> *Randy has practiced the piano every day for the last ten years.*
>
> *Randy has never been bored with practice.*

PAST PERFECT TENSE expresses action or a condition that occurred as a precedent to some other past action or condition.

> *Randy had considered playing clarinet before he discovered the piano.*

PRESENT TENSE: expresses that which is currently happening or is always true

PAST TENSE: expresses action that occurred in a past time

FUTURE TENSE: expresses action or a condition of future time

PRESENT PERFECT TENSE: expresses action or a condition that started in the past and is continued or completed in the present

PAST PERFECT TENSE: expresses action or a condition that occurred as a precedent to some other past action or condition

FUTURE PERFECT TENSE: expresses action that started in the past or the present and will conclude at some time in the future

FUTURE PERFECT TENSE expresses action that started in the past or the present and will conclude at some time in the future.

> *By the time he goes to college, Randy will have been an accomplished pianist for more than half of his life.*

Use of verbs: mood

Indicative mood is used to make unconditional statements; subjunctive mood is used for conditional clauses or wish statements that pose conditions that are untrue. Verbs in subjunctive mood are plural with both singular and plural subjects.

> *If I were a bird, I would fly.*
>
> *I wish I were as rich as Donald Trump.*

Use of verbs: voice

ACTIVE VOICE: when the subject of the verb is the doer of the action

PASSIVE VOICE: when the subject of the verb is the receiver of the action

A verb is in the ACTIVE VOICE when its subject is the doer of the action. A verb is in the PASSIVE VOICE when its subject is the receiver of the action.

Active Voice	Passive Voice
The director adjourned the meeting. The subject, *director*, performs the action, *adjourned*.	**The meeting was adjourned by the director.** The subject, *meeting*, is not performing the action; instead, it is receiving the action, *was adjourned*.
The mechanic at the Shell station inspected Mrs. Johnson's automobile. The subject, *mechanic*, performed the action, *inspected*.	**Mrs. Johnson's automobile was inspected by the mechanic at the Shell station.** The subject, *automobile*, is not acting; it is receiving the action, *was inspected*.

How do you recognize passive voice? Look at the verb. A passive-voice verb has at least two parts:

1. A form of the verb to be (am, is, are, was, were, be, been)

> *The computer was installed by Datacorp.*

2. A past participle form of the main verb (thrown, driven, planted, talked)

> *The computer was <u>installed</u> by Datacorp.*

– Sometimes the subject is in an object position in the sentence.

> *The computer was installed by <u>Datacorp</u>. (object of preposition)*

– Watch for a "by" statement between the verb phrase and the object.

> *The computer was installed <u>by</u> Datacorp. (preposition)*

– Sometimes the doer is not even present.

> *The computer was installed. (By whom?)*

Verb conjugation

The conjugation of verbs follows the patterns used in the discussion of tense above. However, the most common errors in verb use stem from the improper formation of the past and past participial forms.

Regular verb:	*believe, believed, (have) believed*
Irregular verbs:	*run, ran, run; sit, sat, sat; teach, taught, taught*

Other errors stem from the use of verbs that are the same in some tenses but have different forms and different meanings in other tenses.

> *I lie on the ground. I lay on the ground yesterday. I have lain down. I lay the blanket on the bed. I laid the blanket there yesterday. I have laid the blanket down every night.*
>
> *The sun rises. The sun rose. The sun has risen.*
>
> *He raises the flag. He raised the flag. He had raised the flag.*
>
> *I sit on the porch. I sat on the porch. I have sat in the porch swing.*
>
> *I set the plate on the table. I set the plate there yesterday. I had set the table before dinner.*

Two other common verb problems stem from misusing the preposition *of* for the verb auxiliary have and misusing the verb ought (now rare).

Incorrect: *I should of gone to bed.*

Correct: *I should have gone to bed.*

Incorrect: *He hadn't ought to get so angry.*

Correct: *He ought not to get so angry.*

Use of pronouns

A pronoun used as a subject of predicate nominative is in nominative case.

> *She was the drum majorette. The lead trombonists were Joe and he. The band director accepted whoever could march in step.*

A pronoun used as a direct object, indirect object, or object of a preposition is in objective case.

> *The teacher praised him. She gave him an A on the test. Her praise of him was appreciated. The students whom she did not praise will work harder next time.*

Some common pronoun errors occur from the misuse of reflexive pronouns:

> *Singular: myself, yourself, herself, himself, itself*
> *Plural: ourselves, yourselves, themselves*

Incorrect: *Jack cut hisself shaving.*

Correct: *Jack cut himself shaving.*

Incorrect: *They backed theirselves into a corner.*

Correct: *They backed themselves into a corner.*

Use of adjectives

An adjective should agree with its antecedent in number.

> *Those apples are rotten.*
> *This one is ripe.*
> *These peaches are hard.*

Comparative adjectives end in -er and superlatives in -est, with some exceptions like worse and worst. Some adjectives that cannot easily make comparative inflections are preceded by more and most.

Avoid double comparisons.

> Mrs. Carmichael is the better of the two basketball coaches.
>
> That is the hastiest excuse you have ever contrived.

Incorrect: *This is the worstest headache I ever had.*

Correct: *This is the worst headache I ever had.*

When comparing one thing to others in a group, exclude the thing under comparison from the rest of the group.

Incorrect: *Joey is larger than any baby I have ever seen. (Since you have seen him, he cannot be larger than himself.)*

Correct: *Joey is larger than <u>any other</u> baby I have ever seen.*

Include all the words necessary to make a comparison clear in meaning.

> I am as tall as my mother. I am as tall as she (is).
>
> My cats are better behaved than those of my neighbor.

Sample Test Questions and Rationale

(Average)

1. **Which combination of words produces an irregular contraction?**

   A. did + not

   B. you + are

   C. I + will

   D. will + not

Answer: D. will + not

The contraction for will + not is won't. Choices A, B, and C are all regular combinations where the first word doesn't change when making the contraction; didn't, you're, I'll.

Sample Test Questions and Rationale (cont.)

(Easy)

2. What is the plural of the word *rose*?

   A. Rosis

   B. Rosses

   C. Roses

   D. Rose's

Answer: C. Roses

When making a word that ends in *e* plural, add an *s*.

(Rigorous)

3. Which word needs to be corrected in the sentence below?

   The presents on the table is wrapped in beautiful wrapping paper.

   A. presents

   B. is

   C. wrapped

   D. beautiful

Answer: B. is

Is needs to be replaced with the word *are*. *Is* should be used in the singular form. *Are* is used in the plural form and there is more than one present. Therefore, the sentence should read, "The presents on the table are wrapped in beautiful wrapping paper."

(Rigorous)

4. What type of sentence is the sentence below?

   Jarrett and Austin like to read and write.

   A. Simple

   B. Compound

   C. Complex

   D. Compound/complex

Answer: A. Simple

The sentence has a compound subject and a compound predicate but it still consists of one subject and one verb. The conjunction, *and*, does not join two or more independent clauses so it cannot be a compound sentence.

(Rigorous)

5. What must be done to make this sentence correct?

   Before the children were allowed to go outside.

   A. Place a comma after before

   B. Change the word *children* to *child*

   C. Change the period to a comma and add an independent clause

   D. Nothing, it is fine the way it is

Answer: C. Change the period to a comma and add an independent clause

This is a dependent clause that needs additional information. Therefore, an independent clause must be added. For example, "Before the children were allowed to go outside, they had to clean their rooms." "They had to clean their rooms" is an independent clause and can stand alone or be proceeded by a dependent clause.

(Easy)

6. Which sentence is punctuated incorrectly?

   A. Tomorrow night we'll have pizza for dinner?

   B. Close the door please.

   C. Go away!

   D. What time does the movie begin?

Answer: A. Tomorrow night we'll have pizza for dinner?

Alone, this is a statement and should be punctuated with a period—not a question mark.

Sample Test Questions and Rationale (cont.)

(Easy)

7. Which punctuation mark is required, if any, in the sentence?

   Let's have some chocolate graham crackers and marshmallows for dessert.

   A. !

   B. ?

   C. ,

   D. None

   Answer: C. ,

   A comma placed between chocolate and graham crackers now suggests that three items are needed for dessert rather than two (chocolate graham crackers and marshmallows).

(Rigorous)

8. What type of sentence is the sentence below?

   Millie and Max seemed tired and bored.

   A. Simple

   B. Compound

   C. Complex

   D. Compound/complex

   Answer: A. Simple

   The sentence has a compound subject but there is only one verb. Therefore, it is a simple sentence.

(Rigorous)

9. Which word needs to be corrected in the sentence below?

   The Biggilow family were concerned with the appearance of their home.

   A. family

   B. were

   C. appearance

   D. their

   Answer: B. were

   The Biggilow family is considered a singular. Therefore, the correct word is *was*.

SKILL 1.9 Progression and stages of writing development

Stages of Writing Development

Young children develop writing in stages just as they do reading. As with reading, writing development is not a linear progression, but rather an overlapping one. Though many label the scribbling that children start out with as prewriting, it is actually one of the stages of writing development.

Each writing stage has unique characteristics involving the areas of spelling, penmanship, print/mechanics concepts, and content. The following table explains the requisite skill for each stage and area.

Each writing stage has unique characteristics involving the areas of spelling, penmanship, print/mechanics concepts, and content.

	SPELLING	PENMANSHIP	PRINT/MECHANICS CONCEPTS	CONTENT
Role Play Writer	Scribbles and uses writing-like behavior; scribbles to represent words; no phonetic association.	Develops pencil position and traces words and letters	Develops awareness of environmental print	Uses pictures and scribble writing
Emergent Writer	Writes initial consonants; correlates some letter/sounds; each syllable has a letter	Can write on line; incorrectly mixes upper and lower case letters	Makes some letters and words; attempts to write name	Copies words and uses pattern sentences
Developing Writer	Left/right correspondence; invented spelling with initial/final consonants; few vowels	Correctly uses upper and lowercase letters	Directional writing and one-to-one writing/reading words; writes word patterns	Uses invented spelling and simple sentences
Beginning Writer	Correct spelling for most words; uses resources and decoding for spelling	Sentence structure; only focuses on one writing component at a time, i.e., spelling or punctuation	Chooses personally significant topics for writing assignments	Organizes paragraphs using complete sentences
Expanding Writer	Edits for mechanics during and after writing	Varies writing components based on writing task	Uses organization and variety of word choices	Writes in a variety of formats: poetry, stories, reports.

The stages of writing development are:

- Role Play Writer
- Emergent Writer
- Developing Writer
- Beginning Writer
- Expanding Writer

See samples of the stages of writing development:

http://cfbstaff.cfbisd.edu/ chienv/stages_of_writing_ development.htm

Spelling and Writing

Spelling is very important in the writing process. At first, young children will use invented spelling, in which they write the words according to letter sounds. There are several factors that influence the development of spelling, such as:

- Surrounding students with an environment rich in print

- Understanding the developmental stages of spelling

- Understanding that learning to spell is problem solving

- Teaching the rules of spelling

- Promoting an awareness about spelling

Spelling in context

Spelling should be taught within the context of meaningful language experiences. Giving a child a list of words to learn to spell and then testing the child on the words every Friday will not aid in the development of spelling. The child must be able to use the words in context and the words must have some meaning for the child. The assessment of how well a child can spell or where there are problems also has to be done within a meaningful environment.

The child must be able to use the words in context and the words must have some meaning for the child. The assessment of how well a child can spell or where there are problems also has to be done within a meaningful environment.

Assessing spelling

The main reasons for assessing spelling are:

- To find out what the child knows about spelling patterns and strategies

- To determine what the teacher needs to teach

- To develop spelling growth over a period of time

In order for spelling assessment to be authentic, it must have meaning for the child. Taking a list of words that a child misspells from a piece of writing is one example of a spelling list that the teacher can use. If the teacher keeps a list of words the children ask to spell, this can also be the basis for a word list.

Since spelling words correctly is something that does happen over time, teachers may notice that the child keeps spelling the same words incorrectly again and again. Through explicit teaching of strategies and even tricks to help spell the words, eventually they will see success in spelling. Assessment is something that has to happen over the course of a grade. Correct spelling is not something that children learn and retain automatically.

The process of learning to spell

FIVE DEVELOPMENTAL STAGES IN LEARNING TO SPELL	
Pre-phonemic Spelling	Children know that letters stand for a message, but they do not know the relationship between spelling and pronunciation.
Early Phonemic Spelling	Children are beginning to understand spelling. They usually write the beginning letter correctly, with the rest consonants or long vowels.
Letter-name Spelling	Some words are consistently spelled correctly. The student is developing a sight vocabulary and a stable understanding of letters as representing sounds. Long vowels are usually used accurately, but silent vowels are omitted. The child spells unknown words by attempting to match the name of the letter to the sound.
Transitional Spelling	This phase is typically entered in late elementary school. Short vowel sounds are mastered and some spelling rules known. The students are developing a sense of which spellings are correct and which are not.
Derivational Spelling	This is usually reached from high school to adulthood. This is the stage at which spelling rules are mastered.

SKILL 1.10 Interrelatedness of reading, writing, listening, speaking, and viewing

Current Trends in Literacy

In the current teaching of literacy, it is not uncommon for reading and writing and thinking, listening, viewing, and discussing to be developed and nurtured simultaneously and interactively. Such an integrated framework reflects the reality of our relationship to language and facilitates student learning in all areas.

A student's developmental writing skills parallel their reading development stages of reading. Print awareness develops in young children as a result of listening to a story read to them by adults, and recognizing that words on a page symbolize meaning. PRINT AWARENESS is the realization that writing is created with instruments such as pens, pencils, crayons, and markers. Children begin to imitate the shapes and letters they see in a book or in text. Children soon learn that the power of writing is expressing one's own ideas in print form and that these ideas can be understood by others.

A student's developmental writing skills parallel their reading development stages of reading.

PRINT AWARENESS: the realization that writing is created with instruments such as pens, pencils, crayons, and markers

Due to the social nature of children's learning, early instruction must provide rich demonstrations, interactions, and models of literacy. Children learn about the relation between oral and written language and the relation between letters, sounds, and words. Classrooms should include a wide variety of print and writing activities that involve students interacting with each other by:

- Talking
- Reading
- Writing
- Playing
- Listening

Books, papers, writing tools, and functional signs should be visible everywhere in the classroom so that children can see and use literacy for multiple purposes.

Aspects of speaking and listening

Listening is a very specific skill for very specific circumstances. There are two aspects to listening that warrant attention: comprehension and purpose. COMPREHENSION involves simply understanding what someone says, the purposes behind the message, and the contexts in which it is said. PURPOSE comes in to play when considering that while someone may completely understand a message, they must also know what to do with it. Are they expected to just nod and smile? Go out and take action?

While listening comprehension is indeed a significant skill in itself, one that deserves a lot of focus in the classroom (much in the same way that reading comprehension does), we will focus on purpose here. Often, when we understand the purpose of listening in various contexts, comprehension will be much easier. Furthermore, when we know the purpose of listening, we can better adjust our comprehension strategies.

Purpose

When complex or new information is provided to us orally, we must analyze and interpret that information. What is the author's most important point? How do the figures of speech impact meaning? How can we arrive at conclusions? Often, making sense of this information can be difficult for oral presentations—first, because we have no way to go back and review material already stated; secondly, because oral language is so much less predictable than written language. However, when we focus on extracting the meaning, message, and speaker's purpose, rather than just "listening" and waiting for things to make sense for us—in other words,

Listening is a very specific skill for very specific circumstances.

COMPREHENSION: involves simply understanding what someone says, the purposes behind the message, and the contexts in which it is said

PURPOSE: comes in to play when considering that while someone may completely understand a message, they must also know what to do with it

when we are more "active" in our listening—we have greater success in interpreting speech.

Listenting for enjoyment

Listening is often done for the purpose of enjoyment. We like to listen to stories, we enjoy poetry, and we like radio dramas and theater. Listening to literature can also be a great pleasure. The problem today is that students have not learned how to extract great pleasure on a widespread scale from simply listening. Perhaps that is because we have not done a good enough job of showing students how listening to literature, for example, can indeed be more interesting than television or video games. In the classrooms of exceptional teachers, we will often find that students are captivated by the reading aloud of good literature. It is refreshing and enjoyable to just sit and soak in the language, story, and poetry of literature being read aloud. Therefore, we must teach students how to listen and enjoy such work. We do this by making it fun and giving many possibilities and alternatives to capture the wide array of interests in each classroom.

Group discussions

Let us consider listening in large and small group conversations. The difference here is that conversation requires more than just listening: it involves feedback and active involvement. This can be particularly challenging, as in our culture, we are trained to move conversations along, to discourage silence in a conversation, and to always get the last word in. This poses significant problems for the art of listening. In a discussion, for example, when we are instead preparing our next response—rather than listening to what others are saying—we do a large disservice to the entire discussion. Students need to learn how listening carefully to others in discussions actually promotes better responses on the part of subsequent speakers. One way teachers can encourage this in both large and small group discussions is to expect students to respond directly to the previous student's comments before moving ahead with their new comments. This will encourage them to pose their new comments in light of the comments that came just before them.

Making Sense of Oral Language

Oral speech can also be much less structured than written language. Yet, aside from re-reading, many of the skills and strategies that help us in reading comprehension can help us in listening comprehension. For example, as soon as we start listening to something new, we should tap into our prior knowledge in order to attach new information to what we already know. This will not only help us to understand the new information more quickly, but it will also assist us in remembering the material.

We can also look for transitions between ideas. Sometimes, in oral speech, this is pretty simple, such as when voice tone or body language changes; as listeners, we have access to the animation that comes along with live speech. Human beings have to try very hard to be completely nonexpressive in their speech. Listeners should take advantage of this and notice how the speaker changes character and voice in order to signal a transition of ideas.

Nonverbal cues

Listeners can also better comprehend the underlying intent of the author when they notice nonverbal cues. In oral speech, unlike written text, elements like irony are not indicated by the actual words, but rather by the tone and nonverbal cues. Simply looking to see the expression on the face of a speaker can often do more to signal irony than trying to extract irony from actual words.

Utilizing Appropriate Communication

In public speaking, not all speeches call for the same type of speaking style. For example, when providing a humorous speech, it is important to utilize body language that accents the humorous moments. However, when giving instructions, it is extremely important to speak clearly and slowly, carefully noting the mood of the audience, so that if there is general confusion on peoples' faces, you can go back and review something. In group discussions, it is important to ensure that you are listening to others carefully and tailoring your messages so that what you say fits into the general mood and location of the discussion at hand. When giving an oral presentation, the mood should be both serious and friendly; you should focus on ensuring that the content is covered, while also relating to audience members as much as possible.

Adjusting speaking styles

It used to be that we thought of speaking and communication only in terms of what is effective and what is not effective. Today, we realize that there is more to communication than just good and bad. We must take into consideration that we must adjust our communication styles for various audiences. While we should not stereotype audiences, we can still recognize that certain methods of communication are more appropriate with certain people than with others. Age is an easy one to consider: Adults know that when they talk to children, they should come across as pleasant and non-threatening, and they should use vocabulary that is simple for children to understand. On the other hand, teenagers realize that they should not speak to their grandmothers the way they speak with their peers. When dealing with communications between cultures and genders, people must be sensitive, considerate, and appropriate.

It used to be that we thought of speaking and communication only in terms of what is effective and what is not effective. Today, we realize that there is more to communication than just good and bad.

Teachers and communication

How do teachers help students to understand these "unspoken" rules of communication? Well, these rules are not easy to communicate in regular classroom lessons. Instead, teachers must model these behaviors, and they must have high expectations for students (clearly communicated, of course) inside and outside the classroom walls.

Teachers must also consider these aspects as they deal with colleagues, parents, community members, and even students. They must realize that all communication should be tailored so that it conveys appropriate messages and tones to listeners.

INFORMAL LANGUAGE: communication used at informal events, such as parties or friendly gatherings

FORMAL LANGUAGE: communication used at formal events, such as business meetings; formal language uses fewer or no contractions, less slang, longer sentences, and more organization in longer segments

The differences between INFORMAL LANGUAGE and FORMAL LANGUAGE are distinctions made on the basis of the occasion as well as the audience. At a "formal" occasion (for example, a meeting of executives or of government officials), even conversational exchanges are likely to be formal. At a cocktail party or a golf game, the language is likely to be much more informal. Formal language uses fewer or no contractions, less slang, longer sentences, and more organization in longer segments. Speeches delivered to executives, college professors, government officials, etc., are likely to be formal. Speeches made to fellow employees are likely to be informal. Sermons tend to be formal; Bible lessons tend to be informal.

Combining Oral and Written Communication

The art of debating, discussion, and conversation is different from the basic writing forms of discourse. The ability to use language and logic to convince the audience to accept your reasoning and to side with you is an art.

The art of debating, discussion, and conversation is different from the basic writing forms of discourse. The ability to use language and logic to convince the audience to accept your reasoning and to side with you is an art. This form of writing/speaking is extremely confined and structured, logically sequenced, and contains supporting reasons and evidence. At its best, it is the highest form of propaganda. Position statements, evidence, reason, evaluation, and refutation are integral parts of this writing schema.

Using written and oral communication in the classroom

Interviewing provides opportunities for students to engage in expository and informative communication. It teaches them how to structure questions to evoke fact-filled responses. Compiling the information from an interview into a biographical essay or speech helps students to list, sort, and arrange details in an orderly fashion.

Speeches that encourage them to describe persons, places, or events in their own lives as well as oral interpretations of literature help students to sense the creativity and effort used by professional writers.

Sample Test Question and Rationale

(Rigorous)

1. How would a letter to the editor be written?

    A. Using formal language

    B. Using informal/slang language

    C. Using informal language with informal mechanics

    D. Using words from the dialect of its intended audience

Answer: A. Using formal language

Normally, a letter to the editor is written to persuade others to think in one way or defend a position. Therefore, it is most likely going to be written using formal language.

COMPETENCY 2
READING AND LANGUAGE ARTS INSTRUCTION

SKILL 2.1 Teaching phonemic awareness

Theorist Marilyn Jager Adams, who researches early reading, has outlined five basic types of phonemic awareness tasks.

The five types of phonemic awareness:

Task 1: Ability to hear rhymes and alliteration. Children would listen to a poem, rhyming picture book or song and identify the rhyming words they hear, while the teacher records or lists them on an experiential chart.

Task 2: Ability to do oddity tasks (recognize the member of a set that is different [odd] among the group.) The children would look at the pictures of (a blade of) grass, a garden and a rose and be able to tell which starts with a different sound.

Task 3: **The ability to orally blend words and split syllables.** The children can say the first sound of a word and then the rest of the word and put it together as a single word.

Task 4: **The ability to orally segment words.** This is the ability to count sounds. The children would be asked as a group to count the sounds in "hamburger."

Task 5: **The ability to do phonics manipulation tasks.** The children would replace the "r" sound in rose with a "p" sound to get the word "pose."

Instructional methods that may be effective for teaching phonemic awareness can include:

- Clapping syllables in words

- Distinguishing between a word and a sound

- Using visual cues and movements to help children understand when the speaker goes from one sound to another

- Oral segmentation activities that focus on easily distinguished syllables rather than sounds

- Singing familiar songs (e.g., Happy Birthday, Knick Knack Paddy Wack) and replacing key words in the song with words having a different ending or middle sound (oral segmentation)

- Dealing children a deck of picture cards and having them sound out the words for the pictures on their cards or calling for a picture by asking for its first and second sound.

APPLIED EXAMPLES OF COMMON PHONEMES:			
Phoneme	**Uses**	**Phoneme**	**Uses**
/A/	a (table), a_e (bake), ai (train), ay (say)	/t/	t (time)
/a/	a (flat)	/U/	u (future), u_e (use), ew (few)
/b/	b (ball)	/u/	u (thumb), a (about)
/k/	c (cake), k (key), ck (back)	/v/	v (voice)

Table continued on next page

Phoneme	Uses	Phoneme	Uses
/d/	d (door)	/w/	w (wash)
/E/	e (me), ee (feet), ea (leap), y (baby)	/gz/	x (exam)
/e/	e (pet), ea (head)	/ks/	x (box)
/f/	f (fix), ph (phone)	/y/	y (yes)
/g/	g (gas)	/z/	z (zoo), s (nose)
/h/	h (hot)	/OO/	oo (boot), u (truth), u_e (rude), ew (chew)
/I/	i (lie), i_e (bite), igh (light), y (sky)	/oo/	oo (book), u (put)
/i/	i (sit)	/oi/	oi (soil), oy (toy)
/j/	j (jet), dge (edge), g (gem)	/ou/	ou (out), ow (cow)
/l/	l (lamp)	/aw/	aw (saw), au (caught), al (tall)
/m/	m (map)	/ar/	ar (car)
/n/	n (no), kn (knock)	/sh/	sh (ship), ti (nation), ci (special)
/O/	o (okay), o_e (bone), oa (soap), ow (low)	/hw/	wh (white)
/o/	o (hot)	/ch/	ch (chest), tch (catch)
/p/	p (pie)	/th/	th (thick)
/kw/	qu (quick)	/th/	th (this)
/r/	r (road), wr (wrong), er (her), ir (sir), ur (fur)	/ng/	ng (sing)
/s/	s (say), c (cent)	/zh/	s (measure)

Sample Test Question and Rationale

(Easy)

1. How many syllables does the word *chocolate* have?

    A. 1
    B. 2
    C. 3
    D. 4

Answer: C. 3

Although we may pronounce *chocolate* using two syllables, it technically has three; *choc-o-late*.

SKILL 2.2 Teaching phonics and spelling

Strategies for Teaching Phonics

The one-letter book

Provide children with a sample of a single letter book (or create one from environmental sources, newspapers, coupons, circulars, magazines, or your own text ideas). Make sure that your already published or created sample includes a printed version of the letter in both upper and lower case forms. Make certain that each page contains a picture of something that starts with that specific letter and also has the word for the picture. The book you select or create should be a predictable one in that when the picture is identified, the word can be read.

Once the children have been provided with your sample and have listened to it being read, challenge them to each make a one-letter book. Often it is best to focus on familiar consonants for the single letter book or the first letter of the child's first name. Use of the first letter of the child's first name invites the child to develop a book that tells about him or her and the words that he or she finds. This is an excellent way to have the reading workshop aspect of the teacher's instruction of the alphabetic principle complement and enhance the writing workshop. Encourage children to be active writers and readers by finding words for their book on the classroom word wall, in alphabet books in the special alphabet book bin, and in grade- and age-appropriate pictionaries (dictionaries for younger children which are filled with pictures).

Practicing the Four Basic Word Types

Practice techniques for student development of the four basic word types can include speed drills in which they read lists of isolated words with contrasting vowel sounds that are signaled by the syllable type. For example, several closed syllable and vowel-consonant-"e" words containing the vowel *a* are arranged randomly on pages containing about twelve lines and read for one minute. Individual goals are established and charts are kept of the number of words read correctly in successive sessions. The same word lists are repeated in sessions until the goal has been achieved for several succeeding sessions. When selecting words for these lists, the use of high-frequency words within a syllable category increases the likelihood of generalization to text reading.

Various techniques are useful with students who have acquired some proficiency in decoding skill but whose levels of skill are lower than their oral language abilities. Such techniques have certain, common features:

- Students listen to text as they follow along with the book

- Students follow the print using their fingers as guides

- Reading materials are used that students would be unable to read independently

> **TRADITIONAL APPROACH:** adheres strictly to a phonics-based approach to spelling

Teaching Spelling

There are basically four approaches for teaching spelling. These are the traditional spelling instruction, whole language, developmental, and the structured language approaches.

The TRADITIONAL APPROACH adheres strictly to a phonics-based approach to spelling. The student uses invented spelling, using known sounds and skipping others. The teacher sequentially teaches phonics rules and their application to spelling, including those words that don't adhere to the rules. In the traditional approach, the student learns to spell by phonemes and word families. Spelling instruction is direct, systematic, and intensive and is believed to be the best way to ensure student success. This approach utilizes the traditional basal speller, rote drill, repeated copying, especially of missed words, and weekly spelling tests.

> *In the traditional approach, the student learns to spell by phonemes and word families. Spelling instruction is direct, systematic, and intensive and is believed to be the best way to ensure student success.*

The WHOLE LANGUAGE APPROACH for teaching spelling supports the idea that the student learns to spell by remembering what the word looks like rather than by remembering how it sounds. Rebecca Sitton, who has developed a whole spelling series, spearheads this group. Proponents of this group believe student success lies in learning to spell words as they need them for their personal writing. Students

> **WHOLE LANGUAGE APPROACH:** supports the idea that the student learns to spell by remembering what the word looks like rather than by remembering how it sounds

are directed in word wall study, both seeing, chanting, writing, and then using the words in their own personal writing. They are then taught to analyze the structure of words and learn what the base words, prefixes, and suffixes look like and mean. Classrooms are print-rich, exposing the student to the sight of many utilitarian words. It is believed that the student learns spelling best by using the words in their own reading/writing tasks. Though a few words and word structures are taught, children mainly learn as they use the word.

The **DEVELOPMENTAL APPROACH** suggests several stages of development that students go through in their development from invented spelling to conventional spelling. This approach holds that students should be allowed to just develop without overt instruction, as they will eventually develop to traditional spelling. Different studies have suggested different numbers of stages, but benchmark stages through the continuum are:

- Precommunicative: Random letters are heard that may match beginning sound
- Semiphonetic: One or more letters representing sounds are heard, usually without medial vowels
- Phonetic: More letters are included, as are more vowels. They are usually spelled exactly as the child perceives the sounds, i.e., the letter /u/ might be represented as 'you'
- Transitional: Letters are included for all sounds, words contain the correct number of syllables although some vowels may be misrepresented, i.e., '-er' might be represented as '-ur'
- Conventional: Mostly correct spelling with only errors in difficult spelling patterns

The **STRUCTURED LANGUAGE APPROACH**, which is considered to have been developed by Samual Orton, involves an in-depth focus on letter/sound relationships and progresses through letters, phonemes, blended syllables, to whole words. There are only 40-plus phonemes used to represent every speech sound made and these are spelled with only 26 letters, so variations have to be learned (as secondary sounds). Orton also associated spelling difficulties with reading difficulties and reasoned that a focus on spelling the 40-plus phonemes would also improve the reading ability of the student.

Each method of teaching spelling has shown documented success. It appears that the key to success is to actively address spelling issues, either in a structured format or based on words needed by individual students.

It is believed that the student learns spelling best by using the words in their own reading/writing tasks.

DEVELOPMENTAL APPROACH: students go through several stages of development from invented spelling to conventional spelling

STRUCTURED LANGUAGE APPROACH: involves an in-depth focus on letter/sound relationships and progresses through letters, phonemes, blended syllables, to whole words

Each method of teaching spelling has shown documented success. It appears that the key to success is to actively address spelling issues, either in a structured format or based on words needed by individual students.

SPELLING PATTERN WORD WALL

Create in your classroom a spelling pattern word wall. Wylie and Durrell have identified spelling patterns that are in their classic thirty-seven "dependable" rhymes. The spelling word wall can be created by stapling a piece of 3" x 5" butcher block paper to the bulletin board. Then attach spelling pattern cards around the border with thumbtacks, so that the cards can be easily removed to use at the meeting area.

Once you decide on a spelling pattern for instruction, remove the corresponding card from the word wall. Then take a 1"x 3" piece of a contrasting color of butcher block paper and tape the card to the top end of a sheet the children will use for their investigation. Next, read one of Wylie and Durrell's short rhymes with the children and have them identify the pattern.

After the pattern is identified, the children can try to come up with other words that have the same spelling pattern. The teacher can write these on the spelling pattern sheet, using a different color marker to highlight the spelling pattern within the word. The children have to add to the list until the sheet is full, which might take two days or more.

After the sheet is full, the completed spelling pattern is attached to the wall.

Spelling in the Classroom

Some of the techniques teachers use to determine the words students need to spell include:

- Lists of misspelled words from student writing

- Lists of theme words

- Lists of words from the content areas

- Word banks

It is important for beginning writers to know that spelling is an important part of the writing process. However, insisting on correct spelling right from the beginning may actually hamper the efforts of beginning writers. In early spelling development, children should be allowed to experiment with words and use invented spelling. Spelling development is something that occurs over time as a developmental process. It does develop in clearly defined stages, which the teacher should take into consideration when planning lessons. Teachers should assess students' spelling knowledge and then plan mini-lessons to the whole class and small groups as they are necessary.

Some of the ways teachers can provide spelling instruction in the context of meaningful reading and writing activities include:

- Shared reading
- Guided reading
- Shared writing
- Guided writing
- Poetry reading using rhyming words with the same spelling patterns

- Reading chants
- Writing lists
- Writing daily news in the classroom
- Writing letters
- Writing invitations

By planning spelling instruction, teachers help children recognize word patterns, help them discern spelling rules and help them develop their own tricks for remembering how to spell words.

By planning spelling instruction, teachers help children recognize word patterns, help them discern spelling rules and help them develop their own tricks for remembering how to spell words. Direct instruction is necessary for students to develop the knowledge they need regarding the morphological structure of words and thus the relationships between words. Students also need to be taught graphophonic relationships to know the relationship between letters and sounds, the probability of letter sequences, and the different letter patterns.

Developing visual methods of recognizing correct spelling is also an aid to helping students learn to spell when they can trace around the shape of a word. This helps them develop a visual memory as to whether or not the word looks as if it is spelled correctly. Memory aids (mnemonics) also facilitate spelling development, such as in the word PAINT—Pat Added Ink Not Tar.

See Wylie and Durrell's 40 phonemes:

http://www.mrs.norris. net/Language/Language/ phonograms.htm

Activities for teaching spelling

Along with direct teaching of spelling, teachers should model the process at all times. By talking about spelling and having students assist in class writing, they will help students develop the awareness that spelling is important. Some activities where teachers can use this approach include:

- Experience charts
- Writing notes to parents
- Writing class poems and stories
- Editing writing with students

For more strategies for teaching spelling:

http://www.readingrockets. org/article/80

Students also need to be encouraged to take risks with spelling. Rather than have students constantly asking how words are spelled, the teacher can use "Have a Go" Sheets. These sheets consist of three columns in which the students write the word as they think it is spelled. Then the student asks the teacher or another student if it is spelled correctly. If it is incorrect, the teacher or student approached will tell the student which letters are in the correct place, and the student will try again. After the third try, the teacher can either tell the student how to spell the word and add this to the list of words the student has to learn or work on the necessary spelling strategy.

Have a Go Sheet

HAVE A GO SHEET		This list belongs to: _____
How I spelled the word in my writing	Have a Go	Teacher or helper writes correct words in this column

Sample Test Question and Rationale

(Rigorous)

1. What is the best strategy to help students alphabetize words?

   A. Have students write random words in alphabetical order

   B. Have students pick a favorite letter in the alphabet

   C. Have students count the number of letters in their name

   D. Have students alphabetize the class names

Answer: D. Have students alphabetize the class names

Students need to use meaningful information in their learning. At a young age students are interested in their names and the names of their classmates. Counting the number of letters in their name (Choice C) is a great math activity, but will not help students with their alphabetizing.

SKILL 2.3 Developing fluency

Techniques for Developing Automaticity

One of the most useful devices for developing automaticity in young students is through the visual pattern provided in the six syllable types.

EXAMPLES OF THE SIX SYLLABLE TYPES	
Not (Closed)	<u>Closed</u> in by a consonant—vowel makes its **short** sound
No (Open)	<u>Ends</u> in a vowel—vowel makes its **long** sound
Note (Silent "E")	<u>Ends</u> in vowel consonant "e"—vowel makes its **long** sound
Nail (Vowel Combination)	<u>Two vowels together</u> make the sound
Bird ("R" Controlled)	<u>Contains</u> a vowel plus R—vowel sound is changed by the r
Table (Consonant "L"-"E")	<u>Applied</u> at the end of a word

These orthographic (letter) patterns signal vowel pronunciation to the reader. Students must become able to apply their knowledge of these patterns to recognize the syllable types and to see these patterns automatically and ultimately, to read words as wholes. The move from decoding letter symbols to identifying recognizable terms, to automatic word recognition is a substantial move toward fluency.

Activities for automaticity

A significant aid for helping students move through this phase was developed by Anna Gillingham when she incorporated the Phonetic Word Cards activity into the Orton-Gillingham lesson plan (Gillingham and Stillman, 1997). This activity involves having the students practice reading words (and some non words) on cards as wholes, beginning with simple syllables and moving systematically through the syllable types to complex syllables and two-syllable words. The words are divided into groups that correspond to the specific sequence of skills being taught.

Prosody

In their article for *Perspectives* (Winter 2002), Pamela Hook and Sandra Jones proposed that teachers can begin to develop awareness of the prosodic features of language by introducing a short three-word sentence with each of the three different words underlined for stress (e.g., *He is sick. He is sick. He is sick.*). The teacher can then model the three sentences while discussing the possible meaning for each variation. The students can practice reading them with different stress until they are fluent. These simple three-word sentences can be modified and expanded to include various verbs, pronouns, and tenses (e.g., *You are sick. I am sick. They are sick.*). This strategy can also be used while increasing the length of phrases and emphasizing the different meanings (e.g., *Get out of bed. Get out of bed. Get out of bed now.*) Teachers can also practice fluency with common phrases that frequently occur in text.

Using prepositional phrases

Prepositional phrases are good syntactic structures for this type of work (e.g., *on the _____, in the _____, over the _____*). Teachers can pair these printed phrases to oral intonation patterns that include variations of rate, intensity, and pitch. Students can infer the intended meaning as the teacher presents different prosodic variations of a sentence. For example, when speakers want to stress a concept they often slow their rate of speech and may speak in a louder voice (e.g., *Joshua, get-out-of-bed-NOW!*). Often, the only text marker for this sentence will be the exclamation point (!) but the speaker's intent will affect the manner in which it is delivered.

Using the alphabet

Practicing oral variations and then mapping the prosodic features onto the text will assist students in making the connection when reading. This strategy can also be used to alert students to the prosodic features present in punctuation marks. In the early stages, using the alphabet helps to focus a student on the punctuation marks without having to deal with meaning. The teacher models for the students and then has them practice the combinations using the correct intonation patterns to fit the punctuation mark (e.g., ABC. DE? FGH! IJKL? or ABCD! EFGHI? KL.).

Using two- or three-word sentences

Teachers can then move to simple two-word or three-word sentences. The sentences are punctuated with a period, question mark and exclamation point and the differences in meaning that occur with each different punctuation mark (e.g., *Chris hops. Chris hops? Chris hops!*) are discussed. It may help students to point out that the printed words convey the fact that someone named Chris is engaged in the physical activity of hopping, but the intonation patterns get their cue from the punctuation mark. The meaning extracted from an encounter with a punctuation mark is dependent upon a reader's prior experiences or background knowledge in order to project an appropriate intonation pattern onto the printed text. Keeping the text static while changing the punctuation marks helps students to attend to prosodic patterns.

Using chunking

Students who read word-for-word may benefit initially from practicing phrasing with the alphabet rather than words since letters do not tax the meaning system. The letters are grouped, an arc is drawn underneath, and students recite the alphabet in chunks (e.g., ABC DE FGH IJK LM NOP QRS TU VW XYZ). Once students understand the concept of phrasing, it is recommended that teachers help students chunk text into syntactic (noun phrases, verb phrases, prepositional phrases) or meaning units until they are proficient themselves. There are no hard and fast rules for chunking, but syntactic units are most commonly used.

Using slashes

For better readers, teachers can mark the phrasal boundaries with slashes for short passages. Eventually, the slashes are used only at the beginning of long passages and then students are asked to continue "phrase reading" even after the marks end. Marking phrases can be done together with students or those on an independent level may divide passages into phrases themselves. Comparisons can be made to clarify reasons for differences in phrasing. Another way to encourage students to focus on phrase meaning and prosody in addition to word identification is to provide tasks that require them to identify or supply a paraphrase of an original statement.

Using rate

A word count is obtained for each reading episode, then mean speed of words per second is computed within each episode and the entire text. Participant miscue and the accuracy rates are then examined.

At some point it is crucial that, just as the nervous, novice bike rider finally relaxes and speeds happily off; so too must the early reader integrate graphophonic cues with semantic and structural ones and move toward fluency. Before this is done, the oral quality of early readers has a stilted beat to it, which of course, does not promote reading engagement and enjoyment.

Using theatrics

The teacher needs to be at his/her most theatrical to model for children the beauties of voice and nuance that are contained in the texts whose print they are tracking so anxiously. Children love nothing more than to mimic their teacher and can do so legitimately and without hesitation if the teacher takes time each day to theatrically recite a poem with them. The poem might be posted on chart paper and be up on the board for a week.

First the teacher can model the fluent and expressive reading of this poem. Then with a pointer, the class can recite it with the teacher. As the week progresses, the class can recite it on their own.

At some point it is crucial that, just as the nervous, novice bike rider finally relaxes and speeds happily off; so too must the early reader integrate graphophonic cues with semantic and structural ones and move toward fluency.

The teacher needs to be at his/her most theatrical to model for children the beauties of voice and nuance that are contained in the texts whose print they are tracking so anxiously.

Sample Test Question and Rationale

(Average)

1. **What pattern in spelling does C-V-C represent?**

    A. Consonant vowel combination

    B. Compare verbs critically

    C. Consonant vowel consonant

    D. Continent vowel component

Answer: C. Consonant vowel consonant

Consonants are all letters that are NOT vowels. When talking about spelling patterns, C stands for consonant and V stands for vowel.

SKILL 2.4 Teaching vocabulary

There are many methods for directly and explicitly teaching words. In fact, the National Reading Panel identified twenty-one methods that have been found effective in research projects. Many emphasize the underlying concept of a word and its connections to other words such as semantic mapping and diagrams that use graphics. The KEYWORD METHOD uses words and illustrations that highlight salient features of meaning. Visualizing or drawing a picture either by the student or by the teacher was found to be effective. Many words cannot be learned in this way, of course, so it should be used as only one method among others. Effective classrooms provide multiple ways for students to learn and interact with words. The panel also found that computer-assisted activities can have a very positive role in the development of vocabulary.

> **KEYWORD METHOD:** uses words and illustrations that highlight salient features of meaning

Context Clues

Children who learn to read on schedule and who are avid readers have been seen to have superior vocabularies compared to other children their age. The reason for this is that in order to understand what they read, they often must determine the meaning for a word based on its context. Children who constantly turn to a dictionary for the meaning of a word they don't know will not have this advantage.

This is an important clue for providing students the kinds of exercises and help they need in order to develop their vocabularies. Learning vocabulary lists is useful, of course, but much less efficient than exercises in determining meaning on the basis of context. It requires an entirely different kind of thinking and learning. Poetry is also useful for developing vocabulary exercises for children, especially rhymed poetry, where the pronunciation of a term may be deduced by what the poet intended for it to rhyme with. In some poems of earlier periods, the teacher may need to intervene because some of the words that would have rhymed when the poem was written do not rhyme in today's English. Even so, this is a good opportunity to help children understand some of the important principles about their constantly changing language.

Crossword puzzles

Another good exercise for developing vocabulary is the crossword puzzle. A child's ability to think in terms of analogy is a step upward toward mature language understanding and use. The teacher may construct crossword puzzles using items from the class such as students' names or the terms from their literature or language lessons.

Sample Test Questions and Rationale

(Rigorous)

1. When is the best time for a teacher to introduce vocabulary words to readers?

    A. Before reading

    B. During reading

    C. After reading

    D. All of the above

    Answer: D. All of the above

    Before reading is not the only time that teachers can introduce vocabulary. Teachers can assign certain words for students to hunt for during reading, and can give them focus vocabulary words to examine after reading.

(Average)

2. Context clues refer to:

    A. Defining new words using the dictionary

    B. Choosing the meaning of words from pre-selected choices

    C. Creating a list of vocabulary from the text

    D. Defining unknown words based on the surrounding text

    Answer: D. Defining unknown words based on the surrounding text

    Context clues are clues given within the text that allow readers to determine the meaning of unknown words. Good readers use this strategy rather than consulting a dictionary while in the middle of reading.

SKILL 2.5 Enhancing comprehension

The point of comprehension instruction is not necessarily to focus just on the text(s) students are using at the very moment of instruction, but rather to help them learn the strategies that they can use independently with any text.

COMMON METHODS OF TEACHING INSTRUCTION	
Summarization	This is where, either in writing or verbally, students go over the main point of the text, along with strategically chosen details that highlight the main point. This is not the same as paraphrasing, which is saying the same thing in different words. Teaching students how to summarize is very important, as it will help them look for the most critical areas in a text and in nonfiction. For example, it will help them distinguish between main arguments and examples. In fiction, it helps students to learn how to focus on the main characters and events and distinguish those from the lesser characters and events.

Table continued on next page

Question Answering	While this tends to be overused in many classrooms, it is still a valid method of teaching students to comprehend. As the name implies, students answer questions regarding a text, either out loud, in small groups, or individually on paper. The best questions are those that require students to think about the text (rather than just find an answer within the text).
Question Generating	This is the opposite of question answering, although students can then be asked to answer their own questions or the questions of their classmates. In general, we want students to constantly question texts as they read. This is important because it causes students to become more critical readers. To teach students to generate questions helps them to learn the types of questions they can ask, and it gets them thinking about the best way to be critical of texts.
Graphic Organizers	Graphic organizers are graphical representations of content within a text. For example, Venn diagrams can be used to highlight the difference between two characters in a novel or two similar political concepts in a social studies textbook. Or, a teacher can use flow-charts with students to talk about the steps in a process (for example, the steps of setting up a science experiment or the chronological events of a story). Semantic organizers are similar in that they graphically display information. The difference, usually, is that semantic organizers focus on words or concepts. For example, a word web can help students make sense of a word by mapping from the central word all the similar and related concepts to that word.
Text Structure	Often in nonfiction, particularly in textbooks and sometimes in fiction, text structures will give important clues to readers about what to look for. Often, students do not know how to make sense of all the types of headings in a textbook and do not realize that, for example, the sidebar story about a character in history is not the main text on a particular page in the history textbook. Teaching students how to interpret text structures gives them tools in which to tackle other similar texts.
Monitoring Comprehension	Students need to be aware of their comprehension, or lack of it, in particular texts. It is important to teach students what to do when text suddenly stops making sense. For example, students can go back and reread the description of a character. Or, they can go back to the table of contents or the first paragraph of a chapter to see where they are headed.
Textual Marking	This is where students interact with the text as they read. For example, armed with Post-it notes, students can insert questions or comments regarding specific sentences or paragraphs within the text. This helps students focus on the importance of the small things, particularly when they are reading larger works (such as novels in high school). It also gives students a reference point on which to go back into the text when they need to review something.
Discussion	Small group or whole class discussion stimulates thoughts about texts and gives students a larger picture of the impact of those texts. For example, teachers can strategically encourage students to discuss concepts related to the text. This helps students learn to consider texts within larger societal and social concepts, or teachers can encourage students to provide personal opinions in discussion. By listening to various students' opinions, this will help all students in a class to see the wide range of possible interpretations and thoughts regarding one text.

Strategies for Monitoring and Facilitating Comprehension

Before reading

Making predictions

One theory or approach to the teaching of reading that gained currency in the late 1960s and the early 1970s was the importance of asking inferential and critical thinking questions of the reader meant to challenge and engage the children in the text. This approach to reading went beyond the literal level of what was stated in the text to an inferential level of using text clues to make predictions and to a critical level of involving the child in evaluating the text.

While asking engaging and thought-provoking questions is still viewed as part of the teaching of reading, it is only viewed currently as a component of the teaching of reading.

PRIOR KNOWLEDGE can be defined as all of an individual's prior experiences, education, and development that precede his or her entrance into a specific learning situation or his or her attempts to comprehend a specific text. Sometimes, prior knowledge can be erroneous or incomplete. Obviously, if there are misconceptions in a child's prior knowledge, these must be corrected so that the child's overall comprehension skills can continue to progress. Even kindergarteners display prior knowledge, which typically includes their accumulated positive and negative experiences both in and out of school. Prior knowledge activities and opportunities might range from traveling with family, watching television, visiting museums, and visiting libraries to staying in hospitals, visiting prisons, and surviving poverty.

Literary response skills are dependent on prior knowledge, schemata, and background. SCHEMATA (the plural of schema) are those structures that represent generic concepts stored in our memories. Effective comprehenders of text, whether they are adults or children, use both their schemata and prior knowledge plus the ideas from the printed text for reading comprehension, and graphic organizers help organize this information.

During reading

Graphic organizers

Graphic organizers solidify, in a chart format, a visual relationship among various reading and writing ideas. The content of a graphic organizer may include:

- Sequence
- Timelines
- Character traits

> **PRIOR KNOWLEDGE:** all of an individual's prior experiences, education, and development that precede his or her entrance into a specific learning situation or his or her attempts to comprehend a specific text

> **SCHEMATA:** (the plural of schema) those structures that represent generic concepts stored in our memories

> *Effective comprehenders of text, whether they are adults or children, use both their schemata and prior knowledge plus the ideas from the printed text for reading comprehension, and graphic organizers help organize this information.*

- Fact and opinion

- Main idea and details

- Differences and likenesses (generally done using a Venn diagram of interlocking circles, a KWL Chart, etc.)

These charts and formats are essential for providing scaffolding for instruction through activating pertinent prior knowledge.

KWL strategy

KWL charts are exceptionally useful for reading comprehension, as they outline what children KNOW, what they WANT to know, and what they've LEARNED after reading. Students are asked to activate prior knowledge about a topic and further develop their knowledge about a topic using this organizer. Teachers often opt to display and maintain KWL charts throughout a text to continually record pertinent information about students' reading.

SPIDER KWL		
What I know	**What I want to know**	**What I have learned**
•	•	•
•	•	•
•	•	•
The most interesting fact I learned was:		
_____		
_____		

This strategy involves the children in actually gaining experience in note taking and in having a concrete record of new data and information gleaned from the passage.

When the teacher first introduces the KWL strategy, the children should be allowed sufficient time to brainstorm what they all actually know about the topic. The children should have a three-columned KWL worksheet template for their journals, and there should be a chart to record the responses from class or group discussion. The children can write under each column in their own journal; they should also help the teacher with notations on the chart. This strategy involves the children in actually gaining experience in note taking and in having a concrete record of new data and information gleaned from the passage.

Depending on the grade level of the participating children, the teacher may also want to channel them into considering categories of information they hope to find out from the expository passage. For instance, they may be reading a book on animals to find out more about the animals' habitats during the winter or about the animals' mating habits.

When children are working on the middle (the *what I want to know* section of their KWL strategy sheet), the teacher may want to give them a chance to share what they would like to learn further about the topic and help them to express it in question format.

KWL can even be introduced as early as second grade with extensive teacher discussion support. It not only serves to support the child's comprehension of a particular expository text, but it also models for children a format for note taking. Additionally, when the teacher wants to introduce report writing, the KWL format provides excellent outlines and question introductions for at least three paragraphs of a report.

Cooper (2004) recommends this strategy for use with thematic units and with reading chapters in required science, social studies, or health textbooks. In addition to its usefulness with thematic unit study, KWL is wonderful for providing the teacher with a concrete format to assess how well children have absorbed pertinent new knowledge within the passage (by looking at the third L section). Ultimately it is hoped that students will learn to use this strategy, not only under explicit teacher direction with templates of KWL sheets, but also on their own by informally writing questions they want to find out about in their journals and then going back to their own questions and answering them after the reading.

Note taking

Older children take notes in their reading journals, while younger children and those more in need of explicit teacher support contribute their ideas and responses as part of the discussion in class. Their responses can be recorded on an experiential chart.

After reading

Connecting texts

The concept of readiness is generally regarded as a developmentally based phenomenon. Various abilities, whether cognitive, affective, or psychomotor, are perceived to be dependent upon the mastery or development of certain prerequisite skills or abilities. Readiness, then, implies that the necessary prior knowledge, experience, and readiness prerequisites should be present before the child engages in the new task.

Readiness for subject area learning is dependent not only on prior knowledge but also on affective factors such as interest, motivation, and attitude. These factors are often more influential on student learning than the preexisting cognitive base.

Readiness for subject area learning is dependent not only on prior knowledge but also on affective factors such as interest, motivation, and attitude.

When texts relate to a student's life, to other reading materials, or to additional areas of study, they become more meaningful and relevant to students' learning. Students enjoy seeing reading material that they can connect to on a deeper level.

Discussing the text

Discussion is an activity in which the children concentrate on a particular text. Among the prompts, the teacher-coach might suggest that the children focus on words of interest they encountered in the text. These can also be words that they heard if the text was read aloud. Children can be asked to share something funny or upsetting or unusual about the words they have read. Through this focus on children's responses to words as the center of the discussion circle, peers become more interested in word study.

Using illustrations in a text

Illustrations can be key supports for emergent and early readers. Teachers should not only use wordless stories (books which tell their narratives through pictures alone), but can also make targeted use of Big Books for read-alouds, so that young children become habituated in the use of illustrations as an important component for constructing meaning. The teacher should model for the child how to reference an illustration for help in identifying a word in the text the child does not recognize.

Of course, children can also go on a picture walk with the teacher as part of a mini-lesson or guided reading and anticipate the story (narrative) using the pictures alone to construct meaning.

Sample Test Questions and Rationale

(Rigorous)

1. **A student reads the sentence, "The boy saw a worm in the ground," and says "The boy saw a worm in the grass." What might you say to the student as a paraprofessional?**

   A. "You said grass. Look at this word and tell me why it can't be grass."

   B. "Look at this word again [pointing to ground]. What sound does this word begin with?

   C. "What vowels do you see in this word? [pointing to ground]"

   D. "Where is another place you might see a worm?"

Answer: A. "You said grass. Look at this word and tell me why it can't be grass."

Although D is another good thing to ask the student, A is better. This option draws the student's attention to the word "ground" and makes them analyze the letter sound relationship.

Sample Test Questions and Rationale (cont.)

(Rigorous)

2. According to this Venn Diagram, what fits within all three categories?

Sample Venn Diagram

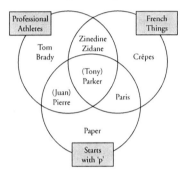

A. Tony Parker

B. Zinedine Zidane

C. Juan Pierre

D. Paris

Answer: A. Tony Parker

Tony Parker is in the middle of three overlapping circles and therefore, meets all three criteria; French Things, Professional Athletes; Starts with "P".

(Rigorous)

3. According to the Venn Diagram, what is true about "Paris"?

A. It starts with "P"

B. It is a French Thing

C. It is the name of a professional athlete

D. It starts with "P", and is a French Thing

Answer: D. It starts with "P", and is a French Thing

The Venn Diagram has three categories represented by three different circles. Paris is in two circles; French Things and Starts with "P".

Sample Test Questions and Rationale (cont.)

(Rigorous)

4. **Before reading a story, what should students use to make predictions?**

   A. The first sentence in the book

   B. The cover and other illustrations in the story

   C. Information from other students

   D. The length of a book or story

   Answer: B. The cover and other illustrations in the story

   Students need to get their minds ready to read and therefore must do a picture walk through a book looking at the cover illustration and other illustrations in the story.

(Rigorous)

5. **When should a KWL chart be filled out?**

   A. After reading only

   B. Before and during reading

   C. During reading only

   D. Before and after reading

   Answer: D. Before and after reading

   The K stands for "What we KNOW," the W stands for "What we WANT to know," L stands for "What we want to LEARN." A KWL chart is filled in before we read and after we read. It may also be completed during reading to monitor reading.

SKILL 2.6 **Methods of teaching writing**

The Writing Process

Learning to write is generally a sequential process. Research confirms that children develop spelling strategies in predictable stages. There is a continuous growth in writing, but the children vary in the development of these stages. A child's writing may show evidence of more than one stage. Children may even skip levels on their way to developing writing competency.

Stage progression

Children progress as writers from one phase to the next, with one set of skills building on the skills acquired earlier. Writing, however, combines many skills, and relies on development in many areas not specific to writing. A child's fine motor control and vocabulary, for example, must improve in order for writing to progress normally.

Cognitive theories of understanding state that learning only takes place when the new learning is based upon previous learning. Struggling students may often lack essential background knowledge necessary to successfully complete a task or use a strategy.

Task analysis

The best way to identify the basic terms and skills necessary for the strategy is to do a task analysis. The task analysis will help teachers to determine if students possess the prerequisite skills necessary to advance to the next stage of writing. After the task analysis is complete, there are many ways that teachers can check students' skills. These include observing student performance, using curriculum-based measures, or simply asking students.

Writing is a process that flows gradually. As you give your students time to explore and experiment with writing, you will begin to see evidence of growth. Since writing is a process and stages are connected, students may show evidence of more than one stage in a single piece of writing.

DEVELOPING EMERGENT WRITING SKILLS	
Assessment	The first step in developing young writers' skills is to know where they are in developmental writing stages. Though skills are overlapping, at any one time a child will fall predominately into one or more skill areas. While the child may be an emergent writer in content, the same child may be a role player writer in penmanship. Teachers need to be aware of where each student falls at any one time in each area of writing. The best means of assessment are writing samples and/or portfolios and journals. Assessment should be ongoing, as a child's writing stage is not static.
Teaching Strategies	Invented spelling is an early writing skill. Teachers should encourage and teach the child invented spelling. The child's name is usually the first meaningful writing the child does. The teacher should focus intensely on teaching the child to write his/her name. Teachers can develop an interest in writing in a young child by guiding the student through meaningful writing tasks such as letters home to parents, thank you notes, and journal writing to share experiences.
Environment	Teachers should set up their classroom environment to encourage meaningful writing, such as having a sign-in sheet, providing pencils and pads for play, for writing traffic tickets, menus, taking restaurant orders, etc. Meaningful writing opportunities should also be provided such as journaling and writing centers, observation journals in science centers, and providing reference charts for alphabet and pattern sentences. Outside writing opportunities should be encouraged with sidewalk chalk, nature journals, and signing library books in and out.
Materials	Teachers should provide a variety of writing materials to inspire all students. Markers and construction paper provide inspiration to some students, while others prefer paints. Sponges cut into letter shapes, stamps, stencils, and hole punchers are some writing materials that can be made available. Shaving cream, sand, jello, rice, and other manipulative materials should be available for those students who need or enjoy the tactile stimulation for writing.

Stages of the Writing Process

Writing is a recursive process. As students engage in the various stages of writing, they develop and improve not only their writing skills, but their thinking skills as well. Students must understand that writing is a process and typically involves many steps when writing quality work. No matter the level of writer, students should be experienced in the following stages of the writing process.

Prewriting

Students gather ideas before writing. PREWRITING may include clustering, listing, brainstorming, mapping, free writing, and charting. Providing many ways for a student to develop ideas on a topic will increase his/her chances for success.

Remind students that as they prewrite, they need to consider their audience.

Prewriting strategies assist students in a variety of ways. Listed below are the most common prewriting strategies students can use to explore, plan and write on a topic. It is important to remember when teaching these strategies that not all prewriting must eventually produce a finished piece of writing. In fact, in the initial lesson of teaching prewriting strategies, it might be more effective to have students practice prewriting strategies without the pressure of having to write a finished product.

- Keep an idea book so that they can jot down ideas that come to mind.

- Write in a daily journal.

- Write down whatever comes to mind; this is called free writing. Students do not stop to make corrections or interrupt the flow of ideas. A variation of this technique is focused free writing—writing on a specific topic—to prepare for an essay.

- Make a list of all ideas connected with their topic; this is called brainstorming. Make sure students know that this technique works best when they let their minds work freely. After completing the list, students should analyze the list to see if a pattern or way to group the ideas emerges.

- Ask the questions Who? What? When? Where? and How? Help the writer approach a topic from several perspectives.

- Create a visual map on paper to gather ideas. Cluster circles and lines to show connections between ideas. Students should try to identify the relationships that exist between their ideas. If they cannot see the relationships, have them pair up, exchange papers and have their partners look for some related ideas.

- Observe details of sight, hearing, taste, touch, and taste.
- Visualize by making mental images of something and write down the details in a list.

After students have practiced each of these prewriting strategies, ask them to pick out the ones they prefer and ask them to discuss how they might use the techniques to help them with future writing assignments. It is important to remember that they can use more than one prewriting strategy at a time. Also they may find that different writing situations may suggest certain techniques.

Drafting

Students compose the first draft. Students should follow their notes/writing plan from the prewriting stage.

Revision and editing

Revision

Revise comes from the Latin word *revidere*, meaning "to see again." REVISION is probably the most important step for the writer in the writing process. Here, students examine their work and make changes in wording, details, and ideas. So many times, students write a draft and then feel they're done. On the contrary, students must be encouraged to develop, change, and enhance their writing as they go, as well as once they've completed a draft.

When discussing revision, begin with discussing the definition of revise. Also, state that all writing must be revised to improve it. After students have revised their writing, it is time for the final editing and proofreading.

Editing

Both teachers and students should be aware of the difference between these two writing processes. Revising typically entails making substantial changes to a written draft, and it is during this process that the look, idea, and feel of a draft may be altered, sometimes significantly. Like revising, EDITING continues to make changes to a draft. However the changes made during the editing process do more to enhance the ideas in the draft, rather than change or alter them. Finally, PROOFREADING is the stage where grammatical and technical errors are addressed.

Effective teachers realize that revision and editing go hand-in-hand and students often move back and forth between these stages during the course of one written work. Also, these stages must be practiced in small groups, pairs and/or

REVISION: a stage of the writing process where students examine their work and make changes in wording, details, and ideas

EDITING: a stage of the writing process where students continue to make changes to a draft, enhancing the ideas rather than altering or changing them

PROOFREADING: a stage of the writing process where grammatical and technical errors are addressed individually. Students must learn to analyze and improve their own work as well as the works of their peers. Some methods to use include:

1. Students, working in pairs, analyze sentences for variety

2. Students work in pairs or groups to ask questions about unclear areas in the writing or to help students add details, information, etc.

3. Students perform final edit

Students need to be trained to become effective at proofreading, revising, and editing strategies. Begin by training them using both desk-side and scheduled conferences. Listed below are some strategies to use to guide students through the final stages of the writing process.

• Provide some guide sheets or forms for students to use during peer responses

• Allow students to work in pairs and limit the agenda

• Model the use of the guide sheet or form for the entire class

• Give students a time limit or number of written pieces to be completed in a specific amount of time

• Have the students read their partners' papers and ask at least three who, what, when, why, how questions; the students answer the questions and use them as a place to begin discussing the piece

• At this point in the writing process, a mini-lesson that focuses on some of the problems your students are having would be appropriate

To help students revise, provide students with a series of questions that will assist them in revising their writing:

• Do the details give a clear picture? Add details that appeal to more than just the sense of sight.

• How effectively are the details organized? Reorder the details if it is needed.

• Are the thoughts and feelings of the writer included? Add personal thoughts and feelings about the subject.

Grammar needs to be taught in the context of the students' own work. Listed below is a series of classroom practices that encourage meaningful context-based grammar instruction, combined with occasional mini-lessons and other language strategies that can be used on a daily basis.

Grammar needs to be taught in the context of the students' own work.

• Connect grammar with the student's own writing while emphasizing grammar as a significant aspect of effective writing

• Emphasize the importance of editing and proofreading as an essential part of classroom activities

- Provide students with an opportunity to practice editing and proofreading cooperatively

- Give instruction in the form of fifteen to twenty minute mini-lessons

- Emphasize the sound of punctuation by connecting it to pitch, stress, and pause

- Involve students in all facets of language learning including reading, writing, listening, speaking and thinking; good use of language comes from exploring all forms of it on a regular basis

There are a number of approaches that involve grammar instruction in the context of the writing.

APPROACHES TO GRAMMAR INSTRUCTION	
Sentence Combining	Try to use the student's own writing as much as possible. The theory behind combining ideas and the correct punctuation should be emphasized.
Sentence and Paragraph Modeling	Provide students with the opportunity to practice imitating the style and syntax of professional writers.
Sentence Transforming	Give students an opportunity to change sentences from one form to another, i.e., from passive to active, inverting the sentence order, changing forms of the words used.
Daily Language Practice	Introduce or clarify common errors using daily language activities. Use actual student examples whenever possible. Correct and discuss the problems with grammar and usage.

Proofreading

Students proofread the draft for punctuation and mechanical errors. There are a few key points to remember when helping students learn to edit and proofread their work.

- It is crucial that students are not taught grammar in isolation, but in context of the writing process

- Ask students to read their writing and check for specific errors such as whether or not every sentence starts with a capital letter and has the correct punctuation at the end

- Provide students with a proofreading checklist to guide them as they edit their work

Publishing

PUBLISHING: a stage in the writing process where students may have their work displayed on a bulletin board, read aloud in class, or printed in a literary magazine or school anthology

PUBLISHING is the last stage of the process. Students may have their work displayed on a bulletin board, read aloud in class, or printed in a literary magazine or school anthology.

It is important to realize that these steps are recursive, as a student engages in each aspect of the writing process. The students may begin with prewriting, then write, revise, write, revise, edit, and publish. They do not engage in this process in a lockstep manner; it is more circular.

Sample Test Questions and Rationale

(Average)

1. **When students just sit down and write about a topic, writing everything that comes to mind, this is called:**

   A. Brainstorming

   B. Outlining

   C. Free writing

   D. Drafting

   Answer: C. Free writing

   Free writing is a great way to get over writer's block. Students just write about whatever comes to mind for a few minutes. This is a great prewriting strategy.

(Rigorous)

2. **What is the difference between drafting and revising?**

   A. Nothing—they are the same thing

   B. Drafting is the first copy and revising is the final copy

   C. Drafting is the first copy and revising corrects spelling errors, etc.

   D. Drafting is the first copy and revising improves the craft of writing

   Answer: D. Drafting is the first copy and revising improves the craft of writing

   Drafting is when students get their ideas down on paper in a semi-coherent piece. Next, students go back and revise their writing to make it better by improving the "craft" of writing.

(Average)

3. **What is the purpose of proofreading?**

   A. To publish a piece of writing for presentation

   B. To rewrite it in one's neatest handwriting

   C. To spell check it in a word processing program

   D. To check it for spelling, correct punctuation, and grammar

   Answer: D. To check it for spelling, correct punctuation, and grammar

   Proofreading is the last step in writing before the piece is ready to be published. This is where the writer checks the spelling, punctuation, and grammar usage.

SKILL 2.7 Theories of language acquisition

Learning Approach

Early theories of language development were formulated from learning theory research. The assumption was that language development evolved from learning the rules of language structures and applying them through imitation and reinforcement. The LEARNING APPROACH also assumed that linguistic, cognitive, and social developments were independent of each other. Thus, children were expected to learn language from patterning after adults who spoke and wrote Standard English. No allowance was made for communication through child jargon, idiomatic expressions, or grammatical and mechanical errors resulting from too strict adherence to the rules of inflection (*childs* instead of *children*) or conjugation (*runned* instead of *ran*). No association was made between physical and operational development and language mastery.

> **LEARNING APPROACH:** a language acquisition theory that assumed that language development evolved from learning the rules of language structures and applying them through imitation and reinforcement

Linguistic Approach

Studies spearheaded by Noam Chomsky in the 1950s formulated the theory that language ability is innate and develops through natural human maturation as environmental stimuli trigger the acquisition of syntactical structures appropriate to each exposure level. This is known as the LINGUISTIC APPROACH. The assumption of a hierarchy of syntax downplayed the significance of semantics. Because of the complexity of syntax and the relative speed with which children acquire language, linguists attributed language development to biological rather than cognitive or social influences.

> **LINGUISTIC APPROACH:** a language acquisition theory that states that language ability is innate and develops through natural human maturation as environmental stimuli trigger the acquisition of syntactical structures appropriate to each exposure level

Cognitive Approach

Researchers in the 1970s proposed that language knowledge derives from both syntactic and semantic structures. Drawing on the studies of Piaget and other cognitive learning theorists, supporters of the COGNITIVE APPROACH maintained that children acquire knowledge of linguistic structures after they have acquired the cognitive structures necessary to process language.

For example, joining words for specific meaning necessitates sensory motor intelligence. The child must be able to coordinate movement and recognize objects before he or she can identify words to name the objects or word groups to describe the actions of these objects. Children must have developed the mental abilities for organizing concepts as well as performing concrete operations, predicting outcomes, and theorizing before they can assimilate and verbalize complex sentence structures, choose vocabulary for particular nuances of meaning, and examine semantic structures for tone and manipulative effect.

> **COGNITIVE APPROACH:** a language acquisition theory that states that children acquire knowledge of linguistic structures after they have acquired the cognitive structures necessary to process language

Sociocognitive Approach

Other theorists in the 1970s proposed that language development results from sociolinguistic competence. This theory finds that the different aspects of linguistic, cognitive, and social knowledge are interactive elements of total human development. Emphasis on verbal communication as the medium for language expression resulted in the inclusion of speech activities in most language arts curricula.

SOCIOCOGNITIVE APPROACH: a language acquisition theory that states that the different aspects of linguistic, cognitive, and social knowledge are interactive elements of total human development

Unlike previous approaches, the SOCIOCOGNITIVE APPROACH allows that determining the appropriateness of language in given situations for specific listeners is as important as understanding semantic and syntactic structures. By engaging in conversation, children at all stages of development have opportunities to test their language skills, receive feedback, and make modifications. As a social activity, conversation is as structured by social order as grammar is structured by the rules of syntax. Conversation satisfies the learner's need to be heard, to be understood, and to influence others. Thus, his or her choices of vocabulary, tone, and content are dictated by the ability to assess the linguistic knowledge of his or her listeners. The learner is constantly applying cognitive skills in using language as a form of social interaction. Although the capacity to acquire language is inborn, a child would not pass beyond grunts and gestures without an environment in which to practice language.

Of course, the varying degrees of environmental stimuli to which children are exposed at all age levels create a slower or faster development of language. Some children are prepared to articulate concepts and recognize symbolism by the time they enter fifth grade, either because they have been exposed to challenging reading and conversations with well-spoken adults at home, or in their social groups. Others are still trying to master the sight recognition skills and are not yet ready to combine words in complex patterns.

Second Language Learners

Any student who is not in an environment where English phonology operates may have difficulty perceiving and demonstrating the differences between English language phonemes.

Students who are raised in homes where English is not the first language and/or where standard English is not spoken, may have difficulty with hearing the difference between similar sounding words like "send" and "sent." Any student who is not in an environment where English phonology operates may have difficulty perceiving and demonstrating the differences between English language phonemes. If students cannot hear the difference between words that sound the same like "grow" and "glow," they will be confused when these words appear in a print context. This confusion will of course, sadly, impact their comprehension.

Considerations for teaching to English Language Learners (ELL) include recognition by the teacher that what works for the English language speaking student from an English language speaking family, does not necessarily work in other languages.

Research recommends that ELL students learn to read initially in their first language. It has been found that a priority for ELL should be learning to speak English before being taught to read English. Research supports oral language development, since it lays the foundation for phonological awareness.

COMPETENCY 3
READING AND LANGUAGE ARTS ASSESSMENT

**SKILL Assessing phonemic awareness
3.1**

Phonemic awareness is a critical skill for beginning readers. PHONEMIC AWARE-NESS involves the understanding that language is made up of sounds and that these sounds can be manipulated to make different words. Often, phonemic awareness skills are described as skills that can be demonstrated in the dark. They are described this way because there is no visual component to them. They are in fact, all oral and auditory in nature.

PHONEMIC AWARENESS: involves the understanding that language is made up of sounds and that these sounds can be manipulated to make different words

Different Phonemic Awareness Skills

Rhyming
The assessment of phonemic awareness skills begins with very young children, even preschool-aged children. One of the earliest phonemic awareness skills is rhyming. Rhyming involves the understanding that words sound the same (cat and hat rhyme but cat and dog do not rhyme because they do not have the same ending sound). To assess this skill teachers use multiple methods. One method is to present the child with two words and have the child identify with a yes or no whether they rhyme. Another method of assessing rhyming skills is to present the child with a word and have him/her produce a word that rhymes with the word presented.

The assessment of phonemic awareness skills begins with very young children, even preschool-aged children.

Following rhyming in the hierarchy of phonemic awareness skills would be segmenting words into syllables (to-mor-row), onset and rhyme (/c/ /at/), or individual sounds (/d/ /o/ /g/). Teachers assess these skills by asking the students to orally segment to the level they want presented words.

Beginning word sounds

Another phonemic awareness skill involves beginning sounds of words. In this skill, teachers can show a picture or say a word and have the students identify the sound that is said at the beginning of the word/picture. For example, the word fish begins with the sound /f/. This skill can become more complicated when teachers ask the students to make substitutions or deletions of beginning sounds. For example, change the /f/ sound in fish to a /d/ and what new word do you have? The answer would be dish. This is an example of a way to assess the substitution of beginning sounds. The same can be done for deletion. For example, what do you have left if you remove the /d/ sound from drug? The answer would be rug.

Substitutions and deletions are more complex skills within the realm of phonemic awareness. They require the students to manipulate sounds within words and require higher level thinking about phonemic awareness activities. In complexity, it is typically easier for students to make substitutions before they are able to make deletions. Additionally, it is usually less complicated for students to make substitutions and deletions at the beginning or end of a word before they are able to demonstrate this skill in the middle of a word.

The assessment of phonemic awareness skills is almost always an individual oral task. It can be completed in a short period of time and requires no materials other than a record sheet for the teacher.

How to Assess Phonemic Awareness

In conclusion, the assessment of phonemic awareness skills is almost always an individual oral task. It can be completed in a short period of time and requires no materials other than a record sheet for the teacher. Students with articulation difficulties might need accommodations or support from a speech and language professional in order to have their phonemic awareness skills adequately measured.

SKILL 3.2 **Assessing phonics skills**

PHONICS: the connection between the sounds of language and the letters

PHONICS is the connection between the sounds of language and the letters. In contrast to phonemic awareness, phonics requires the student to be able to recognize the sound and match it to the correct letter or group of letters that make that sound. Phonics skills help students to be able to sound out unknown words using the sound symbol correspondence.

Phonics Skills

Phonics skills begin with direct sound to one letter correspondence. For example, recognizing that the sound /d/ is made by the letter d and applying that to reading opportunities. Teachers can assess these skills by having the students write the letters that specific sounds make. Another method for assessing this type of skill would be to show the students pictures and have the students write the first letter of the picture or see if the students are able to write all of the sounds they hear in a word.

Beginning readers and writers will often write words with incorrect spellings because in many English words not all letters needed to spell a word correctly produce a sound that can be heard in the word. For example, the word "team" has four letters to spell it correctly, but only three sounds are heard.

How to assess phonics skills

Assessment of phonics skills can also be completed by watching how students use the skills in the context of reading words in stories. Teachers can take informal notes as to the sounds the student is applying correctly and those that they are not applying correctly to help plan future instruction. This type of formative assessment is critical to help students make continuous progress with their reading skills.

In addition to the informal process of assessing students' phonics use, more formalized approaches can be used. This might be a test with multiple choice questions (i.e., which of the following words is spelled correctly: cat or kat?; which two letters combine to make the long *a* sound? Ay, ao, ab, etc.) or pictures where students are required to label the specific letters that make the sounds of the picture.

Any phonics assessment needs to combine the sounds that make up words with the letters that are used to represent those sounds. Phonics assessments do not need to be done individually, but certainly can be. Teachers can find many phonics assessments available through commercial companies or Internet sources, or they can create their own assessments specific to the goals and objectives they are teaching their students. Whether formal or informal, phonics skills are important skills for teachers and students alike to consider as a regular component of beginning reading instruction.

Any phonics assessment needs to combine the sounds that make up words with the letters that are used to represent those sounds.

Sample Test Question and Rationale

(Average)

1. **A student is reading and gets stuck on the word *sure*. All of the following are good ways to help the student decode the word EXCEPT:**

    A. Have the student sound it out

    B. Have the student skip the word and come back to it later

    C. Tell the student *is* rhymes with *lure*

    D. Tell the student that *ur* makes the *er* sound

Answer: A. Have the student sound it out

Sounding out the word won't work for this particular word because normally /*sh*/ makes the "sh" sound, and *u-e* normally makes a long *e* sound.

SKILL 3.3 **Assessing fluency**

The best way to test for fluency is to have a student read something out loud, preferably a few sentences in a row. Most students just learning to read are probably not fluent right away; with practice, they will increase their fluency. Even though fluency is not the same as COMPREHENSION, it is said that fluency is a good predictor of comprehension. Think about it: if a student is focusing too much on sounding out each word, he or she is not going to be paying attention to the meaning.

Determining Reading Rate

The simplest means of determining a student's reading rate is to have the student read aloud from a prescribed passage that is at the appropriate reading level for age and grade and contains a specified number of words. The passage should not be too familiar for the student (some will try to memorize or "work out" difficult bits ahead of time) and should not contain more words than can be read comfortably and accurately by a normal reader in one or two minutes. Count only the words *correctly* pronounced on the first reading, and divide this word count into the elapsed time to determine the student's reading rate. To determine the student's standing and progress, compare this rate with the norm for the class and the average for all students who read fluently at that specific age/grade level.

The following general guidelines can be applied for reading lists of words with a speed drill and a one-minute timing:

APPROXIMATE WORDS PER MINUTE BY GRADE	
30 Correct WPM	First- and second-grade children
40 Correct WPM	Third-grade children
60 Correct WPM	Mid-third-grade
80 Correct WPM	Fourth grade and higher

Accuracy

One way to evaluate reading fluency is to look at student accuracy, and one way to do this is to record running records of students during oral reading. Calculating the reading level lets you know if the book is at the level from which the child can read it independently or comfortably with guidance or if the book is at a level where reading it frustrates the child.

As part of the informal assessment of primary grade reading, it is important to record the child's word insertions, omissions, requests for help, and attempts to get the word. In informal assessment the rate of accuracy can be estimated from the ratio of errors to total words read.

The results of running record informal assessments can be used for teaching based on text accuracy, by using the following table:

As part of the informal assessment of primary grade reading, it is important to record the child's word insertions, omissions, requests for help, and attempts to get the word.

ACCURACY RATES AND READING ACTIVITIES	
95–100 Percent Correct	The child is ready for independent reading
92–97 Percent Correct	The child is ready for guided reading
Below 92 Percent Correct	The child needs a read-aloud or shared reading activity

Independent, Instructional, and Frustration Reading Levels

Instructional reading is generally judged to be at the 95 percent accuracy level although Taberski places it at between 92 and 97 percent. Taberski tries to enhance the independent reading levels by making sure that readers on the instructional reading levels read a variety of genres and have a range of available and interesting books with a particular genre to read.

Taberski's availability for reading conferences helps her to both assess first hand her children's frustration levels and to model ongoing teacher/reader book conversations by scheduling child-initiated reading conferences where she personally replenishes their book bags.

In order to allay children's frustration levels in their reading and to foster their independent reading, it is important to some children that the teacher personally take time out to hear them read aloud and to check for fluency and expression.

In order to allay children's frustration levels in their reading and to foster their independent reading, it is important to some children that the teacher personally take time out to hear them read aloud and to check for fluency and expression. Children's frustration level can be immeasurably lessened if they are explicitly told by the teacher after they have read aloud that they need to read without pointing and that they should try chunking words into phrases that mimic their natural speech.

Assessment of the reading development of individual students

Using pictures and illustrations

For young readers who are from ELL backgrounds, even if they have been born in the United States, the use of pictures validates their story-authoring and story-telling skills and provides them with access and equity to the literary discussion and book talk of their native, English-speaking peers. These children can also demonstrate their story-telling abilities by drawing sequels or prequels to the story detailed in the illustrations alone. They might even be given the opportunity to share the story aloud in their native language or to comment on the illustrations in their native language.

Since many stories today are recorded in two or even three languages at once, discussing story events or analyzing pictures in a different native language is a beneficial practice.

Use of pictures and illustrations can also help the K-3 educator assess the capabilities of children who are struggling readers because they are children whose learning strength is spatial.

Use of pictures and illustrations can also help the K–3 educator assess the capabilities of children who are struggling readers because they are children whose learning strength is spatial. Through targeted questions about how the pictures would change if different plot twists occurred or how the child might transform the story through changing the illustrations, the teacher can begin to assess struggling reader deficits and strengths.

Using recorded readings

Children from ELL backgrounds can benefit from listening to a recorded tape version of a particular story with which they can read along. This gives them another opportunity to "hear" the story correctly pronounced and presented and to begin to internalize its language structures. In the absence of taped versions of some key stories or texts, the teacher may want to make sound recordings.

Highly proficient readers can also be involved in creating these literature recordings for use with ELL peers or younger peers. This, of course, develops oral language proficiency, but also introduces these skilled readers into the intricacies of supporting ELL English language reading instruction. When they actually see their tapes being used by children they will be tremendously gratified.

Assessing Reading Errors

Reading errors or miscues can be classified into one of nine categories. Categorizing the errors helps the teacher determine the appropriate intervention.

CATEGORIES OF READING ERRORS	
Dialect Variation	Pronunciation difference due to dialect, i.e., caw for car
Intonation Shift or Prosody	Stress or emphasis changes meaning, i.e., The girl WAS in the house vs. The GIRL was in the house
Graphic Similarity	Word looks similar to correct one, i.e., horse for house
Sound Similarity	i.e., cook for look
Grammatical Similarity	i.e., *the blue book* is read as *the red book*
Syntactic Acceptability	Same as grammatical similarity
Semantic Acceptability	Meaning is the same, i.e., child is read as baby
Meaning Change	i.e., he rode the horse read as he wrote the horse
Self-Correction with Semantic Acceptability	Self-corrects based on meaning, i.e., as in example above, reader would change *wrote* to rode because it doesn't make sense otherwise

If the miscues are due to orthographic mistakes, the teacher should stress phonics instruction. If miscues are due to semantic mistakes, the teacher should teach the child to read for meaning. Syntactic miscues means the teacher needs to address grammar, such as parts of speech and sentence structure.

Sample Test Questions and Rationale

(Average)

1. A teacher has letter tiles and she distributes some to students so they can participate in a making and breaking words activity. This activity is especially helpful in supporting which phase of reading?

   A. Orthographic phase

   B. Analyzing phase

   C. Logographic phase

   D. Emergent reader phase

   Answer: A. Orthographic phase

   During the orthographic phase, students are able to use what they know about spelling patterns and letter relationships to help them with what they don't know.

(Rigorous)

2. When a teacher refers to one-to-one corresponding in reading what is she referring to?

   A. One-to-one reading conferences with students

   B. One-to-one letter sound relationship in spelling

   C. One-to-one reading/pointing of a word to what is on the page

   D. One-to-one matching of students to an appropriate text

   Answer: C. One-to-one reading/pointing of a word to what is on the page

   When students read they move from left to right and match each spoken word to a word that appears on the page.

SKILL 3.4 Assessing vocabulary

Vocabulary Self-Collection

VOCABULARY SELF-COLLECTION: a student-centered strategy in which children, even from grade two, take responsibility for their vocabulary learning

The strategy of VOCABULARY SELF-COLLECTION is one in which children, even from grade 2, take responsibility for their learning. It is also by definition, a student-centered strategy, which demonstrates student ownership of their chosen vocabulary. It provides the teacher with built-in assessment information as well.

This strategy is one that can be introduced by the teacher early in the year, perhaps even the first day or week. The format for self-collection can then be started by the children. It may take the form of a journal with photocopied template pages. It can be continued throughout the year.

Activity for vocabulary self-collection

To start, ask the children to read a required text or story. Invite them to select one word for the class to study from this text or story. The children can work individually, in teams, or in small groups. The teacher can also do the self-collecting so that this becomes the joint effort of the class community of literate readers. Tell the children that they should select words that particularly interest them or are unique in some way.

After the children have had time to make their selections and to reflect on them, make certain that they have time to share them with their peers as a whole class. When each child shares the word he/she has selected, have them provide a definition for the word. Each word that is given should be listed on a large experiential chart or even in a big book format, if that is age and grade appropriate. The teacher should also share the word he/she selected and provide a definition. The teacher's definition and sharing should be somewhere in the middle of the children's recitations.

The dictionary should be used to verify the definitions. When all the definitions have been checked, a final list of child-selected and teacher-selected words should be made.

Once this final list has been compiled, the children can choose to record all or part of the list in their word journals. Some students may record only those words they find interesting. It is up to the teacher at the onset of the vocabulary self-collection activity to decide whether the children have to record all the words on the final list or can eliminate some. The decision made at the beginning by the teacher must be adhered to throughout the year.

Adapting this activity for higher levels
To further enhance this strategy, children, particularly those in grades 3 and beyond, can be encouraged to use their collected words as part of their writings or to record and clip these words as they appear in newspaper stories or online. This type of additional recording demonstrates that the child has truly incorporated the word into his/her reading and writing. It also habituates children to be lifelong readers, writers, and researchers.

One of the nice things about this simple but versatile strategy is that it works equally well with either expository or narrative texts. It also provides children with an opportunity to use the dictionary.

Assessment of vocabulary self-collection
Assessment is built into the strategy. As the children select the word for the list, they share how they used contextual clues. Further, as children respond to definitions offered by their peers, their prior knowledge can be assessed.

What is most useful about this strategy is that it documents that children can learn to read and write by reading and writing. The children take ownership of

> What is most useful about this strategy is that it documents that children can learn to read and write by reading and writing. The children take ownership of the words in the self-collection journals, which can be used later to develop writer observation journals.

the words in the self-collection journals, which can be used later to develop writer observation journals. Children also use the word lists as a start for writers' commonplace books. These books are filled with newspaper, magazine, and functional document clippings using the journal words.

This activity is a good one for demonstrating the balanced literacy belief that vocabulary study works best when the words studied are chosen by the child.

SKILL 3.5 Assessing comprehension

Retelling

RETELLING: a comprehension assessment strategy in which the student retells a story that they have read to highlight the main themes

RETELLING needs to be very clearly defined so that the child reader does not think that the teacher wants him or her to repeat verbatim the WHOLE story back in the retelling. A child should be able to talk comfortably and fluently about the story he/she has just read. He/she should be able to tell the main things that have happened in the story.

When a child retells a story to a teacher, the teacher needs ways to help in assessing the child's understanding. Ironically, the teacher can use some of the same strategies he/she suggests to the child to assess the child's understanding of a book with which the teacher is not familiar. These strategies include:

- Back cover reading

- Scanning the table of contents

- Looking at the pictures

- Reading the book jacket

If the child can explain how the story turned out and provide examples to support these explanations, the teacher should try not to interrupt the child with too many questions. Children can use the text of the book to reinforce what they are saying and they can even read from it if they wish. It is also important to note that some children need to reread the text twice with the second reading being for enjoyment.

Assessing a student's retelling

When the teacher plans to use the retelling as a way of assessing the child, then the following ground rules have to be set and made clear to the child. The teacher explains the purpose of the retelling to determine how well the child is reading at the outset of the conference.

The teacher maintains in the child's assessment notebook or in his/her assessment record what the child is saying in phrases, not sentences. Just enough is recorded to indicate whether the child actually understood the story. The teacher also tries to analyze from the retelling why the child cannot comprehend a given text. If the child's accuracy rate with the text is below 95 percent, then the problem is at the word level, but if the accuracy rate for the text is above 95 percent, the difficulty lies at the text level.

Word Map Strategy

Although also a teaching strategy, this approach provides useful assessment data for teachers. This strategy is helpful for children in grades 3–6 and beyond. The target group of children for the WORD MAP STRATEGY includes those who need to improve their independent vocabulary acquisition abilities. The strategy is essentially teacher-directed learning where children are "walked through" the process. The teacher helps the children to identify the type of information that makes a definition. Children are also assisted in using context clues and background understanding to construct meaning.

The word map graphic organizer is the tool teachers use to complete this strategy with children. Word map templates are available online from the Houghton Mifflin website and from *ReadWriteThink*, the website of the NCTE. The word map helps children to visually represent the elements of a given concept.

WORD MAP STRATEGY: a comprehension assessment strategy that features teacher-directed learning where children are "walked through" the process of identifying the type of information that makes a definition. Children are also assisted in using context clues and background understanding to construct meaning

Word Map

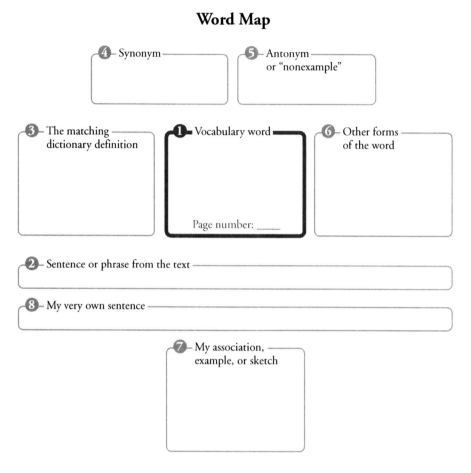

Example of word mapping

The children's literal articulation of the concept can be prompted by three key questions:

- What is it?

- What is it like?

- What are some examples?

For instance, the word "oatmeal" might yield a word map with boxes that have the answers to each of the three key questions. What is it? (A hot cereal) What's it like? (Hot and Mushy) What are some examples? (Instant or Irish)

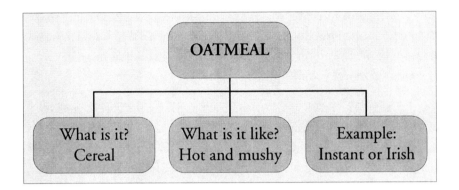

Implementing mapping in class

To share this strategy with children, the teacher selects three concepts familiar to the children and shows them the template of a word map with the three questions asked on the map. The teacher then helps the children to fill in at least two word maps with the topic in the top box and the answers in the three question boxes. The children should then independently complete the word map for the third topic. To reinforce the lesson, the teacher has the children select a concept of their own to map either independently or in a small group. As the final task for this first part of the strategy, the children, in teams or individually, write a definition for at least one of the concepts using the key things about it listed on the map. The children share these definitions aloud and talk about how they used the word maps to help them with the definitions.

For the next part of this strategy, the teacher picks an expository text or a textbook the children are already using to study mathematics, science, or social studies. The teacher either locates a short excerpt where a particular concept is defined or uses the content to write original model passages of definition.

After the passages are selected or authored, the teacher duplicates them. Then they are distributed to the children along with blank word map templates. The children will be asked to read each passage and then to complete the word map for the concept in each passage. Finally, the children share the word maps they have developed for each passage, and explain how they used the word in the passage to help them fill out their word map. Lastly, the teacher reminds the children that the three components of the concept—class, description, and example—are just three of the many components for any given concept.

Word mapping as assessment

This strategy has assessment potential because the teacher can literally see how the students understand specific concepts by looking at their maps and hearing their explanations. The maps that the students develop on their own demonstrate whether they have really understood the concepts in the passages. This strategy

> *This word map strategy can be adapted by the teacher to suit the specific needs and goals of instruction.*

serves to ready students for inferring word meanings on their own. By using the word map strategy, children develop concepts of what they need to know to begin to figure out an unknown word on their own. It assists the children in grades three and beyond to connect prior knowledge with new knowledge.

This word map strategy can be adapted by the teacher to suit the specific needs and goals of instruction. Illustrations of the concept and the comparisons to other concepts can be included in the word mapping for children grades five and beyond. This particular strategy is also one that can be used with a research theme in other content areas.

Sample Test Questions and Rationale

(Average)

1. If a teacher gives students a concept and asks students to formulate questions about that concept during reading and answer those questions after reading, what strategy is the teacher using?

   A. Preview in context

   B. Predicting

   C. Word mapping

   D. Hierarchical and linear arrays

   Answer: C. Word mapping

   When students preview in context students are taught vocabulary directly prior to reading. Choice B, predicting, is a reading strategy, but students predict before and during reading. A word map, Choice C, is when students are given a theme idea and ask questions about it and answer those questions during reading. With heirarchical and linear arrays, students rank vocabulary words.

(Average)

2. What is the best way to assess student's comprehension of reading material?

   A. Have students read a page from the text aloud

   B. Have students write definitions of words using the dictionary

   C. Have students write a summary of what they have read

   D. Have students recommend a book to a classmate

   Answer: C. Have students write a summary of what they have read

   A summary will check the comprehension of students to see if they understood the characters and their problem, the major events in the plot and the resolution.

Sample Test Questions and Rationale (cont.)

(Average)

3. Which choice shows the best way to check a student's comprehension of a non-fiction reading selection?

   A. Have the student point out the headings

   B. Have the student identify the main idea

   C. Have the student read all of the captions

   D. Have the student complete a vocabulary quiz

Answer: B. Have the student identify the main idea

If a student can identify the main idea of a non-fiction reading selection, then they are showing that they were able to comprehend the text. Students should preview headings and captions (Choice A and C) before reading. Vocabulary should always be taught authentically; therefore Choice D is not the best answer.

SKILL 3.6 Assessing writing skills

Writer's Workshops

Many teachers introduce WRITER'S WORKSHOP to their students to maximize learning about the writing process. The workshop also provides various opportunities for assessing students' abilities with writing. A basic writer's workshop will include a block of classroom time committed to writing various projects (i.e., narratives, memoirs, book summaries, fiction, book reports, etc.). Students use this time to write, meet with others to review/edit writing, make comments on writing, revise their own work, proofread, meet with the teacher, and publish their work.

> **WRITER'S WORKSHOP:** a writing skill assessment strategy that consists of a block of classroom time committed to writing various projects

Teachers who facilitate effective writer's workshops are able to meet with students one at a time and can guide that student in their individual writing needs. This approach allows the teacher to differentiate instruction for each student's writing level.

Spelling

When assessing spelling, teachers should look for the following behaviors:

- Knowledge of sounds and symbols
- Development of visual memory

- Development of morphemic knowledge

- Mastery of high frequency words at specific grade levels

- Location and knowledge of how to use spelling resources

- Attempts at spelling unknown words

- Risk taking attempts in using invented spelling

Sample Test Question and Rationale

(Rigorous)

1. **Students in a classroom are asked to keep a Writer's Notebook which they write in every day. What is the purpose of this notebook?**

   A. To write down ideas for poems that students might want to write

   B. To keep lists of ideas on certain topics that might be developed later

   C. To draw quick sketches and then write about them in greater detail

   D. All of the above

Answer: D. All of the above

A Writer's Notebook is a great place to keep prewriting ideas that can later be developed into drafts and perhaps published/finished pieces of writing.

SKILL 3.7 Student presentations and rubrics

Literacy Portfolios

LITERACY PORTFOLIOS: a student assessment strategy where students collect all of their reading and writing products so that teachers can track growth

Compiling LITERACY PORTFOLIOS is an increasingly popular and meaningful form of informal assessment. It is particularly compelling because artists, television directors, authors, architects, and photographers use portfolios in their careers and jobs. It is also a most authentic format for documenting children's literacy growth over time. The portfolio is not only a significant professional informal assessment tool for the teacher, but a vehicle and format for the child reader to take ownership of his/her progress over time. It models a way of compiling one's reading and writing products as a lifelong learner, which is the ultimate goal of reading instruction.

FOUR CATEGORIES OF MATERIALS IN LITERACY PORTFOLIOS	
Work Samples	These can include children's story maps, webs, KWL charts, pictures, illustrations, storyboards, and writings about the stories they have read.
Records of Independent Reading and Writing	These can include the children's journals, notebooks, or logs of books read with the names of the authors, titles of the books, date completed, and pieces related to books completed or in progress.
Checklists and Surveys	These include checklists designed by the teacher for reading development, writing development, ownership checklists, and general interest surveys.
Self-Evaluation Forms	These are the children's own evaluations of their reading and writing process framed in their own words. They can be simple templates with starting sentences such as: • I am really proud of the way I • I feel one of my strengths as a reader is • To improve the way I read aloud I need to • To improve my reading I should

Generally, a child's portfolio in grade three or above begins with a letter to the reader explaining the work that will be found in the portfolio. In grade four and up, children write a brief reflection detailing their feelings and judgments about their growth as readers and writers.

Uses for literacy portfolios

When teachers maintain student portfolios for mandated school administrative review, district review, or even for their own research, they often prepare portfolio summary sheets. These provide identifying data on the children and then a timeline of their review of the portfolio contents. The summary sheets also contain professional comments on the extent to which the portfolio documents demonstrate satisfactory and ongoing growth in reading.

Portfolios can be used beneficially for child-teacher and parent/teacher conversations to:

• Review the child's progress

• Discuss areas of strength

• Set future goals

- Make plans for future learning activities

- Evaluate what should remain in the portfolio and what needs to be cleared out for new materials.

Rubrics

Holistic scoring involves assessing a child's ability to construct meaning through writing. It uses a scale called a *rubric* and usually ranges can range from 0 to 4:

RUBRIC SCALE	
0	Indicates the piece cannot be scored. It does not respond to the topic or is illegible.
1	The writing responds to the topic but does not cover it accurately.
2	The writing responds to the topic but lacks sufficient details or elaboration.
3	This piece fulfills the purpose of the writing assignment and has sufficient development (which refers to details, examples, and elaboration of ideas).
4	This response has the most details, best organization, and presents a well-expressed reaction to the original writer's piece.

Sample Test Question and Rationale

(Rigorous)

1. What does "Story Mapping" have children do?

   A. The students retell the story details

   B. Identify the characters, setting, problem and solution

   C. Identify the main idea and supporting details

   D. Draw a map to show what the characters did

Answer: B. Identify the characters, setting, problem, and solution

When students map a story, they identify the characters, setting, problem, and solution. It is best to use this strategy with stories that have only a few characters and have obvious problems and solutions.

Sample Test Questions and Rationale

Directions: For Questions 1-3, read the following passage and choose the best answer for each question.

You might think that an easy-going, laid back, unstructured summer is good for children. But chances are, due to our lack of routine and structure, children's sleep habits often suffer. Don't let your summer turn into the "dog days of summer" like mine have before. Be sure that your children get enough sleep even during the unstructured months of June, July, and August.

Of course not all children are the same and do not require the same amount of sleep. I was surprised to learn that a 5-year old still needs about 11 hours of sleep a night. That means that if Rachel goes to bed at 8:00 then she should sleep until about 7:00 the next morning. Or if she goes to bed at 9:30 she should sleep until about 8:30 the next morning. If this isn't the case, there are a couple of things that can be done to help a child catch up. Options include taking a nap during the day, putting children to bed at an early hour, never waking a sleeping child, and keeping daily activities limited. Remember, children who are well rested have better temperaments and are much more enjoyable to be around.

(Rigorous)

1. **What is MOST LIKELY true based on the above passage?**

   A. The author is a parent

   B. The author is a pediatrician

   C. The author is a teacher

   D. The author has twins

   Answer: A. The author is a parent

   The author sounds like they have experience handling tired children over the summer. Choice B might be true, but it isn't the best answer because the author doesn't offer any clinical information.

(Easy)

2. **What will most likely happen if a young child does not get enough sleep?**

   A. They won't be able to sleep well at night

   B. They will be fine and make it through the day

   C. They will get sick more easily

   D. They will misbehave and act irrational

   Answer: D. They will misbehave and act irrational

   The author puts the saying, "The dog days of summer" in quotes to indicate that children who do not get enough sleep will most likely act like wild dogs.

(Average)

3. **The author was surprised to learn that a 5-year-old still needs about 11 hours of sleep. Does this sentence contain a fact or an opinion?**

   A. Fact

   B. Opinion

   Answer: A. Fact

   "A 5-year-old requires about 11 hours sleep" is a fact because it is verifiable.

Sample Test Questions and Rationale (cont.)

Directions: For Question 4, read the following passage and choose the best answer.

Many people say that the story *The Ugly Duckling* mirrors Hans Christian Andersen's childhood. He was an odd child and did not fit in well with other children. Hans was often older than other children and because of this felt alienated. He was interested in the stage and visited the playhouse outside of Copenhagen with his father. However, eventually he was sent away to a boarding school. His experience there was dreadful. He lived with the schoolmaster where he was abused. The headmaster had said it was a way to improve his character.

(Rigorous)

4. **Which detail supports the main idea, "Hans Christian Andersen had a difficult childhood"?**

   A. Hans Christian Andersen's headmaster abused him

   B. Hans' life mirrored that of *The Ugly Duckling*

   C. Hans was often older than other children

   D. Hans enjoyed the theatre as a child

   Answer: A. Hans Christian Andersen's headmaster abused him

   B draws a comparison between one of his stories and his childhood. Choices C and D are details, but they do not support the main idea that Andersen had a difficult childhood.

Directions: For Question 5, read the following passage and choose the best answer.

Time seemed to be passing so slowly. Leslie looked at the clock for at least the hundredth time in the past hour. She turned back and looked the other way. Soon this became uncomfortable too and she turned and laid on her back. This position also didn't feel right so she turned back toward the clock. Twenty minutes had passed. "Umph," Leslie grunted closing her eyes again.

(Average)

5. **From Leslie's actions we can determine that:**

   A. Leslie is laying on the beach somewhere

   B. Leslie is at the doctor's office waiting her turn

   C. Leslie is excited about an upcoming event

   D. Leslie is having a difficult time sleeping

   Answer: D. Leslie is having a difficult time sleeping

   The clock, trying to find a satisfying position, and the frustration are all clues that Leslie is having a hard time sleeping.

Sample Test Questions and Rationale (cont.)

Directions: For Question 6, read the following passage and choose the best answer.

Molly slid into her gorgeous dress. She had imagined this day since she was a young girl living in Hartford, Connecticut. Checking herself in the mirror one last time, she decided that this was as good as it was going to get. Her hair was perfect, just the way she had imagined—the hairdresser had definitely earned her fee this morning. As did the make-up specialist Molly thought to herself as she examined her face in the mirror. Then she heard the anthem of the orchestra. She turned from the mirror and headed toward the aisle.

(Average)

6. **It can be inferred from the passage above that Molly is:**

   A. A runway model

   B. About to get married

   C. Shopping at a store

   D. A Broadway performer

Answer: B. About to get married

The clues that allow us to decide that Molly is about to get married are that she puts on a gorgeous dress, has imagined this day since she was young, and had her hair done and her make-up done. She then hears the orchestra begin to play and she heads toward the aisle.

DOMAIN II
MATHEMATICS

PERSONALIZED STUDY PLAN

COMPETENCY 4

MATHEMATICS CURRICULUM

Place Value

Place value is the basis of our entire number system. A PLACE VALUE SYSTEM is one in which the position of a digit in a number determines its value. In the standard system, called base ten, each place represents ten times the value of the place to its right. You can think of this as making groups of ten of the smaller unit and combining them to make a new unit.

> **PLACE VALUE SYSTEM:** one in which the position of a digit in a number determines its value

Base ten

Ten ones make up one of the next larger unit, tens. Ten of those units make up one of the next larger unit, hundreds. This pattern continues for greater values (ten hundreds = one thousand, ten thousands = one ten thousand, etc.), and lesser, decimal values (ten tenths = 1, ten hundredths = one tenth, etc.).

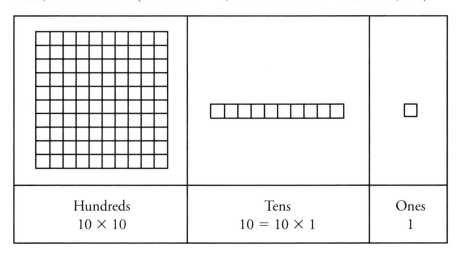

| Hundreds 10×10 | Tens $10 = 10 \times 1$ | Ones 1 |

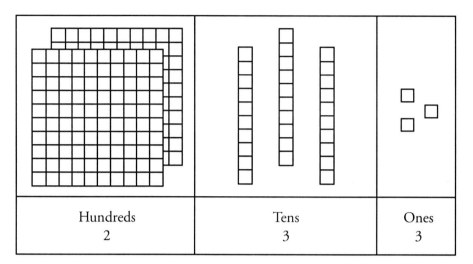

| Hundreds 2 | Tens 3 | Ones 3 |

In standard form, the number modeled above is 233.

Teaching place value

A place value chart is a way to make sure digits are in the correct places. The value of each digit depends on its position or place. A great way to see the place value relationships in a number is to model the number with actual objects (place value blocks, bundles of craft sticks, etc.), write the digits in the chart, and then write the number in the usual, or standard, form.

Place value is vitally important to all later mathematics. Without it, keeping track of greater numbers rapidly becomes impossible. (Can you imagine trying to write 999 with only ones?) A thorough mastery of place value is essential to learning the operations with greater numbers. It is the foundation for regrouping ("borrowing" and "carrying") in addition, subtraction, multiplication, and division.

Preschool children and place value

Preschool children should develop an understanding of one-to-one correspondence, being able to link a single number name with one object, and only one, at a time. This concept is needed in order for children to formalize the meaning of a whole number. An example would be for a child to count four blocks in a row, saying the number as each block is touched. Another example would be for a child to get a carton of milk for each of the other children at a table.

Preschool children should also be able to use one-to-one correspondence to compare the size of a group of objects. For example, students should be able to compare the number of cars they have with the number another child has and say, "I have more…or less."

Preschool children should develop an understanding of one-to-one correspondence, being able to link a single number name with one object, and only one, at a time.

Number sense

Number sense develops into the further understanding of place value and how numbers are related. This involves identifying and explaining how numbers can be grouped into tens, ones, and eventually hundreds or more. Using trading games, place value mats, and base ten blocks students can develop these skills. These activities will progress until the student understands that the one in sixteen represents ten, not simply one.

Children first learn to count using the counting numbers (1, 2, 3 . . .). Preschool children should be able to recite the names of the numerals in order or sequence (rote counting). This might be accomplished by singing a counting song. This should progress to being able to attach a number name to a series of objects. A preschool child should understand that the last number spoken when counting a group of objects represents the total number of objects.

In kindergarten, children should learn to read the numbers 0 through 10, and in first grade, they should be able to read through the number 20. At first, this could involve connecting a pictorial representation of the number with a corresponding number of items. This exercise may or may not involve assistive technology. As students advance, they should be able to read the numbers as sight words.

In kindergarten, children should learn to read the numbers 0 through 10, and in first grade, they should be able to read through the number 20.

Naming procedure

Students should be taught that there is a naming procedure for our number system. The numbers 0, 1 . . . 12 all have unique names. The numbers 13, 14 . . . 19 are the "teens." These names are a combination of earlier names, with the ones place named first. For example, fourteen is short for "four ten" which means "ten plus four." The numbers 20, 21 . . . 99 are also combinations of earlier names, but the tens place is named first. For example, 48 is "forty-eight," which means "four tens plus eight." The numbers 100, 101 . . . 999 are combinations of hundreds and previous names. Once a number has more than three digits, groups of three digits are usually set off by commas.

Real-life application of numbers

As students gain an understanding of numbers and are able to read them, they should be taught to apply these concepts to everyday life applications. For example, once children can read the numbers 1 through 12, they can begin to learn how to tell time. At the very basic level, if shown a clock or a diagram of a clock, a child needs to understand that the big hand represents minutes and the little hand represents hours. The child begins to recognize that when the big hand is on the twelve and the little hand is on the two, it is 2 o'clock. As the child learns to count by fives, the concept may be expanded so that the child understands that the distance between two consecutive numbers is an interval of five minutes. The child

As students gain an understanding of numbers and are able to read them, they should be taught to apply these concepts to everyday life applications.

then begins to recognize by counting by fives that when the big hand is on the 4 and the little hand is on the 2, it is twenty minutes after the hour of 2 o'clock.

Money

Another real-life application is money. In kindergarten, students learn to recognize a penny, nickel, dime, quarter, and one-dollar bill. In first grade, they learn how different combinations of coins have equivalent values, for example, that 10 pennies are the same as 1 dime and 10 dimes are the same as 1 dollar. Teaching children that money has value can start with a simple exercise of counting pennies to understand their monetary value. From here, students can advance to counting nickels, dimes, and so on. The next step might be to have students combine different coins and compute the value of the combination. As students advance in their understanding of the value of money, shopping math can be introduced where students see that money has value in exchange for goods. They can also learn to make change and count change.

Teaching children that money has value can start with a simple exercise of counting pennies to understand their monetary value.

Number Systems

The real number system includes all rational and irrational numbers.

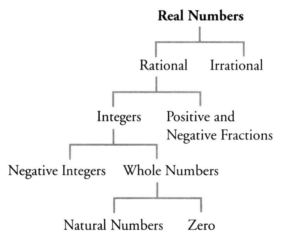

Real Numbers

RATIONAL NUMBERS can be expressed as the ratio of two integers, $\frac{a}{b}$, where $b \neq 0$. For example: $\frac{2}{3}, -\frac{4}{5}, \frac{5}{1} = 5$.

RATIONAL NUMBERS: can be expressed as the ratio of two integers, $\frac{a}{b}$, where $b \neq 0$

The rational numbers include integers, fractions and mixed numbers, and terminating and repeating decimals. Every rational number can be expressed as a repeating or terminating decimal and can be shown on a number line.

INTEGERS are the positive and negative whole numbers and zero.

...-6, -5, -4, -3, -2, -1, 0, 1, 2, 3, 4, 5, 6,...

INTEGERS: the positive and negative whole numbers and zero

WHOLE NUMBERS are the natural numbers and zero.

0, 1, 2, 3, 4, 5, 6...

WHOLE NUMBERS: the natural numbers and zero

NATURAL NUMBERS are the counting numbers.

 1, 2, 3, 4, 5, 6...

IRRATIONAL NUMBERS are real numbers that cannot be written as the ratio of two integers. They are infinite, nonrepeating decimals.

Examples:
 $\sqrt{5} = 2.2360$, pi $= \pi = 3.1415927...$

PERCENT $=$ per 100 (written with the symbol %). Thus $10\% = \frac{10}{100} = \frac{1}{10}$.

DECIMALS $=$ deci $=$ part of ten. To find the decimal equivalent of a fraction, use the denominator to divide the numerator as shown in the following examples.

Example: Find the decimal equivalent of $\frac{7}{10}$:

$$\begin{array}{r} .7 \\ 10\overline{)7.0} \\ \underline{70} \\ 00 \end{array}$$

Since 10 cannot divide into 7 evenly, put a decimal point in the answer row on top; put a 0 behind 7 to make it 70. Continue the division process. If a remainder occurs, put a 0 by the last digit of the remainder and continue the division.

 Thus $\frac{7}{10} = 0.7$

It is a good idea to write a 0 before the decimal point so that the decimal point is emphasized.

Example: Find the decimal equivalent of $\frac{7}{25}$:

$$\begin{array}{r} .28 \\ 25\overline{)7.000} \\ \underline{500} \\ 200 \\ \underline{200} \\ 0 \end{array}$$

Example: Convert 0.28 to a fraction.

 Multiplying 0.28 by $^{100}\!/_{100}$ to get rid of the decimal point:

 $0.28 \times {}^{100}\!/_{100} = {}^{28}\!/_{100} = \frac{7}{25}$

Example: Find 23% of 1000.

 $= \frac{23}{100} \times \frac{1000}{1} = 23 \times 10 = 230$

NATURAL NUMBERS: the counting numbers

IRRATIONAL NUMBERS: real numbers that cannot be written as the ratio of two integers

PERCENT: a base-ten positional notation system for numbers

DECIMAL: a number written with a whole-number part, a decimal point, and a decimal part

Example: Convert 6.25% to a fraction and to a mixed number.

$$6.25\% = 0.0625 = 0.0625 \times \frac{10000}{10000} = \frac{625}{10000} = \frac{1}{16}$$

A decimal can be converted to a percent by multiplying by 100, or merely moving the decimal point two places to the right. A percent can be converted to a decimal by dividing by 100, or moving the decimal point two places to the left.

> *A decimal can be converted to a percent by multiplying by 100, or merely moving the decimal point two places to the right. A percent can be converted to a decimal by dividing by 100, or moving the decimal point two places to the left.*

Examples:

$0.375 = 37.5\%$	$84\% = 0.84$
$0.7 = 70\%$	$3\% = 0.03$
$0.04 = 4\%$	$60\% = 0.6$
$3.15 = 315\%$	$110\% = 1.1$
	$\frac{1}{2} = 0.5\% = 0.005$

A percent can be converted to a fraction by placing it over 100 and reducing to simplest terms.

Examples:

$$32\% = \frac{32}{100} = \frac{8}{25}$$
$$6\% = \frac{6}{100} = \frac{3}{50}$$
$$111\% = \frac{111}{100} = 1\frac{11}{100}$$

Common Equivalents

COMMON EQUIVALENTS				
$\frac{1}{2}$	=	0.5	=	50%
$\frac{1}{3}$	=	$0.33\frac{1}{3}$	=	$33\frac{1}{3}\%$
$\frac{1}{4}$	=	0.25	=	25%
$\frac{1}{5}$	=	0.2	=	20%
$\frac{1}{6}$	=	$0.16\frac{2}{3}$	=	$16\frac{2}{3}\%$
$\frac{1}{8}$	=	$0.12\frac{1}{2}$	=	$12\frac{1}{2}\%$
$\frac{1}{10}$	=	0.1	=	10%
$\frac{2}{3}$	=	$0.66\frac{2}{3}$	=	$66\frac{2}{3}\%$

Table continued on next page

$\frac{5}{6}$	=	$0.83\frac{1}{3}$	=	$83\frac{1}{3}\%$
$\frac{3}{8}$	=	$0.37\frac{1}{2}$	=	$37\frac{1}{2}\%$
$\frac{5}{8}$	=	$0.62\frac{1}{2}$	=	$62\frac{1}{2}\%$
$\frac{7}{8}$	=	$0.87\frac{1}{2}$	=	$87\frac{1}{2}\%$
1	=	1.0	=	100%

CARDINAL numbers are also known as "counting" numbers because they indicate quantity. Examples of cardinal numbers are 1, 2, and 10.

ORDINAL numbers indicate the order of things in a set; for example, 1st, 2nd, 10th. They do not show quantity, only position.

CARDINAL: also known as "counting" numbers because they indicate quantity

ORDINAL: indicate the order of things in a set

	WORD NAME	STANDARD NUMERAL	PICTORIAL MODE
Decimal	Three-tenths	0.3	
Fraction	One-half	$\frac{1}{2}$	
Integer or Whole Number	Three	3	

Mathematical operations

MATHEMATICAL OPERATIONS include addition, subtraction, multiplication, and division. Addition can be indicated by these expressions: sum, greater than, and, more than, increased by, added to. Subtraction can be expressed by difference, fewer than, minus, less than, and decreased by. Multiplication is shown by product, times, multiplied by, and twice. Division is used for quotient, divided by, and ratio.

MATHEMATICAL OPERATIONS: include addition, subtraction, multiplication, and division

Recognition and understanding of the relationships between concepts and topics is of great value in mathematical problem solving and the explanation of more complex processes.

For instance, multiplication is simply repeated addition. This relationship explains the concept of variable addition. We can show that the expression $4x + 3x = 7x$ is true by rewriting 4 times x and 3 times x as repeated addition, yielding the expression $(x + x + x + x) + (x + x + x)$. Thus, because of the relationship between multiplication and addition, variable addition is accomplished by coefficient addition.

> **PROPERTIES:** rules that apply for addition, subtraction, multiplication, or division of real numbers

PROPERTIES are rules that apply for addition, subtraction, multiplication, or division of real numbers. These properties are:

Commutative	You can change the order of the terms or factors as follows.
	For addition: $\qquad a + b = b + a$
	For multiplication: $\qquad ab = ba$
	Since addition is the inverse operation of subtraction and multiplication is the inverse operation of division, no separate laws are needed for subtraction and division.
	Example: $5 + 8 = 8 + 5 = 13$
	Example: $2 \times 6 = 6 \times 2 = 12$
Associative	You can regroup the terms as you like.
	For addition: $\qquad a + (b + c) = (a + b) + c$
	For multiplication: $\qquad a(bc) = (ab)c$
	This rule does not apply for division and subtraction.
	Example: $(2 + 7) + 5 = 2 + (7 + 5)$ *$\qquad 9 + 5 = 2 + 12 = 14$*
	Example: $(3 \times 7) \times 5 = 3 \times (7 \times 5)$ *$\qquad 21 \times 5 = 3 \times 35 = 105$*
Identity	Finding a number so that when added to a term results in that number (additive identity); finding a number such that when multiplied by a term results in that number (multiplicative identity).
	For addition: $\qquad a + 0 = a$ (zero is the additive identity)
	For multiplication: $\qquad a \times 1 = a$ (one is the multiplicative identity)
	Example: $17 + 0 = 17$
	Example: $34 \times 1 = 34$
	The product of any number and one is that number.

Table continued on next page

Inverse	Finding a number such that when added to the number it results in zero; or when multiplied by the number results in 1.
	For addition: $a - a = 0$
	For multiplication: $a \times \left(\frac{1}{a}\right) = 1$
	$(-a)$ is the additive inverse of a; $\left(\frac{1}{a}\right)$, also called the reciprocal, is the multiplicative inverse of a.
	Example: $25 - 25 = 0$
	Example: $5 \times \frac{1}{5} = 1$
	The product of any number and its reciprocal is one.
Distributive	This technique allows us to operate on terms within parentheses without first performing operations within the parentheses. This is especially helpful when terms within the parentheses cannot be combined.
	$a(b + c) = ab + ac$
	Example: $6 \times (4 + 9) = (6 \times 4) + (6 \times 9)$
	$6 \times 13 = 24 + 54 = 78$
	To multiply a sum by a number, multiply each addend by the number, then add the products.

Addition of Whole Numbers

Example: At the end of a day of shopping, a shopper had $24 remaining in his wallet. He spent $45 on various goods. How much money did the shopper have at the beginning of the day?

The total amount of money the shopper started with is the sum of the amount spent and the amount remaining at the end of the day.

$$\begin{array}{r} \$\ 24 \\ +\ 45 \\ \hline \$\ 69 \end{array}$$ The original total was $69.

Example: A race took the winner 1 hr. 58 min. 12 sec. on the first half of the race and 2 hr. 9 min. 57 sec. on the second half of the race. How much time did the entire race take?

$$\begin{array}{r} 1 \text{ hr } 58 \text{ min } 12 \text{ sec} \\ +\ 2 \text{ hr }\ \ 9 \text{ min } 57 \text{ sec} \\ \hline 3 \text{ hr } 67 \text{ min } 69 \text{ sec} \end{array}$$ Add these numbers.

$$\begin{array}{r} +\ 1 \text{ min } -\ 60 \text{ sec} \\ \hline 3 \text{ hr } 68 \text{ min }\ \ 9 \text{ sec} \end{array}$$ Change 60 sec to 1 min.

$$\begin{array}{r} +\ 1 \text{ hr } -\ 60 \text{ min} \\ \hline 4 \text{ hr } 8 \text{ min } 9 \text{ sec} \end{array}$$ Change 60 min to 1 hr.

Final answer.

Subtraction of Whole Numbers

Example: At the end of his shift, a cashier has $96 in the cash register. At the beginning of his shift, he had $15. How much money did the cashier collect during his shift?

The total collected is the difference between the ending amount and the starting amount.

$96
−15
$81   The total collected was $81.

Multiplication of Whole Numbers

Multiplication is one of the four basic number operations. In simple terms, multiplication is the addition of a number to itself a certain number of times. For example, 4 multiplied by 3 is equal to $4 + 4 + 4$ or $3 + 3 + 3 + 3$. Another way of conceptualizing multiplication is to think in terms of groups. For example, if we have 4 groups of 3 students, the total number of students is 4 multiplied by 3. We call the solution to a multiplication problem the PRODUCT.

> *Another way of conceptualizing multiplication is to think in terms of groups.*

> **PRODUCT:** the answer to a multiplication problem

The basic algorithm for whole number multiplication begins with aligning the numbers by place value, with the number containing more places on top.

172
× 43   Note that we placed 172 on top because it has more places
            than 43 does.

Next, we multiply the ones place of the bottom number by each place value of the top number sequentially.

(2)
172   {$3 \times 2 = 6, 3 \times 7 = 21, 3 \times 1 = 3$}
× 43   Note that we had to carry a 2 to the hundreds column
516   because $3 \times 7 = 21$. Note also that we add carried numbers to
            the product.

Next, we multiply the number in the tens place of the bottom number by each place value of the top number sequentially. Because we are multiplying by a number in the tens place, we place a zero at the end of this product.

(2)
172
× 43   {$4 \times 2 = 8, 4 \times 7 = 28, 4 \times 1 = 4$}
516
6880

Finally, to determine the final product, we add the two partial products.

$$
\begin{array}{r}
172 \\
\times\ 43 \\
\hline
516 \\
+\ 6880 \\
\hline
7396
\end{array}
$$

The product of 172 and 43 is 7396.

Example: A student buys 4 boxes of crayons. Each box contains 16 crayons. How many total crayons does the student have?

The total number of crayons is 16×4.

$$
\begin{array}{r}
(2) \\
16 \\
\times\ 4 \\
\hline
64
\end{array}
$$

The total number of crayons equals 64.

Division of Whole Numbers

Division, the inverse of multiplication, is another of the four basic number operations. When we divide one number by another, we determine how many times we can multiply the divisor (number divided by) before we exceed the number we are dividing (dividend). For example, 8 divided by 2 equals 4 because we can multiply 2 four times to reach 8 ($2 \times 4 = 8$ or $2 + 2 + 2 + 2 = 8$). Using the grouping conceptualization we used with multiplication, we can divide 8 into 4 groups of 2 or 2 groups of 4. We call the answer to a division problem the QUOTIENT.

If the divisor does not divide evenly into the dividend, we express the leftover amount either as a remainder or as a fraction with the divisor as the denominator. For example, 9 divided by 2 equals 4 with a remainder of 1, or $4\frac{1}{2}$.

> **QUOTIENT:** the answer to a division problem

The basic algorithm for division is long division. We start by representing the quotient as follows.

$14\overline{)293} \rightarrow$ 14 is the divisor and 293 is the dividend. This represents $293 \div 14$.

Next, we divide the divisor into the dividend, starting from the left.

$\overset{2}{14\overline{)293}} \rightarrow$ 14 divides into 29 two times with a remainder.

Next, we multiply the partial quotient by the divisor, subtract this value from the first digits of the dividend, and bring down the remaining dividend digits to complete the number.

$$\begin{array}{r} 2 \\ 14\overline{)293} \\ -28\downarrow \\ \hline 13 \end{array}$$ → $2 \times 14 = 28, 29 - 28 = 1$, and bringing down the 3 yields 13.

Finally, we divide again (the divisor into the remaining value) and repeat the preceding process. The number left after the subtraction represents the remainder.

$$\begin{array}{r} 20 \\ 14\overline{)293} \\ -28 \\ \hline 13 \\ -0 \\ \hline 13 \end{array}$$ →

The final quotient is 20 with a remainder of 13. We can also represent this quotient as $20\frac{13}{14}$.

Example: Each box of apples contains 24 apples How many boxes must a grocer purchase to supply a group of 252 people with one apple each?

The grocer needs 252 apples. Because he must buy apples in groups of 24, we divide 252 by 24 to determine how many boxes he needs to buy.

$$\begin{array}{r} 10 \\ 24\overline{)252} \\ -24 \\ \hline 12 \\ -0 \\ \hline 12 \end{array}$$ → The quotient is 10 with a remainder of 12.

Thus, the grocer needs 10 boxes plus 12 more apples. Therefore, the minimum number of boxes the grocer can purchase is 11.

Example: At his job, John gets paid $20 for every hour he works. If John made $940 in a week, how many hours did he work?

This is a division problem. To determine the number of hours John worked, we divide the total amount made ($940) by the hourly rate of pay ($20). Thus, the number of hours worked equals 940 divided by 20.

$$\begin{array}{r} 47 \\ 20\overline{)940} \\ -80 \\ \hline 140 \\ -140 \\ \hline 0 \end{array}$$ → 20 divides into 940 a total of 47 times with no remainder.

John worked 47 hours.

Addition and Subtraction of Decimals

When adding and subtracting decimals, we align the numbers by place value as we do with whole numbers. After adding or subtracting each column, we bring the decimal down, placing it in the same location as in the numbers added or subtracted.

> *When adding and subtracting decimals, we align the numbers by place value as we do with whole numbers.*

Example: Find the sum of 152.3 and 36.342.

```
  152.300
+  36.342
  188.642
```

Note that we placed two zeros after the final place value in 152.3 to clarify the column addition.

Example: Find the difference of 152.3 and 36.342.

```
   2 9 10            (4)11(12)
 152.300          152.300
-  36.342        −  36.342
      58          115.958
```

Note how we borrowed to subtract from the zeros in the hundredths and thousandths places of 152.300.

Sample Test Questions and Rationale

(Easy)

1. **State the number modeled below.**

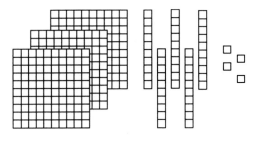

A. 354

B. 345

C. 453

D. 543

Answer: A. 354

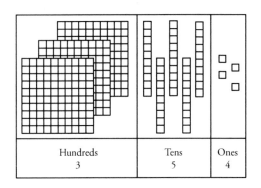

	Hundreds	Tens	Ones
	3	5	4

Sample Test Questions and Rationale (cont.)

(Average)

2. Which of the numbers is an example of an irrational number?

    A. 3

    B. $\sqrt{7}$

    C. 0.5

    D. $\frac{3}{4}$

    Answer: B. $\sqrt{7}$

    An irrational number is a real number that cannot be written as the ratio of two integers. These are infinite, non-repeating decimals. $\sqrt{7}$ = 2.64575...

(Average)

3. Which property is illustrated by the following?

    $(5 \times 4) \times 8 = 5 \times (4 \times 8)$

    A. Associative property of addition

    B. Commutative property of multiplication

    C. Inverse property of multiplication

    D. Associative property of multiplication

    Answer: D. Associative property of multiplication

    With the associative property of multiplication, you can regroup terms as you like.

(Average)

4. Emma had a balance of $236 in her savings account. She deposits the $55 she made babysitting this week. How much money will she have in her savings account?

    A. $181

    B. $55

    C. $291

    D. $236

    Answer: C. $291

    Add the amount deposited into the account to the existing balance.

(Easy)

5. Solve. $463.7 - 51.672$

    A. 412.028

    B. 412.172

    C. 47.035

    D. 412.138

    Answer: A. 412.028

    When subtracting decimals, you align the decimal points. You can add extra zeros after the last number on the right so both numbers have the same number of decimal places. You will have to use borrowing to subtract from zero.

SKILL 4.2 Prealgebra and algebra

In the primary grades, the concept of algebra is significantly different from what an adult remembers as algebra class. As adults, we typically recall the letters being used to hold the place of a number and solving various equations to find the answer for a variable. However, for young children, the basis for this concept is developed through learning about patterns, the attributes of objects, and how to describe objects in detail. These ideas help students to develop the fundamental thinking and concepts behind algebraic reasoning. These patterns may begin through concrete objects but will be further developed into counting patterns and other recognition of the patterns of numbers.

Beginning with the basic understanding of the symbols used throughout math (numerical representations) students can investigate things around them. They can gather this information and begin to report it in a way that means something to others who look at it. These facts related to their own thinking can be expanded. As students look at a variety of situations and manipulate the objects to draw new conclusions, their problem solving skills are advanced. These skills will allow students to begin to solve missing number problems or solve for unknown pieces to a situation. This can be done with the youngest students as well. An example of a preschool missing object problem might be:

Red   yellow   red   _____   red   yellow   red   yellow   red

In this case, the students would be shown real objects of two colors set in a pattern and need to determine which one is missing from the center of the pattern. This type of thinking is more complex than "what comes next" types of questions.

As children begin to compare, sort, order, and demonstrate seriating of objects using various characteristics their thinking changes. These changes are the beginning of algebraic thought. As they add on to patterns, make changes to patterns, build their own patterns, or convert patterns into new formats, they are thinking in more complex ways. Connecting this new thinking with the understanding of the number system is the beginning of using variables to define the relationships between mathematical concepts. This method of problem solving is then defined further into the expression of these relationships in a more traditional mathematical manner. Primary students may solve problems for the number that goes in the box. For example:

$3 + \square = 5$

As children begin to compare, sort, order, and demonstrate seriating of objects using various characteristics their thinking changes. These changes are the beginning of algebraic thought.

Pre-K children should be able to recognize and extend simple repeating patterns using objects and pictures. By patterns, we mean a sequence of symbols, sounds, movements, or objects that follow a simple rule, such as ABBABBABB. Students should be presented with a simple pattern that they try to understand. Once they have an understanding of the pattern, they should copy and extend it. Students at this age are capable of assigning letters to their patterns to verbalize how the pattern repeats. These are the very early fundamental stages of algebra.

Arithmetic Sequences

When given a set of numbers where the common difference between the terms is constant, use the following formula:

$a_n = a_1 + (n - 1)d$

where a_1 = the first term

n = the nth term (general term)

d = the common difference between the terms

Example: Find the eighth term of the arithmetic sequence 5, 8, 11, 14, ...

$a_n = a_1 + (n - 1)d$	
$a_1 = 5$	Identify the 1st term.
$d = 8 - 5 = 3$	Find d.
$a_n = 5 + (8 - 1)3$	Substitute.
$a_n = 26$	

Example: Given two terms of an arithmetic sequence, find a_1 and d.

$a_n = a_1 + (n - 1)d$ $\qquad a_4 = 21, n = 4$

$21 = a_1 + (4 - 1)d$ $\qquad a_6 = 32, n = 6$

$32 = a_1 + (6 - 1)d$

$21 = a_1 + 3d$ $\qquad$ Solve the system of equations.

$32 = a_1 + 5d$

$\begin{aligned} 21 &= a_1 + 3d \\ -32 &= -a_1 - 5d \\ \hline -11 &= -2d \\ 5.5 &= d \end{aligned}$ Multiply by -1.
Add the equations.

$21 = a_1 + 3(5.5)$ $\qquad$ Substitute d = 5.5, into one of the equations.

$21 = a_1 + 16.5$

$a_1 = 4.5$

The sequence begins with 4.5 and has a common difference of 5.5 between numbers.

Sample Test Question and Rationale

(Rigorous)

1. **Find the sixth term in the sequence 3, 7, 11, 15 …**

   A. 19

   B. 23

   C. 27

   D. 31

Answer: B. 23

Use the formula $a_n = a_1 + (n - 1)d$ where $a_1 =$ the first number in the sequence, $n =$ the *nth* term and *d* is the common difference between the terms.

<table>
<tr><td>SKILL
4.3</td><td>**Geometry and measurement**</td></tr>
</table>

Two-Dimensional Geometrical Shapes

A TRIANGLE is a polygon with three sides.

Triangles can be classified by the types of angles or the lengths of their sides.

Classifying by angles:

An ACUTE TRIANGLE has exactly three acute angles.

A RIGHT TRIANGLE has one right angle.

An OBTUSE TRIANGLE has one obtuse angle.

acute

right

obtuse

Classifying by sides:

All three sides of an EQUILATERAL TRIANGLE are the same length.

Two sides of an ISOSCELES TRIANGLE are the same length.

TRIANGLE: a polygon with three sides

ACUTE TRIANGLE: a triangle with exactly three acute angles

RIGHT TRIANGLE: a triangle with one right angle

OBTUSE TRIANGLE: a triangle with one obtuse angle

EQUILATERAL TRIANGLE: a triangle with all three sides the same length

ISOSCELES TRIANGLE: a triangle with two sides the same length

SCALENE TRIANGLE: a triangle with no sides the same length

None of the sides of a SCALENE TRIANGLE are the same length.

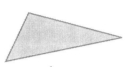

equilateral   isosceles   scalene

Three Dimensional Geometric Shapes

POLYGON: a simple closed figure composed of line segments

A POLYGON is a simple closed figure composed of line segments. In a REGULAR POLYGON all sides are the same length and all angles are the same measure.

REGULAR POLYGON: all sides are the same length and all angles are the same measure

The union of all points on a simple closed surface and all points in its interior form a space figure called a solid. The five regular solids, or polyhedra, are the cube, tetrahedron, octahedron, icosahedron, and dodecahedron. A NET is a two-dimensional figure that can be cut out and folded up to make a three-dimensional solid. Below are models of the five regular solids with their corresponding face polygons and nets.

NET: two-dimensional figure that can be cut out and folded up to make a three-dimensional solid

Cube 6 squares

Tetrahedron 4 equilateral triangles

Octahedron 8 equilateral triangles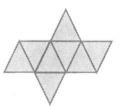

Icosahedron 20 equilateral triangles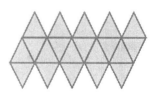

Dodecahedron 12 regular pentagons

Other examples of solids:

A **SPHERE** is a space figure having all its points the same distance from the center.

A **CONE** is a space figure having a circular base and a single vertex.

Tessellations

A **TESSELLATION** is an arrangement of closed shapes that completely covers the plane without overlapping or leaving gaps. Unlike tilings, tessellations do not require the use of regular polygons. In art, the term is used to refer to pictures or tiles mostly in the form of animals and other life forms, which cover the surface of a plane in a symmetrical way without overlapping or leaving gaps. M. C. Escher is known as the "father" of modern tessellations. Tessellations are used for tiling, mosaics, quilts, and art.

If you look at a completed tessellation, you will see the original motif repeats in a pattern. There are seventeen possible ways that a pattern can be used to tile a flat surface, or "wallpaper."

There are four basic transformational symmetries that can be used in tessellations: translation, rotation, reflection, and glide reflection. The transformation of an object is called its image. If the original object was labeled with letters, such as *ABCD*, the image may be labeled with the same letters followed by a prime symbol, *A'B'C'D'*.

The tessellation below is a combination of the four types of transformational symmetry we have discussed:

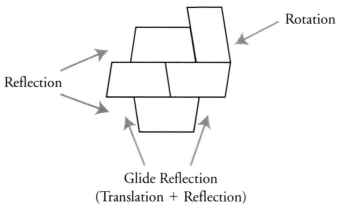

TRANSFORMATION: a change in the position, shape, or size of a geometric figure

A **TRANSFORMATION** is a change in the position, shape, or size of a geometric figure. **TRANSFORMATIONAL GEOMETRY** is the study of manipulating objects by flipping, twisting, turning, and scaling them. **SYMMETRY** is exact similarity between two parts or halves, as if one were a mirror image of the other.

TRANSFORMATIONAL GEOMETRY: the study of manipulating objects by flipping, twisting, turning, and scaling them

A **TRANSLATION** is a transformation that "slides" an object a fixed distance in a given direction. The original object and its translation have the same shape and size, and they face in the same direction.

SYMMETRY: exact similarity between two parts or halves, as if one were a mirror image of the other

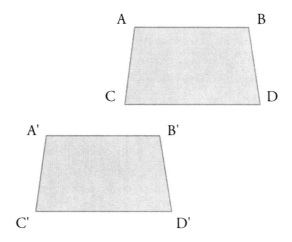

TRANSLATION: a transformation that "slides" an object a fixed distance in a given direction

An example of a translation in architecture is stadium seating. The seats are the same size and the same shape, and they face in the same direction.

A **ROTATION** is a transformation that turns a figure about a fixed point called the center of rotation. An object and its rotation are the same shape and size, but the figures may be turned in different directions. Rotations can occur in either a clockwise or a counterclockwise direction.

ROTATION: a transformation that turns a figure about a fixed point called the center of rotation

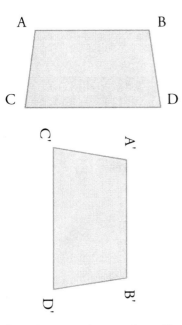

Rotations can be seen in wallpaper and art, and a Ferris wheel is an example of rotation.

An object and its REFLECTION have the same shape and size, but the figures face in opposite directions.

> **REFLECTION:** objects have the same shape and size, but the figures face in opposite directions

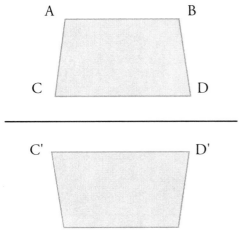

The line (where a mirror may be placed) is called the LINE OF REFLECTION. The distance from a point to the line of reflection is the same as the distance from the point's image to the line of reflection.

> **LINE OF REFLECTION:** the line where a mirror may be placed; the distance from a point to this line is the same as the distance from the points image to this line

Measurement

Students should be able to determine what unit of measurement is appropriate for a particular problem, as indicated by the following table:

PROBLEM TYPE	UNIT (CUSTOMARY SYSTEM)	UNIT (METRIC SYSTEM)
Length	Inch Foot Yard	Millimeter Centimeter Meter
Distance	Mile	Kilometer
Area	Square inches Square feet Square yards Square miles	Square millimeters Square centimeters Square meters Square kilometers
Volume	Cubic inches Cubic feet Cubic yards	Cubic millimeters Cubic centimeters Cubic meters
Liquid Volume	Fluid ounces Cups Pints Quarts Gallons	Milliliters Liters
Mass		Milligrams Centigrams Grams Kilograms
Weight	Ounces Pounds Tons	Milligrams Centigrams Grams Kilograms
Temperature	Degrees Fahrenheit	Degrees Celsius or Kelvin

Sample Test Question and Rationale

(Rigorous)

1. What solid can be made from the following net diagram?

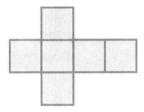

A. Rectangular prism

B. Square

C. Cube

D. Sphere

Answer: C. Cube

A net is a two-dimensional drawing of a three dimensional figure. This net diagram will create a cube.

SKILL **Probability, statistics, and data analysis**
4.4

Methods and Tools to Analyze Data and Describe Shape, Spread, and Center

Mean, median, and mode are three measures of central tendency. The MEAN is the average of the data items. The MEDIAN is found by putting the data items in order from smallest to largest and selecting the item in the middle (or the average of the two items in the middle). The MODE is the most frequently occurring item.

RANGE is a measure of variability. It is found by subtracting the smallest value from the largest value.

Example: Find the mean, median, mode, and range of the test scores listed below:

85	77	65
92	90	54
88	85	70
75	80	69
85	88	60
72	74	95

MEAN: the average of the data items

MEDIAN: found by putting the data items in order from smallest to largest and selecting the item in the middle

MODE: the most frequently occurring item

RANGE: a measure of variability

Mean = sum of all scores ÷ number of scores = 78

Median = Put the numbers in order from smallest to largest. Pick the middle number.

54 60 65 69 70 72 74 75 | 77 80 | 85 85 85 88 88 90 92 95

both in middle

Therefore, the median is the average of two numbers in the middle, 78.5.

Mode = most frequent number
    = 85

Range = the largest number minus the smallest number
    = 95 − 54
    = 41

Example: Different situations require different information. If we examine the circumstances under which an ice cream store owner may use statistics collected in the store, we find different uses for different information.
Over a 7-day period, the store owner collected data on the ice cream flavors sold. He found that the mean number of scoops sold was 174 per day. The most frequently sold flavor was vanilla. This information was useful in determining how much ice cream to order in all and in what amounts for each flavor.

In this case, the median and range had little business value for the owner.

Example: Consider the set of test scores from a math class: 0, 16, 19, 65, 65, 65, 68, 69, 70, 72, 73, 73, 75, 78, 80, 85, 88, and 92. The mean is 64.06 and the median is 71.
Since there are only three scores less than the mean out of the eighteen scores, the median (71) would be a more descriptive score.

Definitions in statistical data

An understanding of the definitions is important in determining the validity and uses of statistical data. All definitions and applications in this section apply to ungrouped data.

Data item: each piece of data is represented by the letter X.

Mean: the average of all data is represented by the symbol $\overline{X}$.

Sum of the Squares: sum of the squares of the differences between each item and the mean.

$$Sx^2 = (X - \overline{X})^2$$

Variance: the sum of the squares quantity divided by the number of items. The lowercase Greek letter sigma squared (σ^2) represents variance.

$$\frac{Sx^2}{N} = \sigma^2$$

The larger the value of the variance, the larger the spread.

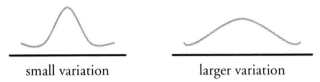

small variation   larger variation

Standard Deviation: the square root of the variance. The lowercase Greek letter sigma (σ) is used to represent standard deviation.

$$\sigma = \sqrt{\sigma^2}$$

Most statistical calculators have standard deviation keys on them and should be used when asked to calculate statistical functions. It is important to become familiar with the calculator and the location of the keys needed.

Example: Given the ungrouped data below, calculate the mean, range, standard deviation, and variance.

| 15 | 22 | 28 | 25 | 34 | 38 |
| 18 | 25 | 30 | 33 | 19 | 23 |

Mean ($\overline{X}$) = 25.8333333
Range: 38 − 15 = 23
Standard deviation (σ) = 6.6936952
Variance (σ^2) = 44.805556

Misuse of statistics

Statistics can be used both to inform and to mislead; thus, it is necessary to be able to discern between appropriate and inappropriate use of statistics. For instance, an improperly chosen measure of central tendency can mislead. Consider a case where a population is divided almost exclusively into extremely poor and extremely rich. In some cases, the mean income (or other measure of wealth) might lead a reader to think that a significant number of people are in the middle class, even if no one qualifies for this categorization, simply because the average income happens to fall between rich and poor. Likewise, extremely broad distributions of particular variables can make measures of central tendency misleading as well.

Statistics can be used both to inform and to mislead; thus, it is necessary to be able to discern between appropriate and inappropriate use of statistics.

In addition to the mathematical considerations associated with appropriate use of statistics, the linguistic aspect must also be considered. The numbers used in a statistical statement are interpreted in light of the language used with them. Thus, to say "Half of population X in this area contracts disease Y, therefore everyone should get tested" might not include the fact that the only ones who contract the particular disease are those who (for instance) work at a certain chemical plant—thus, only those who work at the plant would need testing for the disease. Thus, it is necessary that the use of statistics includes all relevant information.

Another common fallacy of statistics is mistaking association for causation.

Sample Test Question and Rationale

(Average)

1. **Consider the set of test scores from a math test. Find the mean, median, and the mode.**

    90, 92, 83, 83, 83, 90, 90, 83, 90, 93, 90, 97, 80, 67, 90, 85, 63, 60

    A. Mean: 83.83, mode: 90, median: 87.5

    B. Mean: 86.5, mode: 83, 90, median: 83.72

    C. Mean: 1507, mode: 90, median 83

    D. Mean 90, mode 83.72, median 90

Answer: A. Mean: 83.83, mode: 90, median: 87.5

The mean is the sum of the data items divided by the number of items. The mode is the test score that appears the most. The median is found by putting the data items in order from smallest to largest and selecting the item in the middle (or the average of the two items in the middle.

COMPETENCY 5
MATHEMATICS INSTRUCTION

SKILL 5.1 **Teaching methods for mathematics**

Mathematical Development

Typical mathematical development progresses through three main stages. These stages are:

THREE MAIN STAGES OF MATHEMATICAL DEVELOPMENT	
Use of Manipulatives	During this stage, children need to work with real objects to help them solve mathematical problems. It is generally accepted practice and helpful to incorporate the use of real objects of some sort when introducing new concepts to students.
Use of Mental Imagery	During this stage, children begin to use pictures or mental images of the objects to solve the problems.
Use of Abstract Imagery	During this stage, children are able to use their understanding of number sense to complete problems. Children in this stage are no longer thinking of real objects, but are using their understanding of mathematical concepts to make broader generalizations and solve problems.

Awareness of these stages can help teachers determine what teaching strategies to employ at different grade levels and topics.

Number Lines

For addition

A number line may be introduced to help students understand addition and subtraction. Suppose we want to show $6 + 3$ on a number line.

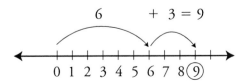

Addition can be thought of as starting from zero and counting 6 units to the right on the line (in the positive direction) and then counting 3 more units to the right. The number line shows that this is the same as counting 9 units to the right.

For subtraction

In the same way, a number line may be used to represent subtraction. Suppose we have $6 - 3$ or rather $6 + (-3)$.

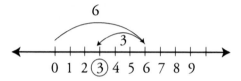

If 3 is shown by counting 3 positions to the right, then -3 can be shown as 3 positions to the left. We start from zero and count 6 positions to the right and then count 3 positions to the left. This illustrates how $6 + (-3) = 3$.

Strategies for Encouraging the Use of Mathematical Concepts and Skills in Everyday Life

One of the easiest ways to incorporate real life mathematical activities is to bring real life activities into the classroom.

One of the easiest ways to incorporate real life mathematical activities is to bring real life activities into the classroom. Working as a class to prepare food, where the students need to measure different ingredients before/after completing lessons on fractions, is an excellent way for the students to understand the importance of the learning, especially if you make a food the children enjoy.

Other mixing activities that involve measuring math skills involve:

- Making play dough

- Making slime

- Creating the perfect bubble blowing mixture

Cooking and mixture activities also have a direct connection to the sciences and allow the teacher to combine subject areas into one lesson.

Other methods to incorporate math activities into more regular parts of students' lives and other subject areas include:

WAYS TO INCORPORATE MATH INTO PRACTICAL ACTIVITIES
Charting/graphing the weather on a regular basis
Predicting temperatures based on a pattern or other information
Helping students keep track of the score of a sporting event using tally marks
Finding the age of other family members or characters in stories
Building race cars or straw structures to represent buildings from stories or having your own race, similar to a NASCAR event
Redesigning the layout of the classroom/cafeteria
Playing cards, dice, and board games with the students (popular games like Pokemon involve a lot of math if played correctly)
Timing activities or determining how long until a special event will occur

In the end, the activity does not really matter. Rather the students need to understand the importance of math in their daily lives. Also, they need to know how the learning in school directly supports their personal interests, ideas, and needs which will make the information most meaningful to the students.

> In the end, the activity you use does not really matter. Rather the students need to understand the importance of math in their daily lives.

Methods for Collection, Organization, and Analysis of Data in the Primary Grades

Collecting, describing, and analyzing data are fun activities in the early childhood classroom. There are numerous exciting and playful methods for collecting data to be used in various classroom lessons. Some fun ways to collect data include:

- Have students drop a piece of cereal into a bowl that is their favorite color

- Have students draw a tally mark under their lunch choice on a bulletin board

- Utilize a thumbs up or thumbs down approach for students' responses when asking whole group questions

- Use wipe boards

- Have the students themselves stand in lines to form a human graph to show a particular set of data

Ideas for collecting data to organize, describe, and analyze:

- Favorite colors

- Birthdays

- Hair/eye/clothing colors

- Favorite foods

- Favorite books

- Ending to a story (like/don't like)

- Shoe size (type/color/style)

- Favorite songs

Once the data have been collected, they need to be organized into a format easily analyzed by the students. This can involve tables, tally charts, and graphs. Using the real objects to form the bars of the graphs can provide the students with immediate results. This can be very important to young children. It also provides a concrete representation, whereas transferring the data to paper to create the graph/table or chart is more abstract of a concept.

Using mathematical language

Once the graph, table, or chart is completed it is important to utilize mathematical language to describe and analyze the information. Comparing two different bars on the graph, finding the greatest, finding the smallest/least, or other types of analysis help students to develop their critical thinking skills. The students need to be exposed to vocabulary terms that mean the same thing (such as smallest and least).

Gathering, organizing and analyzing data are easy to incorporate as a daily routine of the early childhood classroom.

Gathering, organizing and analyzing data are easy to incorporate as a daily routine of the early childhood classroom. An entire activity can be completed in five to ten minutes of the math class on a regular basis and provide students with a fun, real-life, critical thinking activity which increases not only mathematical understanding and skills, but builds vocabulary skills as well. It is also an area of math that can help to tie together many other subject areas in an easy way.

COMPARING TEST RESULTS					
	TEST 1	TEST 2	TEST 3	TEST 4	TEST 5
Evans, Tim	75	66	80	85	97
Miller, Julie	94	93	88	97	98
Thomas, Randy	81	86	88	87	90

BAR GRAPHS are used to compare various quantities.

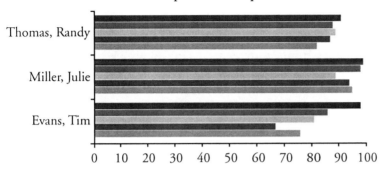

LINE GRAPHS are used to show trends, often over a period of time.

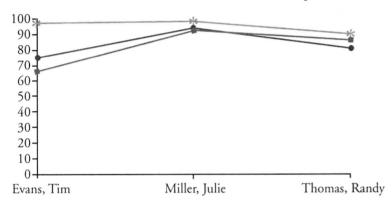

A PICTOGRAPH shows comparison of quantities using symbols. Each symbol represents a number of items.

¶ ¶ ¶ ¶
¶ ¶ ¶ ¶ ¶ ¶ ¶
¶ ¶ ¶
¶ ¶
¶ ¶ ¶ ¶ ¶

To read a bar graph or a pictograph, read the explanation of the scale that was used in the legend. Compare the length of each bar with the dimensions on the axes and calculate the value each bar represents. On a pictograph, count the number of pictures used in the chart and calculate the value of all the pictures.

Measurement Activities

We humans like to reduce everything in the real world to numbers, and the only way to do this with some things is to measure them. The most common things we measure are time, temperature, distance, weight, and angles. Children have been exposed to some or all of these concepts before they start school.

The most common things we measure are time, temperature, distance, weight, and angles.

One of the most important things that must be emphasized when beginning measurement activities is that now we are entering the world of approximations. No measurement can ever be exact, and teachers should refrain from using the word "exact" in connection with measurements. Many adults are confused about this concept, so we should try to be clear from the outset.

The stages of measuring something are:

1. Determine what to measure

2. Decide on an appropriate tool

3. Select a reasonable unit of measure

4. Estimate how much or how long the measurement will be

5. Measure

6. Check the reasonableness of the results

Time

Start with time. Most people measure time with clocks or watches. What are the units? Most children are familiar with hours and minutes. Practice this with them. With older children, you can talk about timed athletic events like running, swimming, horse races, etc. At this point, they would probably see the need for a smaller unit, so you could talk about seconds and even tenths of seconds. Constantly point out that 10.3 seconds only means that the time in question is closer to 10.3 than it is to 10.2 or 10.4.

Temperature

Next could be temperature. Most children are aware of temperature as it is given on television, in Fahrenheit degrees in the United States. Introduce them to the thermometer with an actual thermometer and then with a large reproduction on paper showing the degree marks. Talk about how air temperature is physically measured.

For example, would we want to put the thermometer in direct sunlight? What would be a comfortable temperature? What would be very hot? Very cold? Have them estimate air temperature each day and then measure it with the thermometer. Again point out that to say the temperature is 75 degrees only means that it is closer to 75 than to 74 or 76. Point this out on the paper diagram of a thermometer scale. With older students, this is a good chance to briefly introduce the idea of negative numbers. Also work with the Celsius (or centigrade) scale.

Length/distance

Next could be length. A great deal of time needs to be spent here. First the students need to be convinced that we need a standard unit. Does foot mean the length of just anybody's foot? Get some objects for them to measure that are very close to 3 feet or 5 feet, etc. Then introduce something smaller so that they will see the need for a smaller unit.

Prior to introducing measurement with standard tools such as a ruler, it is appropriate to teach children how to measure with nonstandard units such as paper clips. Students are taught to use the paper clip as a unit by laying the paper clips end to end. They measure an object longer than the paper clip (repetition of a single unit to measure something larger than the unit).

Prior to introducing measurement with standard tools such as a ruler, it is appropriate to teach children how to measure with nonstandard units such as paper clips.

Students should practice measuring objects to the nearest inch. After they have been measuring for a few weeks, introduce the millimeter as a still smaller unit. Most rulers are metric on one side with standard English units on the other.

Introducing the metric system

Teachers should get students used to the metric system as soon as possible, sticking with millimeter and centimeter. Use these interchangeably with inches and feet. Older children can then proceed to yards and meters. Still older ones can work on paper (or the computer) with miles and kilometers. Many activities must be constantly presented to get children familiar with all these units.

Teachers should get students used to the metric system as soon as possible, sticking with millimeter and centimeter.

Weights

Some work can be done occasionally with weights. Pounds would be the obvious starting unit, then ounces for a smaller unit and tons for a larger one. Fairly early on in this work introduce the kilogram and the gram. Guess the weights of objects before actually weighing them.

Another thing students should learn to measure is liquids. Introduce the idea of gallons and quarts, but fairly soon also work with liters and milliliters. Bring in soda bottles and notice that both metric and English units are given. Briefly talk about pints and cups, as used in recipes.

Area

The concept of area is a difficult one for them. Try to get some hint that they are ready to tackle that one. Somewhere about the end of grade two or beginning of grade three would be an appropriate time to introduce this idea. Work with squares and rectangles first, then right triangles.

Angles

Finally teachers can approach the concept of an angle, particularly a right angle because it can be associated with turns. There are many exercises available, both paper-and-pencil and computer software, for working with angles. It is probably not appropriate to introduce the protractor until about grade three.

For all of these measurement activities, bring examples from newspapers and television to class and discuss them. Have the children be on the lookout for such examples. What would they like to measure? What would be easy to measure? What would be hard to measure? Keep harping on the idea that no measurement is ever exact.

Choosing What to Measure

After students decide that there is some object they want to measure, the first question to answer is "what attribute can be measured on this object?" Most physical objects have a length, although even here there are choices to be made. Since the world is three-dimensional, students have to choose which dimension will be the length, which the width, and which the height. We use these words to distinguish the three dimensions from each other, but of course all three are measured in length units. Other measureable attributes of common physical objects are their weight, surface area, volume and temperature.

In PreK-3, volume is not an appropriate topic, except as it might enter into a discussion of liquid measure. Also, the time spent on area concepts will probably be short. Measurement of temperature will normally be confined to air temperature for this age group.

Using the Environment

With the advent of good and inexpensive digital cameras, math teachers have wonderful opportunities to show students how pervasive mathematics and measuring are in their lives.

With the advent of good and inexpensive digital cameras, math teachers have wonderful opportunities to show students how pervasive mathematics and measuring are in their lives. The teacher can go around the immediate area of the school taking pictures of physical objects that illustrate various things they are studying. For example, if you are working on length measures and also geometric figures, before having them measure the length and width of a bunch of rectangles on paper, show them pictures (a PowerPoint demonstration would be ideal here) of different rectangles around the neighborhood. For example, some things they can measure include:

- The walls of the classroom

- Tiles on the floor or ceiling

- Sidewalks
- Exteriors of buildings

Do the same for other geometric figures. Bridges are good examples of triangles. Church windows are often circular. Children are usually quite familiar with circles, but circles introduce some very real problems. With younger students the perimeter can be approximated (remember that all measurements are approximate anyway). Using a piece of string and fitting it around a circle on a piece of paper, then measuring the length of the string that seems to fit, makes a nice little exercise.

Measuring Devices

Every math classroom should be equipped with various measuring devices—a set of rulers, a few meter sticks, some thermometers, a few different scales for weighing objects, clocks and perhaps a stopwatch and protractors. Hands-on exercises are definitely most useful when teaching measurement. When showing pictures of objects we want to measure in the immediate environment, ask the students questions such as:

Hands-on exercises are definitely most useful when teaching measurement.

- How could we measure these objects and what would be an appropriate instrument to use?

- What units would be best to express the measurement?

- What would their guess be about the result of measuring the object?

- Where could they go to find out if their guess was a good approximation to the reported measurement of this object?

Difficulty of Angles

Angles are difficult to teach to young children. They can be introduced by having them stand up, face front, then turn to face sideways right. What if we turned only part way to the right? How could we measure this? They might have some interesting ideas for solving this problem. Eventually, you can tell them about angles and how they are measured. Draw some angles and talk about what exactly is being measured here. Point out that the angle is no bigger if you extend the sides indefinitely. Actual measuring with protractors could be introduced if you feel the children are ready, but getting the idea of what we mean by the concept of angle is more important at first.

Sample Test Questions and Rationale

(Easy)

1. A number line can be used to introduce which two operations?

   A. Addition and multiplication

   B. Subtraction and division

   C. Addition and subtraction

   D. Multiplication and division

   Answer: C. Addition and subtraction

   A number line is a good way to introduce addition and subtraction. You can show the starting number and how many units to move to arrive at the answer. For addition, move to the right in the positive direction. For subtraction, move to the left, in the negative direction.

(Average)

2. **Children use mathematical skills and concepts daily, usually without even realizing it. Which answer does not describe an activity students can do to incorporate math into their daily lives?**

   A. Writing their name 100 times on a piece of paper

   B. Redesigning the layout of their bedroom

   C. Playing the card game cribbage

   D. Making a batch of green slime

   Answer: A. Writing their name 100 times on a piece of paper

   Writing one's name many times over does not show any mathematical skill that is used in daily activities.

(Easy)

3. Emma did a presentation to the class of the data she collected. She organized her data in the following chart.

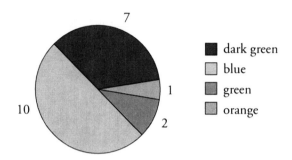

   Which display type did she use to organize her data?

   A. Line graph

   B. Pictograph

   C. Circle graph

   D. Bar graph

   Answer: C. Circle graph

   A circle graph is a way of displaying data as areas of a circle.

(Average)

4. **You are introducing your students to measurement using the metric system. What is a good way to begin the lesson?**

   A. Have students measure items using the metric system

   B. Have students discuss items they have seen that have metric system labels such as measuring cups, thermometers, bottles of juice, mile signs

   C. Have students convert measurements between customary and metric systems

   D. Use metric measurement terms in problem solving

Sample Test Questions and Rationale (cont.)

Answer: B. Have students discuss items they have seen that have metric system labels such as measuring cups, thermometers, bottles of juice, mile signs

Students will have come into contact with the metric measures on items in their lives. By discussing them, students will see the connections between the customary and metric systems.

(Rigorous)

5. **You give your students this problem. What information would you tell them to help them understand and solve the problem?**

Mr. Smith owns 560 acres of farm land. He leases out 430 acres to Mr. Gray for $125 per acre. The property tax is $15 per acre. What is the profit Mr. Smith earns on his property?

A. The problem can be done in one step

B. The profit is the difference between how much Mr. Smith earns in rent and how much he pays in taxes

C. You will need to use addition and division to solve the problem

D. The problem is too difficult to do

Answer: B. The profit is the difference between how much Mr. Smith earns in rent and how much he pays in taxes.

Students need to understand what a profit is before they can know which operations to use to solve the problem.

(Average)

6. **According to this graph, what group of people made up the largest percentage of the unemployed in 2004?**

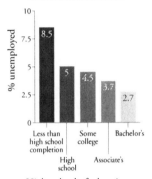

Unemployment rates of persons 25 years old and over, by highest level of education: 2004

U.S. Department of Labor, Bureau of Labor Statistics, Office of Employment and Unemployment Statistics, Current Population Survey (CPS), 2004.

A. Those who did not complete high school

B. Those who completed high school

C. Those who have taken some college credit

D. Those who possess a Bachelor's degree

Answer: A. Those who did not complete high school.

The tallest bar equals 8.5%. The x-axis represents the highest level of education completed and the y-axis represents the % unemployed.

SKILL Problem-solving
5.2

For very young children, almost any mathematical question posed is a problem to be solved. Too often, the term problem solving is misrepresented as word problems. In fact, any problem presented to a child where they are unaware of the answer is a problem to be solved. From the very beginning, children need to experience a variety of mathematical situations across all subject areas. Exposing children to a variety of contexts in which to solve problems allows the child to develop their own constructs upon which they can build new learning. Problem Solving in the Classroom

More than one way

Problem solving is not about one strategy or right way, but rather about allowing students of varying mathematical skills and abilities to look at the same situation presented and find a way to solve it. In a group of five, it may be reasonable to expect five different methods to reach the solution. Providing students with the means to investigate a problem allows them to be flexible in their approach. Often times, teachers limit the abilities of their students to solve problems by restricting them to one mode of reaching a solution.

Incorporating real world problems

Problem solving needs to be incorporated in a real way for students to understand, appreciate, and value the process. Using daily activities or problems can help make problem solving a regular part of a child's day. As situations arise in any subject area, it is important for the teacher to incorporate problem-solving activities. Some examples of ways to include realistic problem solving in the classroom are:

- Having the students help with lunch count

- Attendance

- Counting the number of days left in the school year

- Calculating the time left until recess

- Other daily types of activities

Problem solving in all subject areas

Additionally, problem-solving activities should be incorporated into all subject areas.

POSSIBLE PROBLEM-SOLVING ACTIVITIES	
SUBJECT	**POSSIBLE ACTIVITIES**
Science	Children can graph the daily temperatures and make predictions for future temperatures.
Social Studies	Children can gather, tabulate, and calculate the data related to the topic presented.
Language Arts	Children can solve problems that occur in all types of children's literature.

Charting favorite books, calculating ages of characters in stories, and drawing maps of the setting(s) of books are some beginning ways to connect other subjects to math. There are also numerous exciting books written with a mathematical basis that can be used to cover multiple subjects in a fun manner.

It is important for the teacher to be a role model. Thinking aloud as you come across a problem in the course of the day will help the students begin to realize the necessity and real-world implications of solving problems. Encouraging students to be reflective will also help in building the necessary mathematical language. Also, students can begin to share their ideas and methods with each other, which is an excellent strategy for learning about problem solving.

Four steps for problem solving

Typically, there are four steps to problem solving. Teachers will need to teach each of the steps explicitly and model them regularly. The steps are:

THE FOUR STEPS OF PROBLEM SOLVING	
Understand the Problem	This involves, among other things, understanding all the words in the problem, understanding what you are being asked to find, possibly being able to draw a picture or diagram, knowing if there is enough information, and knowing if there is too much information.
Devise a Plan	This involves being able to choose an appropriate strategy to solve the problem. These strategies include, but are not limited to, guessing and checking, looking for a pattern, using a model, and working backward.
Carry Out the Plan	This is the actual solving of the problem using whatever strategy you have chosen.
Look Back	Included in this step is checking the answer, if possible, to make sure it is correct. This step may be extended to include determining if there might have been an easier way to find the solution.

Nondirect methods for problem solving

The GUESS-AND-CHECK STRATEGY calls for making an initial guess of the solution, checking the answer, and using the outcome of this check to inform the next guess. With each successive guess, one should get closer to the correct answer. Constructing a table from the guesses can help organize the data.

Example: There are 100 coins in a jar: 10 are dimes, and the rest are pennies and nickels. If there are twice as many pennies as nickels, how many pennies and nickels are in the jar?

Based on the given information, there are 90 total nickels and pennies in the jar (100 coins − 10 dimes = 90 nickels and pennies). Also, there are twice as many pennies as nickels. Using this information, guess results that fulfill the criteria and then adjust the guess in accordance with the result. Continue this iterative process until the correct answer is found: 60 pennies and 30 nickels. The table below illustrates this process.

NUMBER OF PENNIES	NUMBER OF NICKELS	TOTAL NUMBER OF PENNIES AND NICKELS
40	20	60
80	40	120
70	35	105
60	30	90

Another nondirect approach to problem solving is WORKING BACKWARD. If the result of a problem is known (for example, in problems that involve proving a particular result), it is sometimes helpful to begin from the conclusion and attempt to work backwards to a particular known starting point. A slight variation of this approach involves both working backward and working forward until a common point is reached somewhere in the middle. The following example from trigonometry illustrates this process.

Example:

Prove that $\sin^2\theta = \frac{1}{2} - \frac{1}{2}\cos^2\theta$.

If the method for proving this result is not clear, one approach is to work backward and forward simultaneously. The following two-column approach organizes the process. Judging from the form of the result, it is apparent that the Pythagorean identity is a potential starting point.

$\sin^2\theta + \cos^2\theta = 1$ $\sin^2\theta = \frac{1}{2} - \frac{1}{2}\cos^2\theta$

$\sin^2\theta = 1 - \cos^2\theta$ $\sin^2\theta = \frac{1}{2} - \frac{1}{2}(2\cos^2\theta - 1)$

$$\sin^2\theta = \frac{1}{2} - \cos^2\theta + \frac{1}{2}$$

$$\sin^2\theta = 1 - \cos^2\theta$$

Thus, a proof is apparent based on the combination of the reasoning in these two columns.

Selection of an appropriate problem-solving strategy depends largely on the type of problem being solved and the particular area of mathematics with which the problem deals. For instance, problems that involve proving a specific result often require different approaches than do problems that involve finding a numerical result.

Estimation as a problem-solving strategy

In order to estimate measurements, it is helpful to have a familiar reference with a known measurement. For instance, you can use the knowledge that a dollar bill is about six inches long or that a nickel weighs about 5 grams to make estimates of weight and length without actually measuring with a ruler or a balance.

Some common equivalents include:

ITEM	APPROXIMATELY EQUAL TO	
	Metric	Customary
large paper clip	1 gram	0.1 ounce
capacity of sports bottle	1 liter	1 quart
average sized adult	75 kilograms	170 pounds
length of an office desk	1 meter	1 yard
math textbook	1 kilogram	2 pounds
length of dollar bill	15 centimeters	6 inches
thickness of a dime	1 millimeter	0.1 inches
area of football field		6,400 sq. yd
temperature of boiling water	100°C	212°F
temperature of ice	0°C	32°F
1 cup of liquid	240 mL	8 fl oz
1 teaspoon	5 ml	

Example: Estimate the measurement of the following items:

The length of an adult cow = ___3___ meters

The thickness of a compact disc = ___2___ millimeters

Your height = ___1.5___ meters

The length of your nose = ___4___ centimeters

The weight of your math textbook = ___1___ kilogram

The weight of an automobile = ___1,000___ kilogram

The weight of an aspirin = ___1___ gram

Depending on the degree of accuracy needed, an object may be measured to different units.

For example, a pencil may be 6 inches to the nearest inch, or $6\frac{3}{8}$ inches to the nearest eighth of an inch. Similarly, it might be 15 cm to the nearest cm or 154 mm to the nearest mm.

Estimation and approximation may be used to check the reasonableness of answers.

Example: Estimate the answer.

$$\frac{58 \times 810}{1989}$$

58 becomes 60, 810 becomes 800, and 1989 becomes 2000.

$$\frac{60 \times 800}{2000} = 24$$

An estimate may sometimes be all that is needed to solve a word problem.

Example: Janet goes into a store to purchase a CD on sale for $13.95. While shopping, she sees two pairs of shoes, prices $19.95 and $14.50. She only has $50. Can she purchase everything, assuming no sales tax?

Solve by rounding:

$19.95 → $20.00

$14.50 → $15.00

$13.95 → $14.00

$49.00   Yes, she can purchase the CD and the shoes.

Solving number problems

Rational numbers include integers, fractions and mixed numbers, and terminating and repeating decimals. Every rational number can be expressed as a repeating or terminating decimal and can be shown on a number line.

Proportions can be used to solve word problems whenever relationships are compared. Some situations include scale drawings and maps, similar polygons, speed, time and distance, cost, and comparison shopping.

Example: Which is the better buy, 6 items for $1.29 or 8 items for $1.69?

Find the unit price.

$$6x = 1.29 \qquad\qquad 8x = 1.69$$
$$x = 0.215 \qquad\qquad x = 0.21125$$

Thus, 8 items for $1.69 is the better buy.

Example: A car travels 125 miles in 2.5 hours. How far will it go in 6 hours?

Write a proportion comparing the distance and time.

Let *x* represent distance in miles. Then,

$\frac{125}{2.5} = \frac{x}{6}$	Set up the proportion.
$2.5x = 6 \times 125$	Cross-multiply.
$2.5x = 750$	Simplify.
$\frac{2.5}{2.5}x = \frac{750}{2.5}$	Divide both sides of the equation by 2.5
$x = 300$ miles	Simplify.

Example: The scale on a map is one inch = 6 miles. What is the actual distance between two cities if they are 2 inches apart on the map?

Write a proportion comparing the scale to the actual distance.

Scale		Actual
x	=	1×6
x	=	6
$2x$	=	12

Thus, the actual distance between the cities is twelve miles.

Word problems involving percentages can be solved by writing the problem as an equation, then solving the equation. Keep in mind that *of* means multiplication and *is* means equals.

> Word problems involving percentages can be solved by writing the problem as an equation, then solving the equation.

Example: The ski club has eighty-five members; 80% of the members are able to attend the meeting. How many members attended the meeting?

Restate the problem:	What is 80% of 85?
Write an equation:	$n = 0.8 \times 85$
Solve:	$n = 68$

Sixty-eight members attended the meeting.

Example: There are sixty-four dogs in the kennel. Forty-eight are collies. What percentage are collies?

Restate the problem:	48 is what percentage of 64?
Write an equation:	$48 = n \times 64$
Solve:	$48 \div 64 = n$
	$n = 75\%$

Seventy-five percent of the dogs are collies.

Example: The auditorium was filled to 90% capacity. There were 558 seats occupied. What is the capacity of the auditorium?

Restate the problem:	90% of what number is 558?
Write an equation:	$0.9n = 558$
Solve:	$n = \frac{558}{0.9}$
	$n = 620$

The capacity of the auditorium is 620 people.

Example: Shoes cost $42.00. Sales tax is 6%. What is the total cost of the shoes?

Restate the problem:	What is 6% of 42?
Write an equation:	$n = 0.06 \times 42$
Solve:	$n = 2.52$
Add the sales tax:	$42.00 + 2.52 = 44.52$

The total cost of the shoes, including sales tax, is $44.52.

Solving problems involving measurement

The units of length in the customary system are inches, feet, yards, and miles.

12 inches (in.)	=	1 foot (ft.)
36 in.	=	1 yard (yd.)
3 ft.	=	1 yd.
5280 ft.	=	1 mile (mi.)
1760 yd.	=	1 mi.

To change from a larger unit to a smaller unit, multiply.

To change from a smaller unit to a larger unit, divide.

Example:

4 mi. = _____ yd.

Since 1760 yd. = 1 mile, multiply 4 × 1760 = 7040 yd.

Example:

21 in. = _____ ft.

21 ÷ 12 = 1.75 ft. (or 1 foot and 9 inches)

The units of weight are ounces, pounds, and tons.

16 ounces (oz.)	=	1 pound (lb.)
2000 lb.	=	1 ton (T.)

Example:

$2\frac{3}{4}$ T. = _____ lb.

$2\frac{3}{4} \times 2000 = 5500$ lb.

The units of capacity are fluid ounces, cups, pints, quarts, and gallons.

8 fluid ounces (fl. oz.)	=	1 cup (c.)
2 c.	=	1 pint (pt.)
4 c.	=	1 quart (qt.)
2 pt.	=	1 qt.
4 qt.	=	1 gallon (gal.)

Example:

3 gal. = _____ qt.

3 × 4 = 12 qt.

Example:

$1\frac{1}{4}$ cups = _____ oz.

$1\frac{1}{4} \times 8 = 10$ oz.

Example:

7 c. = _____ pt.

$7 \div 2 = 3\frac{1}{2}$ pt.

Square Units

Square units can be derived with knowledge of basic units of length by squaring the equivalent measurements.

1 square foot (sq. ft.)	=	144 sq. in.
1 sq. yd.	=	9 sq. ft.
1 sq. yd.	=	1296 sq. in.

Example:

14 sq. yd. = _____ sq. ft.
$14 \times 9 = 126$ sq. ft.

Metric Units

The metric system is based on multiples of ten. Conversions are made by simply moving the decimal point to the left or right.

METRIC PREFIXES AND THEIR MEANING		
kilo-	1000	thousands
hecto-	100	hundreds
deca-	10	tens
deci-	.1	tenths
centi-	.01	hundredths
milli-	.001	thousandths

The basic unit for length is the meter. One meter is approximately one yard.

The basic unit for weight or mass is the gram. A paper clip weighs about one gram.

The basic unit for volume is the liter. One liter is approximately a quart.

These are the most commonly used units.

1 m = 100 cm	1000 mL = 1 L
1 m = 1000 mm	1 kL = 1000 L
1 cm = 10 mm	1000 mg = 1 g
1000 m = 1 km	1 kg = 1000 g

The prefixes are commonly listed from left to right for ease in conversion.

K H D U D C M

Example:

63 km = _____ m

Since there are 3 steps from **K**ilo to **U**nit, move the decimal point 3 places to the right.

63 km = 63,000 m

Example:

14 mL = _____ L

Since there are 3 steps from **M**illi to **U**nit, move the decimal point 3 places to the left.

14 mL = 0.014 L

Example:

56.4 cm = _____ mm

56.4 cm = 564 mm

Example:

9.1 m = _____ km

9.1 m = 0.0091 km

Sample Test Questions and Rationale

(Easy)

1. When students are checking for reasonableness of an answer, which problem solving strategy can be used?

   A. Draw a diagram

   B. Work backwards

   C. Guess and check

   D. Estimation and approximation

   Answer: D. Estimation and approximation

   Sometimes an exact answer is not needed. When checking to see if an answer is reasonable, estimation and approximation are good strategies to use.

(Easy)

2. You are teaching your students how to solve problems using measurement. Items measured in fluid ounces, cups, pints, quarts, and gallons are all units for what type of measurement?

   A. Length

   B. Capacity

   C. Weight

   D. Mass

   Answer: B. Capacity

   Fluid ounces, cups, pints, quarts, and gallons are all units of capacity.

SKILL 5.3 Materials, equipment, texts, and technology in mathematics

The Use of Manipulatives for Teaching Math Concepts

MANIPULATIVES:
materials that students can physically handle and move

MANIPULATIVES are materials that students can physically handle and move. Manipulatives allow students to understand mathematical concepts by allowing them to see concrete examples of abstract processes. Manipulatives are attractive to students because they appeal to the students' visual and tactile senses. Available for all levels of math, manipulatives are useful tools for reinforcing operations and concepts. They are not, however, a substitute for the development of sound computational skills.

A popular activity using ordinary objects as manipulatives can be used to illustrate the base ten number system. This involves counting the days towards the 100th day of school. Students use straws (or small sticks) to represent each day. The students add a straw to their collection each day, and when they have ten, they bundle them with a rubber band. By the time they reach the 100th day, they have 9 bundles of 10, and when they add the last straw, they will have 10 bundles of 10. The students then bundle the 10 bundles of 10 into 1 bundle of 100.

Unifix Cubes are another excellent manipulative for teaching the base ten number system. They can be easily used as base ten blocks for exploring ones and tens. Each color can act as a group of ten when connected.

Technology and math

There are many forms of technology available to math teachers. For example, students can test their understanding of math concepts by working on skill specific computer programs and websites. Graphing calculators can help students visualize the graphs of functions. Teachers can also enhance their lectures and classroom presentations by creating multimedia presentations.

Here are some of the most important technology tools below:

- Computers: It is easy to look past the importance of the computer, itself, in the wake of Internet technology. However, many children from low socioeconomic backgrounds throughout the country lack access to computers and may not have basic computing skills. Indeed, many teachers must be taught to utilize some of the more advanced features that could help them with their daily work. In general, the computer is viewed as a tool for storage and efficient processing. While computers cannot replace teachers, they can be used to enhance the curriculum. Computers may be used to help students practice basic skills. Many excellent programs exist to encourage higher-order thinking skills, creativity and problem solving. Learning to use technology appropriately is an important preparation for adulthood. Computers can also show the connections between mathematics and the real world.

- Internet: There are many websites and options on the Internet for supplementing the teaching of math concepts. Teachers need to be conscientious about staying current with website options and also in evaluating the appropriateness of various sites for students.

- Calculators: Calculators are important tools. Their use should be encouraged in the classroom and at home. They do not replace basic knowledge, but they can relieve the tedium of mathematical computations, assuming that the requisite basic knowledge is already present. Students will be able to use calculators more intelligently if they are taught how. Students need to always check their work by estimating.

- Video Projection: Video in the classroom is a common tool to enhance the learning of students. Indeed, video has become a "text" in itself, much like literature. While the Internet has been a good source for information, video continues to be a great source of refined, carefully structured information for teachers and students.

Sample Test Questions and Rationale

(Average)

1. You are given a set of algebra tiles with your test book. How can you use these tiles to help teach your students equality?

    A. Place them on a scale or balance

    B. Divide the tiles into equal groups

    C. Factoring

    D. Model equations

    Answer: D. Model equations

    Algebra tiles can be used to model equations by taking away tiles from one side and adding them to the other to keep the equality.

(Rigorous)

2. You are teaching a class in probability. You toss a coin and record the number of times heads and tails appear on each toss. How can the use of technology help you arrive at the probability of heads?

    A. You can toss the coin more times by hand

    B. You can run more simulations on the computer than you can in class

    C. You forget to record some of the tosses

    D. The coin used in class may be biased

    Answer: B. You can run more simulations on the computer than you can in class

    Computer models can do many more trials in a matter of seconds than what can be done in class.

COMPETENCY 6
MATHEMATICS ASSESSMENT

SKILL **Analysis of student work in guiding mathematics instruction**
6.1

Formative Assessments

FORMATIVE ASSESSMENT takes place during the process of teaching a lesson. It can be both formal and informal, with the teacher assigning marks or making a simple note in the teacher's grade book. It could also be a note to the student reminding him or her of mistakes to watch out for. On another occasion, the teacher may look for the same things to see whether the student has improved. Formative assessment tells the teacher how well the students have mastered the objectives, and, if students are having difficulties, the teacher can adjust the instruction accordingly.

Teacher-made tests can be very effective in assessing how well students are doing with particular tasks or skills. However, the value of teacher observations cannot be underestimated. It is through the use of observations that the teacher is able to informally assess the needs of the students during instruction. These observations will drive the lesson and determine the direction that the lesson will take based on student activity and behavior.

After a lesson is carefully planned, teacher observation is the single most important component of an instructional presentation. If the teacher observes that a particular student is not on-task, she will change the method of instruction accordingly. She may change from a teacher-directed approach to a more interactive approach. Questioning will increase in order to increase the participation of the students. If appropriate, the teacher will introduce manipulative materials to the lesson. In addition, teachers may switch to a cooperative group activity, or plan a field trip or other external activity.

> **FORMATIVE ASSESSMENT:** a formal or informal way for a teacher to judge how well the students have mastered the objectives of a given assignment or lesson.

> *After a lesson is carefully planned, teacher observation is the single most important component of an instructional presentation*

Sample Test Questions and Rationale

(Easy)

1. You are teaching your students a lesson on adding fractions with and without common denominators. To make sure that students understand the lesson, what types of formal assessment can you add to your lesson?

   A. Quizzes after each concept is presented

   B. Essay questions

   C. Gauge students' reactions

   D. Take a vote

Answer: A. Quizzes after each concept is presented

Adding a one or two question quiz after each concept is presented is a good way to tell if students understand the material.

(Average)

2. You are teaching students a new concept that is related to a previously taught lesson. What is the best way to assess student's readiness for the new lesson?

   A. Jump right into the lesson without any connection to prior material

   B. Begin with a review and assessment of the previous skill

   C. Discuss how the new topic is related to a future topic

   D. Have students read the lesson and answer the exercises at the end of the lesson

Answer: B. Begin with a review and assessment of the previous skill

It is good to begin a new lesson by reviewing and assessing student's knowledge of previously learned skills. The skills of math are like building blocks that are used over and over again with slightly different twists.

(Easy)

3. Your students are having a difficult time understanding how to subtract with borrowing. Some students "just don't get it." Your teaching style tends to be the teacher-directed approach. Which one of the answers is not something you can do to help the students?

   A. Have the students who understand the material help the others

   B. Bring in manipulatives to help the students see the concept

   C. Keep teaching the way you are and hope the students catch up

   D. Switch to a cooperative group activity

Answer: C. Keep teaching the way you are and hope the students catch up

Continuing to teach when students do not understand the material leads to the students falling behind. It also does not help the student's self-esteem and confidence in his/her ability to do math.

Sample Test Questions and Rationale (cont.)

(Rigorous)

4. Why is planning some formal assessment during a lesson important?

   A. It gives the teacher a break from teaching

   B. It allows students a chance to catch up on the material if they are behind

   C. It allows the teacher to make sure all students understand the material. If they do not, it allows the teacher an opportunity to adjust the instruction

   D. It's not a good idea to use formal assessment during a lesson

Answer: C. It allows the teacher to make sure all students understand the material. If they do not, it allows the teacher an opportunity to adjust the instruction

Teachers need a way to make sure students understand the material. One or two questions asked at different parts of the lesson will let the teacher know if students understand the material.

SKILL 6.2 Formal and informal assessment of mathematics knowledge

Direct Observation

When assessing problem solving, the most effective method is direct observation. Teachers need to observe students to determine what strategies are being implemented. Watching students solve problems can provide teachers with insight into future teaching opportunities and skills mastered already by the students. Problem solving alone is difficult to assign a grade, but the information gained from the process is critical to future teaching.

Also, see Skills 18.2 and 18.3

Sample Test Question and Rationale

(Average)

1. **What is the most effective method to assess problem solving skills?**

   A. Informal assessment

   B. Formal assessment

   C. Student portfolios

   D. Direct observation

Answer: D. Direct observation

Teachers need to observe students to determine what strategies are being implemented.

DOMAIN III
SCIENCE

PERSONALIZED STUDY PLAN

COMPETENCY 7
SCIENCE CURRICULUM

Basic Organization of Life

The organization of living systems builds by levels from small to increasingly more large and complex. All living things, whether a cell or an ecosystem, have the same requirements to sustain life. Life is organized from simple to complex in the following ways:

Organelles make up cells. Cells make up tissues, and tissues make up organs. Groups of organs make up organ systems. Organ systems work together to provide life for an organism.

Several characteristics identify living versus nonliving substances.

1. Living things are made of cells; they grow, respond to stimuli and are capable of reproduction

2. Living things must adapt to environmental changes or perish

3. Living things carry on metabolic processes; they use and make energy

All organisms are adapted to life in their unique habitat. The habitat includes all the components of their physical environment and is a necessity for the species' survival. Below are several key components of a complete habitat that all organisms require.

Food and water

Because all biochemical reactions take place in aqueous environments, all organisms must have access to clean water, even if only infrequently. Organisms also require two types of food: a source of energy (fixed carbon) and a source of nutrients. AUTOTROPHS can fix carbon for themselves but must have access to certain inorganic precursors. These organisms must also be able to obtain other nutrients, such as nitrogen, from their environment. HETEROTROPHS, on the other hand, must consume other organisms for both energy and nutrients. The species these organisms use as a food source must be present in their habitat.

> **AUTOTROPHS:** can fix carbon for themselves but must have access to certain inorganic precursors

> **HETEROTROPHS:** must consume other organisms for both energy and nutrients

Sunlight and air

This need is closely related to that for food and water because almost all species derive some needed nutrients from the sun and atmosphere. Plants require carbon dioxide to photosynthesize and oxygen is required for cellular respiration. Sunlight is also necessary for photosynthesis and is used by many animals to synthesize essential nutrients (e.g., vitamin D).

Shelter and space

The need for shelter and space vary greatly between species. Many plants do not need shelter, per se, but must have adequate soil to spread their roots and acquire nutrients. Certain invasive species can threaten native plants by out-competing them for space. Other types of plants and many animals also require protection from environmental hazards. These locations may facilitate reproduction (for instance, nesting sites) or provide seasonal shelter (for example, dens and caves used by hibernating species).

Feeding relationships

DEFINITIONS OF FEEDING RELATIONSHIPS	
Parasitism	When two species occupy a similar place, but the parasite benefits from the relationship while the host is harmed.
Commensalism	When two species occupy a similar place, and neither species is harmed or benefits from the relationship.
Mutualism (Symbiosis)	When two species occupy a similar place and both species benefit from the relationship.
Competition	When two species occupy the same habitat or eat the same food.
Predation	When animals eat other animals. The animals they feed on are called the prey. Population growth depends upon competition for food, water, shelter, and space. The amount of predators determines the amount of prey, which in turn affects the number of predators.
Carrying Capacity	The total amount of life a habitat can support. Once the habitat runs out of food, water, shelter, or space, the carrying capacity decreases and then re-stabilizes.

TROPHIC LEVELS: the feeding relationships that determine energy flow and chemical cycling

TROPHIC LEVELS are based on the feeding relationships that determine energy flow and chemical cycling.

Autotrophs are the primary producers of the ecosystem. Producers mainly consist of plants. Primary consumers are the next trophic level. The primary consumers are the herbivores that eat plants or algae. Secondary consumers are the carnivores that eat the primary consumers. Tertiary consumers eat the secondary consumers. These trophic levels may go higher depending on the ecosystem. Decomposers are consumers that feed off animal waste and dead organisms. This pathway of food transfer is known as the food chain.

The Food Chain

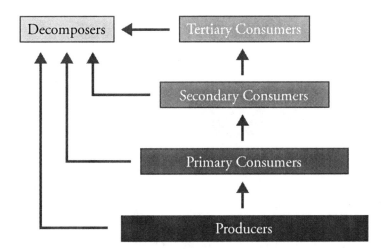

Basic Taxonomy of Organisms: Five Kingdoms

Living organisms are divided into five major kingdoms: Monera, Protista, Fungi, Plantae, and Animalia.

THE FIVE MAJOR KINGDOMS	
Kingdom Monera	Bacteria and blue-green algae; prokaryotic; have no true nucleus; unicellular.
Kingdom Protista	Eukaryotic; unicellular; some are photosynthetic, and some are consumers. Microbiologists use methods of locomotion, reproduction, and how the organism obtains its food to classify protista.
Kingdom Fungi	Eukaryotic; multicellular; absorptive consumers; contain a chitin cell wall.
Kingdom Plantae	Includes nonvascular plants (plants without true leaves, stems, or roots) like some mosses, vascular plants (vascular tissue is xylem and phloem which allows for the transport of water and minerals), and angiosperms, which are the flowering plants that produce true seeds for reproduction.
Kingdom Animalia	Includes annelid (worms), mollusks, arthropods (insects, crustaceans, and spiders), echinoderms (sea urchins and starfish), and all animals with a backbone (the phylum is chordate), which includes many fish, amphibians, reptiles, and mammals.

Life Cycles

A diagram of an organism's life cycle simply reveals the various stages through which it progresses from the time it is conceived until it reaches sexual maturity and reproduces, starting the cycle over again. However, the various types of animals pass through very different phases of life. The different species may either lay eggs or give live birth, pass through metamorphosis or be born in a form similar to that of an adult, and have aquatic and terrestrial phases or spend their entire lives on land. Some classic examples are outlined here.

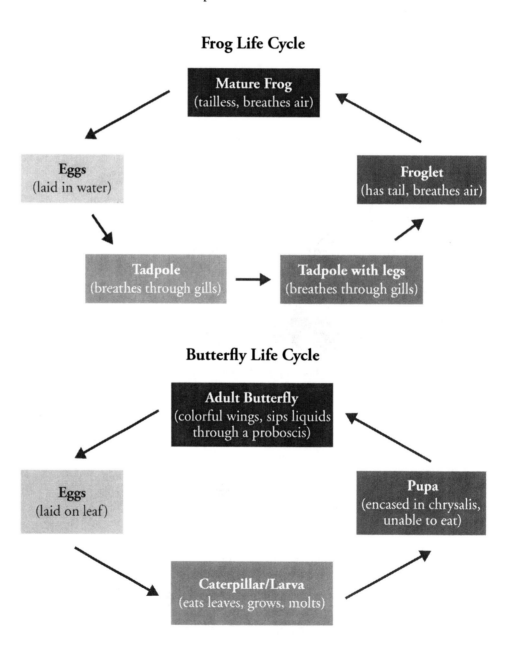

Frog Life Cycle

Mature Frog
(tailless, breathes air)

Eggs
(laid in water)

Froglet
(has tail, breathes air)

Tadpole
(breathes through gills)

Tadpole with legs
(breathes through gills)

Butterfly Life Cycle

Adult Butterfly
(colorful wings, sips liquids through a proboscis)

Eggs
(laid on leaf)

Pupa
(encased in chrysalis, unable to eat)

Caterpillar/Larva
(eats leaves, grows, molts)

Mouse Life Cycle

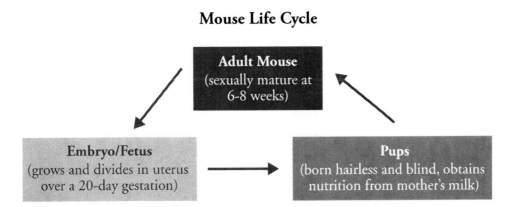

Ecological Problems

Nonrenewable resources are fragile and must be conserved for use in the future. Humankind's impact and knowledge of conservation will control our future. The following are just some of the ways in which the earth's ecology is altered by human interaction.

- Biological magnification: chemicals and pesticides accumulate along the food chain. Tertiary consumers have more accumulated toxins than animals at the bottom of the food chain.

- Simplification of the food web: three major crops feed the world (rice, corn, and wheat). Planting these foods in abundance wipes out habitats and pushes animals residing there into other habitats, causing overpopulation or extinction.

- Fuel sources: strip mining and the overuse of oil reserves have depleted these resources. At the current rate of consumption, the only way to guarantee our future fuel sources is conservation or alternate fuel sources.

- Pollution: although technology gives us many advances, pollution is a side effect of production. Waste disposal and the burning of fossil fuels have polluted our land, water, and air. Global warming and acid rain are two results of the burning of hydrocarbons and sulfur.

- Global warming: rainforest depletion and the use of fossil fuels and aerosols have caused an increase in carbon dioxide production. This leads to a decrease in the amount of oxygen, which is directly proportional to the amount of ozone. As the ozone layer depletes, more heat enters our atmosphere and is trapped. This causes an overall warming effect, which may eventually melt polar ice caps and cause a rise in water levels or changes in climate that will affect weather systems worldwide.

- Endangered species: construction of homes to house people has caused the destruction of habitats for other animals, leading to their extinction.

- Overpopulation: the human race is still growing at an exponential rate. Carrying capacity has not been met due to our ability to use technology to produce more food and housing. However, space and water cannot be manufactured; eventually, our nonrenewable resources will reach a crisis state. Our overuse affects every living thing on this planet.

Sample Test Questions and Rationale

(Easy)

1. Which of the following describes the interaction between community members when one species feeds of another species but does not kill it immediately?

   A. Parasitism

   B. Predation

   C. Commensalism

   D. Mutualism

   Answer: A. Parasitism

   Predation occurs when one species kills another species. In mutualism, both species benefit. In commensalism one species benefits without the other being harmed.

(Easy)

2. An ecosystem can be described as:

   A. The connection between plants, plant eaters, and animal eaters

   B. Relationships between a community and its physical environment

   C. The specific environment or place where an animal or plant lives

   D. Organisms that live and reproduce there

   Answer: B. Relationships between a community and its physical environment

   Animal and plant communities depend on interactions between each other and with the physical environment in general (e.g., air, water, enriched soil, temperature, and light). The sustaining of life through these interrelationships is called an ecosystem.

(Easy)

3. Which is not a characteristic of living organisms?

   A. Sexual reproduction

   B. Ingestion

   C. Synthesis

   D. Respiration

   Answer: A. Sexual reproduction

   Only certain organisms reproduce sexually, that is by mixing DNA. Single-celled organisms generally reproduce by cell division. Ingestion means taking nutrients from outside the cell wall. Synthesis means creating new cellular material. Respiration means generating energy by combining oxygen or some other gas with material in the cell.

Sample Test Questions and Rationale (cont.)

(Average)

4. Which of the following is not a property that eukaryotes have and prokaryotes do not have?

   A. Nucleus

   B. Ribosomes

   C. Chromosomes

   D. Mitochondria

Answer: B. Ribosomes

Prokaryotes do not have a nuclear membrane and the DNA is not packed into chromosomes. Mitochondria are organelles that produce power and are not found in the smaller, simpler cells. Ribosomes are the sites where cells assemble proteins.

SKILL **Earth and space science**
7.2

Minerals and Rocks

MINERALS are natural, nonliving solids with a definite chemical composition and a crystalline structure. ORES are minerals or rock deposits that can be mined for a profit. ROCKS are earth materials made of one or more minerals. A ROCK FACIES is a rock group that differs from comparable rocks (as in composition, age, or fossil content).

There are over 3,000 minerals in Earth's crust. Minerals are classified by composition. The major groups of minerals are

- Silicates
- Oxides
- Sulfates
- Carbonates
- Sulfides
- Halides

The largest group of minerals is the silicates. Silicates are made of silicon, oxygen, and one or more other elements. This is the most abundant class of minerals on Earth and includes quartz, garnets, micas, and feldspars.

Rocks

Rocks are simply aggregates of minerals. Rocks are classified by their differences in chemical composition and mode of formation. Generally, three classes are recognized: igneous, sedimentary, and metamorphic. However, it is common that one type of rock is transformed into another and this is known as the rock cycle.

MINERALS: natural, non-living solids with a definite chemical composition and a crystalline structure

ORES: minerals or rock deposits that can be mined for a profit

ROCKS: earth materials made of one or more minerals

ROCK FACIES: a rock group that differs from comparable rocks

Igneous rocks

IGNEOUS ROCKS: formed from molten magma

IGNEOUS ROCKS are formed from molten magma. There are two types of igneous rock: volcanic and plutonic. As the name suggests, volcanic rock is formed when magma reaches the Earth's surface as lava. Plutonic rock is also derived from magma, but it is formed when magma cools and crystallizes beneath the surface of the Earth. Thus, both types of igneous rock are magma that has cooled either above (volcanic) or below (plutonic) the Earth's crust. Examples of this type of rock include granite and obsidian glass.

Sedimentary rocks

SEDIMENTARY ROCKS: formed by the layered deposition of inorganic and/or organic matter

SEDIMENTARY ROCKS are formed by the layered deposition of inorganic and/or organic matter. Layers, or strata, of rock are laid down horizontally to form sedimentary rocks. Sedimentary rocks that form as mineral solutions (e.g., sea water) evaporate are called precipitate. Those that contain the remains of living organisms are termed biogenic. Finally, those that form from the freed fragments of other rocks are called clastic. Because the layers of sedimentary rocks reveal chronology and often contain fossils, these types of rock have been key in helping scientists understand the history of the earth. Chalk, limestone, sandstone, and shale are all examples of sedimentary rock.

Metamorphic rocks

METAMORPHIC ROCKS: created when rocks are subjected to high temperatures and pressures

METAMORPHIC ROCKS are created when rocks are subjected to high temperatures and pressures. The original rock, or protolith, may have been igneous, sedimentary, or even an older metamorphic rock. The temperatures and pressures necessary to achieve transformation are higher than those observed on the Earth's surface and are high enough to alter the minerals in the protolith. Because these rocks are formed within the Earth's crust, studying metamorphic rocks gives us clues to conditions in the Earth's mantle. In some metamorphic rocks, different colored bands are apparent. These result from strong pressures being applied from specific directions and is termed foliation. Examples of metamorphic rock include slate and marble.

Fossils

FOSSIL: the trace or remains of any once living organism

A FOSSIL is the trace or remains of any once living organism. The preservation of fossils in the environment is not all that common an occurrence. Although there is no formally set time limit to be considered a fossil, the term is not usually applied to remains less than 100 years old. Although soft tissues can be fossilized, they are very rare. If preserved, the fossil is usually found as hard points. Bones and shells are the most fossilized parts of the organism. Rapid burial is a major factor in fossilization. It helps to keep scavengers at bay and bacterial decay at a minimum. Some 99 percent of all fossils are found in sedimentary rock. The heat present in forming igneous and metamorphic rock generally obliterates organic remains.

Water

The unique properties of water are partially responsible for the development of life on Earth. Many of the unique qualities of water stem from the hydrogen bonds that form between the molecules. Hydrogen bonds are particularly strong dipole-dipole interactions that form between the H-atom of one molecule and an F, O, or N atom of an adjacent molecule. The partial positive charge on the hydrogen atom is attracted to the partial negative charge on the electron pair of the other atom. The hydrogen bond between two water molecules is shown as the dashed line below:

The unique properties of water are partially responsible for the development of life on Earth.

Hydrogen Bond

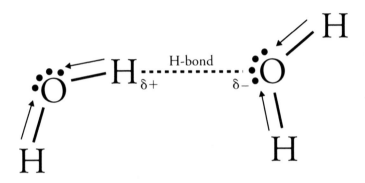

Erosion, weathering, and deposition

EROSION is the inclusion and transportation of surface materials by another moveable material, usually water, wind, or ice. The most important cause of erosion is running water. Streams, rivers, and tides are constantly at work removing weathered fragments of bedrock and carrying them away from their original location.

A stream erodes bedrock by the grinding action of the sand, pebbles and other rock fragments. This grinding against each other is called abrasion. Streams also erode rocks by dissolving or absorbing their minerals. Limestone and marble are readily dissolved by streams.

The breaking down of rocks at or near to the Earth's surface is known as WEATHERING. Weathering breaks down these rocks into smaller and smaller pieces. There are two types of weathering: physical weathering and chemical weathering.

PHYSICAL WEATHERING is the process by which rocks are broken down into smaller fragments without undergoing any change in chemical composition. Physical weathering is mainly caused by the freezing of water, the expansion of rock, and the activities of plants and animals.

EROSION: the inclusion and transportation of surface materials by another moveable material, usually water, wind, or ice

WEATHERING: the breaking down of rocks at or near to the Earth's surface

PHYSICAL WEATHERING: the process by which rocks are broken down into smaller fragments without undergoing any change in chemical composition

CHEMICAL WEATHERING: the breaking down of rocks through changes in their chemical composition

Frost wedging is the cycle of daytime thawing and refreezing at night. This cycle causes large rock masses, especially the rocks exposed on mountaintops, to be broken into smaller pieces.

CHEMICAL WEATHERING is the breaking down of rocks through changes in their chemical composition. An example would be the change of feldspar in granite to clay. Water, oxygen, and carbon dioxide are the main agents of chemical weathering. When water and carbon dioxide combine chemically, they produce a weak acid that breaks down rocks.

DEPOSITION: also known as sedimentation, is the term for the process by which material from one area is slowly deposited into another area

DEPOSITION, also known as sedimentation, is the term for the process by which material from one area is slowly deposited into another area. This is usually due to the movement of wind, water, or ice containing particles of matter. When the rate of movement slows down, particles filter out and remain behind, causing a build up of matter. Note that this is a result of matter being eroded and removed from another site.

Natural Objects in the Sky

There are eight established planets in our solar system. These are Mercury, Venus, Earth, Mars, Jupiter, Saturn, Uranus, and Neptune. Pluto was known as an established planet in our solar system, but as of Summer 2006, its status is being reconsidered. The planets are divided into two groups based on their distance from the Sun. The inner planets include Mercury, Venus, Earth, and Mars. The outer planets include Jupiter, Saturn, Uranus, and Neptune.

Solar System

Montage of planetary images taken by spacecraft managed by the Jet Propulsion Laboratory. Courtesy of NASA Jet Propulsion Laboratory, Pasadena, CA.

The inner planets

- Mercury: The closest planet to the Sun. Its surface has craters and rocks. The atmosphere is composed of hydrogen, helium and sodium. Mercury was named after the Roman messenger god.

- Venus: Has a slow rotation when compared to Earth. Venus and Uranus rotate in opposite directions from the other planets. This opposite rotation is called retrograde rotation. The surface of Venus is not visible due to the extensive cloud cover. The atmosphere is composed mostly of carbon dioxide. Sulfuric acid droplets in the dense cloud cover give Venus a yellow appearance. Venus has a greater greenhouse effect than observed on Earth. The dense clouds combined with carbon dioxide trap heat. Venus was named after the Roman goddess of love.

- Earth: Considered a water planet with 70 percent of its surface covered by water. Gravity holds the masses of water in place. The different temperatures observed on earth allow for the different states (solid, liquid, gas) of water to exist. The atmosphere is composed mainly of oxygen and nitrogen. Earth is the only planet that is known to support life.

- **Mars:** Surface contains numerous craters, active and extinct volcanoes, ridges, and valleys with extremely deep fractures. Iron oxide found in the dusty soil makes the surface seem rust colored and the skies seem pink in color. The atmosphere is composed of carbon dioxide, nitrogen, argon, oxygen and water vapor. Mars has polar regions with ice caps composed of water. Mars has two satellites and was named after the Roman war god.

The outer planets

- **Jupiter:** The largest planet in the solar system. Jupiter has 16 moons. The atmosphere is composed of hydrogen, helium, methane and ammonia. There are white colored bands of clouds indicating rising gas and dark colored bands of clouds indicating descending gases. The gas movement is caused by heat resulting from the energy of Jupiter's core. Jupiter has a Great Red Spot that is thought to be a hurricane type cloud. Jupiter has a strong magnetic field.

- **Saturn:** The second largest planet in the solar system. Saturn has rings of ice, rock, and dust particles circling it. Saturn's atmosphere is composed of hydrogen, helium, methane, and ammonia. Saturn has 20 plus satellites and was named for the Roman god of agriculture.

- **Uranus:** the second largest planet in the solar system with retrograde revolution. Uranus is a gaseous planet. It has 10 dark rings and 15 satellites. Its atmosphere is composed of hydrogen, helium, and methane. Uranus was named after the Greek god of the heavens.

- **Neptune:** Another gaseous planet with an atmosphere consisting of hydrogen, helium, and methane. Neptune has 3 rings and 2 satellites. Neptune was named after the Roman sea god because its atmosphere is the same color as the seas.

Other natural objects

Pluto was once considered the smallest planet in the solar system; its status as a planet is being reconsidered. Pluto's atmosphere probably contains methane, ammonia, and frozen water. Pluto has 1 satellite. Pluto revolves around the Sun every 250 years. Pluto was named after the Roman god of the underworld.

ASTEROIDS are found in the region between Mars and Jupiter. Astronomers believe that these rocky fragments may have been the remains of the birth of the solar system that never formed into a planet.

> **ASTEROIDS:** found in the region between Mars and Jupiter

COMETS: masses of frozen gases, cosmic dust, and small rocky particles

COMETS are masses of frozen gases, cosmic dust, and small rocky particles. Astronomers think that most comets originate in a dense comet cloud beyond Pluto. A comet consists of a nucleus, a coma, and a tail. A comet's tail always points away from the sun. The most famous comet, Halley's Comet, is named after the person whom first discovered it in 240 B.C. It returns to the skies near earth every 75 to 76 years.

METEOROIDS: composed of particles of rock and metal of various sizes

METEOROIDS are composed of particles of rock and metal of various sizes. When a meteoroid travels through the earth's atmosphere, friction causes its surface to heat up and it begins to burn. The burning meteoroid falling through the earth's atmosphere is called a meteor (also known as a "shooting star").

METEORITES: meteors that strike the earth's surface

METEORITES are meteors that strike the earth's surface. A physical example of a meteorite's impact on the earth's surface can be seen in Arizona. The Barringer Crater is a huge meteor crater. There are many other meteor craters throughout the world.

CONSTELLATIONS: groups or patterns of stars

Astronomers use groups or patterns of stars called CONSTELLATIONS as reference points to locate other stars in the sky. Familiar constellations include Ursa Major (also known as the big bear) and Ursa Minor (known as the little bear). Within the Ursa Major, the smaller constellation, the Big Dipper is found. Within the Ursa Minor, the smaller constellation, the Little Dipper is found.

Different constellations appear as the earth continues its revolution around the sun with the seasonal changes. Magnitude stars are 21 of the brightest stars that can be seen from earth. These are the first stars noticed at night. There are 15 commonly observed first magnitude stars in the Northern Hemisphere.

GALAXY: a vast collection of stars

A vast collection of stars is defined as a GALAXY. Galaxies are classified as irregular, elliptical, and spiral. An irregular galaxy has no real structured appearance; most are in their early stages of life. An elliptical galaxy consists of smooth ellipses, containing little dust and gas, but composed of millions or trillion stars. Spiral galaxies are disk-shaped and have extending arms that rotate around its dense center. Earth's galaxy is found in the Milky Way, and it is a spiral galaxy.

Human-made Objects in the Sky

Space satellites

An artificial **SATELLITE** is any object placed into orbit by human endeavor. A satellite revolves around a planet in a circular or elliptical path. Most man-made satellites are useful objects placed in orbit purposely to perform some specific mission or task. Such satellites may include:

- Weather satellites

- Communication satellites

- Navigational satellites

- Reconnaissance satellites

- Scientific study satellites

Satellites are placed into orbit by first riding on a rocket or in the cargo bay of a space shuttle that is launched into space. Once the vessel has reached the satellite's destination, the satellite is released into space and remains in orbit due to the Earth's gravitational pull. The largest artificial satellite currently orbiting the Earth is the International Space Station. Currently, there are approximately 23,000 items of space junk—objects large enough to track with radar that were inadvertently placed in orbit or have outlived their usefulness—floating above Earth.

Airplanes

AIRPLANES or fixed-wing aircraft are heavier than aircraft that utilize the laws of physics to achieve flight. Airplanes achieve flight using the concepts of lift, weight, thrust, and drag. Lift pushes the plane upward and is created by the design of aircraft wings, which have flat bottoms and slightly rounded tops. As the aircraft is propelled forward by thrust from the engines, air moves faster over the top of the wings, and slower under the bottom. The slower airflow beneath the wing generates more pressure, while the faster airflow above generates less. This difference in pressure results in upward lift. Weight is Earth's gravity pulling down on a plane. Planes are designed to remain level, with equal weight in the front and back of the plane. Drag is the opposite force that slows a plane. Planes minimize drag with aerodynamic design.

Humankind's interest in flight is documented as far back as Greek mythology. The first real study of flight, however, is attributed to Leonardo da Vinci, who designed a craft called the orthinopter, on which the modern day helicopter is based. The Wright Brothers achieved the first successful flight off the outer

> **SATELLITE:** any object placed into orbit by human endeavor

Seasonal change on Earth is caused by the orbit and axial tilt of the planet in relation to the Sun's ecliptic, which is the rotational path of the Sun.

SURFACE CURRENTS: caused by winds and classified by temperature

COLD CURRENTS: originate in the polar regions and flow through surrounding water that is measurably warmer

EQUATOR: the imaginary line that runs around the middle of the Earth's surface and is equidistant from the North and South Poles

THUNDERSTORM: a brief, local storm produced by the rapid upward movement of warm, moist air within a cumulonimbus cloud

TORNADO: a severe storm with swirling winds that may reach speeds of hundreds of km per hour.

HURRICANES: storms that develop when warm, moist air carried by trade winds rotates around a low-pressure "eye".

banks of North Carolina. They developed their craft by first studying many early attempts at flight, and then testing their own theories using balloons and kites. The brothers designed gliders to understand craft control and wind effects. Using a wind tunnel, the Wright Brothers tested many different wing and tail shapes. After determining a glider shape that consistently passed flight tests, they began to develop a propulsion system capable of creating lift. Eventually, the brothers constructed an engine capable of generating almost twelve horsepower. On December 17, 1903, the Wright Brother's craft known as the "Flyer" lifted from ground level piloted by brother Orville, and traveled 120 feet.

Weather

Seasonal change on Earth is caused by the orbit and axial tilt of the planet in relation to the Sun's ecliptic, which is the rotational path of the Sun. These factors combine to vary the degree of insolation (distribution of solar energy) at a particular location and thereby change the seasons.

World weather patterns are greatly influenced by ocean surface currents in the upper layer of the ocean. These currents continuously move along the ocean surface in specific directions. SURFACE CURRENTS are caused by winds and classified by temperature. COLD CURRENTS originate in the polar regions and flow through surrounding water that is measurably warmer. Those currents with a higher temperature than the surrounding water are called warm currents and can be found near the EQUATOR. These currents follow swirling routes around the ocean basins and the equator. The Gulf Stream and the California Current are the two main surface currents that flow along the coastlines of the United States. The California Current is a cold current that originates in the Arctic regions and flows southward along the western coast of the United States.

A THUNDERSTORM is a brief, local storm produced by the rapid upward movement of warm, moist air within a cumulonimbus cloud. Thunderstorms always produce lightning and thunder, and are accompanied by strong wind gusts and heavy rain or hail.

A severe storm with swirling winds that may reach speeds of hundreds of km per hour is called a TORNADO. Such a storm is also referred to as a "twister." Large cumulonimbus clouds cover the sky and violent thunderstorms occur. A funnel-shaped swirling cloud may extend downward from a cumulonimbus cloud and reach the ground. Tornadoes are storms that leave a narrow path of destruction on the ground.

HURRICANES are storms that develop when warm, moist air carried by trade winds rotates around a low-pressure "eye." A large, rotating, low-pressure system accompanied by heavy precipitation and strong winds is called a tropical CYCLONE (better known as a hurricane). In the Pacific region, a hurricane is called a typhoon.

Storms that occur only in the winter are known as blizzards or ice storms. A BLIZZARD is a storm with strong winds, blowing snow and frigid temperatures. An ICE STORM consists of falling rain that freezes when it strikes the ground, covering everything with a layer of ice.

CYCLONE: a large, rotating, low-pressure system accompanied by heavy precipitation and strong winds

BLIZZARD: a storm with strong winds, blowing snow and frigid temperatures

ICE STORM: consists of falling rain that freezes when it strikes the ground, covering everything with a layer of ice

Sample Test Questions and Rationale

(Average)

1. **Tornados often happen over the Midwest United States because:**

   A. Warm, dry air is forced to rise over the Rocky Mountains

   B. The maritime polar air mass and continental tropical air mass meet over the Midwest

   C. Cold air from the Rockies sinks rapidly and forces a funnel cloud to the surface

   D. The maritime tropical and continental polar air mass meet over the Midwest

   Answer: D. The maritime tropical and continental polar air mass meet over the Midwest

   The warm moist air mass and the cold dry air mass clash over the middle of the United States. The warm, moist air is forced up and over the dry air mass, condenses forming large, unstable clouds. These clouds can begin to circulate, causing tornadoes.

(Average)

2. **Why is the winter in the Southern Hemisphere colder than winter in the Northern Hemisphere?**

   A. Earth's axis of 24-hour rotation tilts at an angle of 23°

   B. The elliptical orbit of Earth around the Sun changes the distance of the Sun from Earth

   C. The Southern Hemisphere has more water than the Northern Hemisphere

   D. The green house effect is greater for the Northern Hemisphere

   Answer: B. The elliptical orbit of Earth around the Sun changes the distance of the Sun from the Earth

   The tilt of Earth's axis causes the seasons. The Earth is close to the Sun during winter in the Northern Hemisphere. Winter in the Southern Hemisphere occurs six months later when Earth is farther from the Sun. The presence of water explains why winters are harsher inland than by the coast.

Sample Test Questions and Rationale (cont.)

(Easy)

3. **Earth's atmosphere contains mostly:**

   A. Carbon dioxide

   B. Oxygen

   C. Helium

   D. Hydrogen

   Answer: B. Oxygen

   Earth's atmosphere contains mostly oxygen.

(Average)

4. **Which word will complete the sentence?**

   It will be _____ cold for us to camp outside this weekend.

   A. too

   B. to

   C. two

   D. tow

   Answer: A. too

   Too shows extremes or means "also." In this sentence, the weather will be below an acceptable temperature so camping will not be an option.

SKILL **Physical science**
7.3

Matter, Mass, and Weight

MATTER: anything that takes up space and has mass

Everything in our world is made up of MATTER, whether it is a rock, a building, an animal, or a person. Matter is defined by its characteristics: it takes up space and it has mass.

MASS: a measure of the amount of matter in an object

MASS is a measure of the amount of matter in an object. Two objects of equal mass will balance each other on a simple balance scale no matter where the scale is located. For instance, two rocks with the same amount of mass that are in balance on Earth will also be in balance on the Moon. They will feel heavier on Earth than on the Moon because of the gravitational pull of the Earth. So, although the two rocks have the same mass, they will have different weights.

WEIGHT: the measure of the Earth's pull of gravity on an object

WEIGHT is the measure of the Earth's pull of gravity on an object. It can also be defined as the pull of gravity between other bodies. The units of weight measurement commonly used are the pound (English measure) and the kilogram (metric measure).

Properties of matter

Physical properties and chemical properties of matter describe the appearance or behavior of a substance. A physical property can be observed without changing the identity of a substance. For instance, you can describe the color, mass, shape, and volume of a book. Chemical properties describe the ability of a substance to be changed into new substances. Baking powder goes through a chemical change as it changes into carbon dioxide gas during the baking process.

Matter constantly changes. A PHYSICAL CHANGE is a change that does not produce a new substance. The freezing and melting of water is an example of physical change. A CHEMICAL CHANGE (or chemical reaction) is any change of a substance into one or more other substances. Burning materials turn into smoke; a seltzer tablet fizzes into gas bubbles.

The PHASE OF MATTER (solid, liquid, or gas) is identified by its shape and volume.

A solid has a definite shape and volume. A liquid has a definite volume, but no shape. A gas has no shape or volume because it will spread out to occupy the entire space of whatever container it is in.

Energy

ENERGY is the ability to cause change in matter. Applying heat to a frozen liquid changes it from solid back to liquid. Continue heating it, and it will boil and give off steam, a gas. EVAPORATION is the change in phase from liquid to gas. CONDENSATION is the change in phase from gas to liquid.

Magnets

A MAGNET is a material or object that attracts certain metals, such as cobalt, nickel, and iron and can also repel or attract another magnet. All magnets have poles: a North-seeking (N) and a South-seeking (S). In a compass, the side marked N will point toward the Earth's North magnetic pole, which is different from the North Pole (they are actually several hundred miles apart). If you cut a magnet into parts, each part will have both North and South poles. If you place magnets near each other, the opposite poles will attract and the like poles will repel each other. Therefore, a North pole will repel a North pole and attract a South pole.

The first true application of a magnet was the compass, which not only helps in navigation but also can help in detecting small magnetic fields. Magnets are also

PHYSICAL CHANGE: a change that does not produce a new substance

CHEMICAL CHANGE: (or chemical reaction) is any change of a substance into one or more other substances

PHASE OF MATTER: (solid, liquid, or gas) is identified by its shape and volume

ENERGY: the ability to cause change in matter

EVAPORATION: the change in phase from liquid to gas

CONDENSATION: the change in phase from gas to liquid

MAGNET: a material or object that attracts certain metals, such as cobalt, nickel, and iron and can also repel or attract another magnet

The first true application of a magnet was the compass, which not only helps in navigation but also can help in detecting small magnetic fields.

found in loudspeakers, electrical generators, and electrical motors. A very common use of magnets is to stick things to the refrigerator.

A **MAGNETIC FIELD** is made up of imaginary lines of flux resulting from moving or spinning electrically charged particles. These lines of magnetic flux move from one end of a magnetic object to the other, or rather, from the North-seeking pole to the South-seeking pole.

Magnetic and electric fields are similar in that in electricity, like charges repel, and in magnetism, like poles repel. They are different in that a magnet must have two poles, but an electrical charge, positive or negative, can stand alone.

> **MAGNETIC FIELD:** made up of imaginary lines of flux resulting from moving or spinning electrically charged particles

Heat

> **HEAT:** a measure of energy

Heat and temperature are different physical quantities. **HEAT** is a measure of energy. **TEMPERATURE** is the measure of how hot (or cold) a body is with respect to a standard object.

> **TEMPERATURE:** the measure of how hot (or cold) a body is with respect to a standard object

We cannot rely on our sense of touch to determine temperature because the heat from a hand may be conducted more efficiently by certain objects, making them feel colder. **THERMOMETERS** are used to measure temperature. A small amount of mercury in a capillary tube will expand when heated. The thermometer and the object whose temperature it is measuring are put in contact long enough for them to reach thermal equilibrium. Then the temperature can be read from the thermometer scale. Three temperature scales are used. These are Celsius, Fahrenheit, and Kelvin.

> **THERMOMETERS:** used to measure temperature

Sample Test Questions and Rationale

(Easy)

1. **Which statement is true about temperature?**

   A. Temperature is a measurement of heat

   B. Temperature is how hot or cold an object is

   C. The coldest temperature ever measured is zero degrees Kelvin

   D. The temperature of a molecule is its kinetic energy

   Answer: B. Temperature is how hot or cold an object is

Temperature is a physical property of objects relating to how they feel when touched. Zero degrees Celsius or −32 degrees Fahrenheit is defined as the temperature of ice water. Heat is a form of energy that flows from hot objects in thermal contact with cold objects. The greater the temperature of an object, the greater the kinetic energy of the molecules making up the object, but a single molecule does not have a temperature.

Sample Test Questions and Rationale (cont.)

(Rigorous)

2. **Which statement best explains why a balance scale is used to measure both weight and mass?**

   A. The weight and mass of an object are identical concepts

   B. The force of gravity between two objects depends on the mass of the two objects

   C. Inertial mass and gravitational mass are identical

   D. A balance scale compares the weight of two objects

Answer: C. Inertial mass and gravitational mass are identical

The mass of an object is a fundamental property of matter and is measured in kilograms. The weight is the force of gravity between Earth and an object near Earth's surface and is measured in Newtons or pounds. Newton's second law ($F = ma$) and the universal law of gravity ($F = G \frac{m_{earth} m}{d^2}$) determine the weight of an object. The mass in Newton's second law is called the inertial mass and the mass in the universal law of gravity is called the gravitational mass. The two kinds of masses are identical.

SKILL 7.4 Health

Overview of Systems in the Human Body

The function of the SKELETAL SYSTEM is support. Vertebrates have an endoskeleton, with muscles attached to bones. Skeletal proportions are controlled by area to volume relationships. Body size and shape is limited due to the forces of gravity. Surface area is increased to improve efficiency in all organ systems.

SKELETAL SYSTEM: the system concerned with support

The function of the MUSCULAR SYSTEM is movement. There are three types of muscle tissue. Skeletal muscle is voluntary. These muscles are attached to bones. Smooth muscle is involuntary. It is found in organs and enable functions such as digestion and respiration. Cardiac muscle is a specialized type of smooth muscle.

MUSCULAR SYSTEM: the system concerned with movement

The neuron is the basic unit of the NERVOUS SYSTEM. It consists of an axon, which carries impulses away from the cell body, the dendrite, which carries impulses toward the cell body, and the cell body, which contains the nucleus. Synapses are spaces between neurons. Chemicals called neurotransmitters are found close to the synapse. The myelin sheath, composed of Schwann cells, covers the neurons and provides insulation.

NERVOUS SYSTEM: the system that carries signals between different parts of

DIGESTIVE SYSTEM: the system that breaks down food and absorbs it into the blood stream

The function of the DIGESTIVE SYSTEM is to break down food and absorb it into the blood stream where it can be delivered to all cells of the body for use in cellular respiration. As animals evolved, digestive systems changed from simple absorption to a system with a separate mouth and anus, capable of allowing the animal to become independent of a host.

The RESPIRATORY SYSTEM functions in the gas exchange of oxygen (needed) and carbon dioxide (waste). It delivers oxygen to the bloodstream and picks up carbon dioxide for release out of the body. Simple animals diffuse gases from and to their environment. Gills allow aquatic animals to exchange gases in a fluid medium by removing dissolved oxygen from the water. Lungs maintain a fluid environment for gas exchange in terrestrial animals.

The function of the CIRCULATORY SYSTEM is to carry oxygenated blood and nutrients to all cells of the body and return carbon dioxide waste to be expelled from the lungs. Animals evolved from an open system to a closed system with vessels leading to and from the heart.

Nutrition and Exercise

The components of nutrition are carbohydrates, proteins, fats, vitamins and minerals, and water.

CARBOHYDRATES are the main source of energy (glucose) in the human diet. The two types of carbohydrates are simple and complex. Complex carbohydrates have greater nutritional value because they take longer to digest, contain dietary fiber, and do not excessively elevate blood sugar levels. Common sources of carbohydrates are fruits, vegetables, grains, dairy products, and legumes.

PROTEINS are necessary for growth, development, and cellular function. The body breaks down consumed protein into component amino acids for future use. Major sources of protein are meat, poultry, fish, legumes, eggs, dairy products, grains, and legumes.

FATS are a concentrated energy source and important component of the human body. The different types of fats are saturated, monounsaturated, and polyunsaturated. Polyunsaturated fats are the healthiest because they may lower cholesterol levels, while saturated fats increase cholesterol levels. Common sources of saturated fats include dairy products, meat, coconut oil, and palm oil. Common sources of unsaturated fats include nuts, most vegetable oils, and fish.

VITAMINS AND MINERALS are organic substances that the body requires in small quantities for proper functioning. People acquire vitamins and minerals in their diets and in supplements. Important vitamins include A, B, C, D, E, and K. Important minerals include calcium, phosphorus, magnesium, potassium,

RESPIRATORY SYSTEM: the system that functions in the gas exchange of oxygen and carbon dioxide

CIRCULATORY SYSTEM: the system that carries oxygenated blood and nutrients to all cells of the body and returns carbon dioxide waste to be expelled from the lungs

CARBOHYDRATES: the main source of energy (glucose) in the human diet

PROTEINS: necessary for growth, development, and cellular function

FATS: a concentrated energy source and important component of the human body

VITAMINS AND MINERALS: organic substances that the body requires in small quantities for proper functioning

sodium, chlorine, and sulfur.

WATER makes up fifty-five to seventy-five percent of the human body and is essential for most bodily functions. It is obtained through foods and liquids.

WATER: makes up fifty-five to seventy-five percent of the human body and is essential for most bodily functions

Determining the adequacy of diets in meeting the nutritional needs of students

Nutritional requirements vary from person-to-person. General guidelines for meeting adequate nutritional needs are:

Nutritional requirements vary from person-to-person.

- No more than 30 percent total caloric intake from fats (preferably 10 percent from saturated fats, 10 percent from monounsaturated fats, 10 percent from polyunsaturated fats)

- No more than 15 percent total caloric intake from protein (complete)

- At least 55 percent of caloric intake from carbohydrates (mainly complex carbohydrates)

Exercise and diet help maintain proper body weight by equalizing caloric intake and caloric output.

Regular exercise improves overall health. Benefits of regular exercise include:

- Stronger immune system
- Stronger muscles, bones, and joints
- Reduced risk of premature death
- Reduced risk of heart disease
- Improved psychological well-being
- Weight management

The health risk factors improved by physical activity include:

- Cholesterol levels
- Blood pressure
- Stress-related disorders
- Heart diseases
- Weight and obesity disorders
- Early death
- Certain types of cancer
- Musculoskeletal problems
- Mental health
- Susceptibility to infectious diseases

COMPETENCY 8
SCIENCE INSTRUCTION

SKILL **Scientific concepts and processes**
8.1

The History of Science

Science began with the agricultural revolution 10,000 years ago because there was apparently a body of knowledge that enabled humans to increase production. Pythagoras' theorem (circa 490 B.C.) was actually recorded on Mesopotamian cuneiform tablets in 1800 B.C. Ancient Greeks discovered the principle behind buoyancy and the approximate radius of Earth. Indians made considerable discoveries in mathematics and astronomy from the 5th to 15th centuries A.D. During this period, there were many pure and applied scientific discoveries in China:

- Compasses
- Movable-type printing
- Atlases of stars
- Cast iron
- The iron plough

- The wheelbarrow
- The suspension bridge
- Solid fuel rocket
- Many more

The scientific method began with Muslim scientists in the Middle Ages, not only because of their achievements in optics, mathematics, chemistry, and astronomy, but because philosophers of the Arab Empire explicitly advocated the need for experiments, observations, and measurements.

The rise of science in the West began with the rise of universities in the 12th century. Roger Bacon (1224–1294) is considered one of the early advocates of the scientific method. In the 14th century, there was scientific progress in kinematics, but the Scientific Revolution began in the 16th century with the heliocentric theory of Nicolaus Copernicus. In 1605, Johannes Kepler discovered that planets orbit the sun in elliptical, not circular paths. In 1677, Isaac Newton derived Kepler's laws from the second law of motion.

In the 19th century, science became a profession and an institution in Western nation-states. The economic progress was due in part to the technological advances made possible by science, and scientific progress was made possible by the economic progress. The rise in science in the West was caused by the cultural and institutional circumstances that existed in Western countries. The increase in the number of women scientists and other minority groups in recent years was caused by the changing values of individuals and changes in institutional structures.

Equilibrium

Math, science, and technology have common themes in how they are applied and understood. All three use models, diagrams, and graphs to simplify a concept for analysis and interpretation. Patterns observed in these systems lead to predictions based on these observations. Another common theme among these three systems is equilibrium. EQUILIBRIUM is a state in which forces are balanced, resulting in stability. STATIC EQUILIBRIUM is stability due to a lack of changes and DYNAMIC EQUILIBRIUM is stability due to a balance between opposite forces.

The fundamental relationship between the natural and social sciences is the use of the scientific method and the rigorous standards of proof that both disciplines require. This emphasis on organization and evidence separates the sciences from the arts and humanities. Natural science, particularly biology, is closely related to social science, the study of human behavior. Biological and environmental factors often dictate human behavior; an accurate assessment of behavior requires a sound understanding of biological factors.

Technology, Data, and Science

The combination of science, mathematics, and technology forms the scientific endeavor and makes science a success. It is impossible to study science on its own without the support of other disciplines like mathematics, technology, geology, physics, and other disciplines.

Science is tentative. By definition, it is searching for information by making educated guesses. It must be replicable. Another scientist must be able to achieve the same results under the same conditions at a later time. The term EMPIRICAL means a phenomenon must be assessed through tests and observations. Science changes over time. Science is limited by the available technology. An example of this would be the relationship of the discovery of the cell and the invention of the microscope. As our technology improves, more hypotheses will become theories and possibly laws.

Science is also limited by the data that is able to be collected. Data may be interpreted differently on different occasions. Science limitations cause explanations to be changeable as new technologies emerge. New technologies gather previously unavailable data and enable us to build upon current theories with new information.

EQUILIBRIUM: a state in which forces are balanced, resulting in stability

STATIC EQUILIBRIUM: stability due to a lack of changes

DYNAMIC EQUILIBRIUM: stability due to a balance between opposite forces

The fundamental relationship between the natural and social sciences is the use of the scientific method and the rigorous standards of proof that both disciplines require.

EMPIRICAL: means a phenomenon must be assessed through tests and observations

The combination of science, mathematics, and technology forms the scientific endeavor and makes science a success.

SKILL **Scientific inquiry**
8.2

> Science may be defined as a body of knowledge that is systematically derived from study, observations, and experimentation.

Science may be defined as a body of knowledge that is systematically derived from study, observations, and experimentation. Its goal is to identify and establish principles and theories that may be applied to solve problems. Pseudoscience, on the other hand, is a belief that is not warranted. There is no scientific methodology or application. Some of the more classic examples of pseudoscience include witchcraft, alien encounters, or any topics that are explained by hearsay.

The Process of Scientific Inquiry

Observation

SCIENTIFIC INQUIRY: the process by which one attempts to discover scientific fact through observation and experimentation

SCIENTIFIC INQUIRY starts with observation. Observation is a very important skill by itself, as it leads to experimentation and communicating the experimental findings to the public. After observing, a question is formed, which starts with "why" or "how." To answer these questions, experimentation is necessary. Between observation and experimentation there are three more important steps. These are:

- Gathering information (or researching the problem)
- Forming a hypothesis
- Designing the experiment

CONTROL: something we compare our results with at the end of the experiment

Experimentation

CONSTANTS: the factors that are kept the same in an experiment to get reliable results

Designing an experiment is very important since it involves identifying control, constants, independent variables, and dependent variables. A CONTROL is something we compare our results with at the end of the experiment. It is like a reference. CONSTANTS are the factors that are kept the same in an experiment to get reliable results. INDEPENDENT VARIABLES are factors we change in an experiment. DEPENDENT VARIABLES are the changes that arise from the experiment. It is very important to bear in mind that there should be more constants than variables to obtain reproducible results in an experiment.

INDEPENDENT VARIABLES: factors we change in an experiment

DEPENDENT VARIABLES: the changes that arise from the experiment

Communication

After the experiment is done, it is repeated and results are graphically presented. The results are then analyzed and conclusions drawn. After the conclusion is drawn, the final step is communication. It is the responsibility of scientists to share the knowledge they obtain through their research. In this age, much emphasis is put on the way and the method of communication. The conclusions must be communicated by clearly describing the information using accurate data and visual presentations like graphs (bar/line/pie), tables/charts, diagrams, artwork, and other appropriate media. Modern technology should be used whenever it is necessary. The method of communication must be suitable to the audience.

Written communication is as important as oral communication. This is essential for submitting research papers to scientific journals, newspapers, and other magazines.

Drawing conclusions and interpreting data

Whenever scientists begin an experiment or project, they must decide what pieces of data they are going to collect. This data could be qualitative or quantitative. Scientists use a variety of methods to gather and analyze this data. Some possibilities include storing the data in a table or analyzing the data using a graph. Scientists also make notes of their observations (what they see, hear, smell, etc.), throughout the experiment. Scientists are then able to use the data and observations to make inferences and draw conclusions about a question or problem.

Several steps should be followed in the interpretation and evaluation of data.

1. First, the scientist should apply critical analysis and thinking strategies asking questions about the accuracy of the data and the procedures of the experiment and procurement of the data.

2. Second is to determine the importance of information and its relevance to the essential question. Any experiment may produce a plethora of data, not all of which is necessary to consider when analyzing the hypothesis. The useful information must then be separated into component parts.

3. At this point, the scientist may then make inferences, identify trends, and interpret data. The final step is to determine the most appropriate method of communicating these inferences and conclusions to the intended audience.

The scientific attitude is to be curious, open to new ideas, and skeptical. In science, there is always new research, new discoveries, and new theories proposed. Sometimes, old theories are disproved. To view these changes rationally, one must have openness, curiosity, and skepticism. (Skepticism is a Greek word, meaning a method of obtaining knowledge through systematic doubt and continual testing. A scientific skeptic is one who refuses to accept certain types of claims without subjecting them to a systematic investigation.) The students may not have these attitudes inherently, but it is the responsibility of the teacher to encourage, nurture, and practice these attitudes so that students will have a good role model.

A SCIENTIFIC THEORY is an explanation of a set of related observations based on a proven hypothesis. A SCIENTIFIC LAW usually lasts longer than a scientific theory and has more experimental data to support it.

The scientific attitude is to be curious, open to new ideas, and skeptical.

SCIENTIFIC THEORY: an explanation of a set of related observations based on a proven hypothesis

SCIENTIFIC LAW: usually lasts longer than a scientific theory and has more experimental data to support it

Simple Investigations

The scientific method is the basic process behind science. It involves several steps, beginning with hypothesis formulation and working through to the conclusion.

THE STEPS OF SCIENTIFIC METHOD	
Posing a Question	Although many discoveries happen by chance, the standard thought process of a scientist begins with forming a question to research. The more limited the question, the easier it is to set up an experiment to answer it.
Form a Hypothesis	Once the question is formulated, researchers should make an educated guess about the answer to the problem or question. This "best guess" is the hypothesis.
Do the Test	To make a test fair, data from an experiment must have a variable or any condition that can be changed, such as temperature or mass. A good test will try to manipulate as few variables as possible to see which variable is responsible for the result. This requires a second example of a control. A control is an extra setup in which all the conditions are the same except for the variable being tested.
Observe and Record the Data	Reporting the data should include the specifics of how measurements were calculated. For example, a graduated cylinder needs to be read with proper procedures. As beginning students, technique must be part of the instructional process so as to give validity to the data.
Drawing a Conclusion	After recording data, compare your data with that of other groups. A conclusion is the judgment derived from the data results.
Graphing Data	Graphing utilizes numbers to demonstrate patterns. The patterns offer a visual representation, making it easier to draw conclusions.
Apply Knowledge of Designing and Performing Investigations	Normally, knowledge is integrated in the form of a lab report. A report has many sections. It should include a specific title that tells exactly what is being studied. The abstract is a summary of the report written at the beginning of the paper. The purpose should always be defined to state the problem. The purpose should include the hypothesis (educated guess) of what is expected from the outcome of the experiment. The entire experiment should relate to this problem.

> *It is important to describe exactly what was done to prove or disprove a hypothesis.*

It is important to describe exactly what was done to prove or disprove a hypothesis. A control is necessary to prove that the results occurred from the changed conditions and would not have happened normally. Only one variable should be manipulated at a time. Observations and results of the experiment, including all results from data, should be recorded. Drawings, graphs, and illustrations should be included to support information. Observations are objective, whereas analysis and interpretation are subjective. A conclusion should explain why the results of the experiment either proved or disproved the hypothesis.

Sample Test Questions and Rationale

(Easy)

1. Which of the following is placed on the y-axis when plotting a graph?

   A. The control

   B. The independent variable

   C. The dependent variable

   D. The inference

   Answer: C. The dependent variable

   The dependent variable or the variable that is affected by the experiment is placed on the y-axis and the independent variable is placed on the x-axis

(Rigorous)

2. Stars near Earth can be seen to move relative to fixed stars. In observing the motion of a nearby star over a period of decades, an astronomer notices that the path is not a straight line, but wobbles about a straight line. The astronomer reports in a peer-reviewed journal that a planet is rotating around the star, causing it to wobble. Which of the following statements best describes the proposition that the star has a planet?

   A. Observation

   B. Hypothesis

   C. Theory

   D. Inference

   Answer: D. Inference

   The observation in the report was the wobbly path of the star. It would be a hypothesis if this was the basis of a further experiment or observation about the existence of the planet. A theory would be more speculative. The astronomer didn't just suggest that the planet was there, the report stated that the star has a planet.

Scientific data

Common Measurements in a Laboratory

Graduated cylinders and beakers are used for measuring the volume of liquids. There are many sizes and shapes. The surface of the liquid will be curved and this curve is called the meniscus. For water, the meniscus is concaved and for mercury the meniscus is convex. Measurements are made by holding the graduated cylinder at eye-level and reading it from the top or the bottom of the meniscus.

Masses are measured with a triple-beam balance or electronic balance. Temperatures are measured with thermometers, time is measured with a stopwatch, and length is measured with a meter stick. A multimeter is used to measure electric currents and voltages.

Organizing Data

Data from research or experiments is usually obtained in a way that is unrelated to the hypothesis or problem that is being investigated. This is called raw data. The raw data should be organized on a data table with column headings in a way that promotes the purpose of the investigation. There may be more than one column heading depending on the investigation. Also, categories for the data may be selected, and the data is put under the defined categories. The data can also be presented in various kinds of graphs, including line graphs, bar graphs, pie graphs, etc.

Sampling

In cases where the number of events or individuals is too large to collect data on each one, scientists collect information from only a small percentage. This is known as SAMPLING or surveying. If sampling is done correctly, it should give the investigator nearly the same information s/he would have obtained by testing the entire population. The survey must be carefully designed, considering both the sampling technique and the size of the sample.

BIAS occurs in a sample when some members or opinions of a population are less likely to be included than others. The method by which a survey is taken can contribute to bias in a survey.

Sampling techniques

There are a variety of sampling techniques: random, systematic, stratified, cluster, and quota are just a few. A truly random sample must include events or

SAMPLING: when the number of events or individuals is too large to collect data on each one, scientists collect information from only a small percentage

BIAS: when some members or opinions in a sample population are less likely to be included than others

individuals without regard to time, place, or result. Random samples are least likely to be biased because they are most likely to represent the population from which they are taken.

Stratified sampling, quota sampling, and cluster sampling all involve the definition of sub-populations. Those subpopulations are then sampled randomly in an attempt to represent many segments of a data population evenly. While random sampling is typically viewed as the "gold standard," sometimes compromises must be made to save time, money, or effort. For instance, when conducting a phone survey, calls are typically only made in a certain geographical area and at a certain time of day. This is an example of cluster sampling. There are three stages to cluster or area sampling:

1. The target population is divided into many regional clusters (groups)

2. A few clusters are randomly selected for study

3. A few subjects are randomly chosen from within a cluster

Systematic sampling involves the collection of a sample at defined intervals (for instance, every tenth part to come off a manufacturing line).

Convenience sampling is the method of choosing items arbitrarily and in an unstructured manner from the frame. Convenience samples are most likely to be biased because they are likely to exclude some members of a population.

Sample size

Another important consideration in sampling is sample size. Again, a large sample will yield the most accurate information but other factors often limit sample size. Statistical methods may be used to determine how large a sample is necessary to give an investigator a specified level of certainty (95 percent is a typical confidence interval).

Conversely, if a scientist has a sample of a certain size, those same statistical methods can be used to determine how confident the scientist can be that the sample accurately reflects the whole population. The smaller the sample size, the more likely the sample is biased.

Example: Brittany called 500 different phone numbers from the phone book to ask people which candidate they were voting for. Which type of sample did Brittany use? Is the sample biased?

Brittany used a random sample. The sample is not biased because it is random and the sample size is appropriate.

Example: Jacob surveyed the girls' softball team on their favorite foods. Which type of sample did he use? Is the sample biased?

Jacob used a convenience sample. The sample is biased because it only sampled a small population of girls.

SKILL Model building and forecasting
8.4

Modeling

Types of models

Much progress in science is due to the construction and use of models and modeling. A simple kind of model scales up or down the target. Examples are wooden cars, models of bridges, globes to represent Earth, models of molecules, etc. The discovery of the double-helix shape of DNA was the discovery of the correct model of DNA.

> Much progress in science is due to the construction and use of models and modeling.

Another kind of modeling involves the simplification of reality. In studying gravity, for example, we assume the Earth is an infinitesimally small point located 4,000 miles away from Earth's surface. In kinematics, we assume there is no friction and that all objects fall down at 9.8 m/s². In fact, Newton's laws only apply to point masses. There are separate equations for describing the rotation of three-dimensional objects. These equations are derived from Newton's laws. This is done by assuming the objects are made up of point masses connected by massless rods. Newton's equations themselves can be considered models because they explain a wide variety of phenomena.

There are also models by analogy. For example, the gas laws can be derived by assuming atoms behave like billiard balls. Carnot's heat engine is an imaginary engine that does work by taking heat from a reservoir. It is used to prove that machines cannot be 100 percent efficient. Water flowing in a system of pipes is analogous to an electric current flowing in a circuit.

Shortcomings of models

In using models, it is important to understand their shortcomings. Newton's laws for example, only apply for speeds small compared to the speed of light. The drift velocity of electrons in a wire is only about one meter per hour, much less than the speed of water flowing in a pipe. But a battery increases the electrical potential energy of an electron, just as a water pump can increase the gravitational potential energy of water. Also, the amount of water flowing is conserved, just as charge is conserved in an electric circuit.

Another type of modeling takes place when we construct best-fit continuous lines from a grid filled with data points. Some models can be considered fictions. For example, in the plum pudding model of the atom electrons were assumed to be placed in some kind of soup of positive charge. The Bohr model of the atom is fictitious because it assumes the electrons are particles without wavelike properties.

Computer simulations have become important in science in recent years. In connection with global warming, for example, computers are used to predict future temperatures on Earth. These calculations are called computer simulations and are based on climate models. A climate model makes various assumptions about the atmosphere, oceans, land, energy from the sun, etc.

Computer simulations have become important in science in recent years.

Teaching methods in science

Alternative Methods of Teaching Science
While a certain amount of information will always be presented in lecture form or using traditional written materials (i.e., textbooks), there are also many alternative resources available for teaching science at the elementary level. Several examples are listed below:

Hands-on experiments and games
Some simple experiments in the life and environmental sciences may be appropriate for elementary-aged students. For instance, they might examine samples of pond water under a microscope or assist with dissection of plants or lower animals. Students can also model environmental scenarios, perhaps with students playing either predatory or prey animals. Such interactive experiences help students visualize principles explained elsewhere and help them become more involved with the subject matter.

When hands-on experiments are costly, complicated, dangerous, or otherwise not possible, students may benefit from software programs that simulate them.

Software and simulations
When hands-on experiments are costly, complicated, dangerous, or otherwise not possible, students may benefit from software programs that simulate them. Multimedia software packages can be used to expose students to the sounds of the life forms and the environmental settings they are studying.

For more information about publishers of multimedia software:

http://www.educational-software-directory.net/science/

Natural history museums, zoos, and wildlife preserves

Visits to facilities that aim to spread information about the life and environmental sciences, such as museums and zoos, can be an exciting change from classroom learning. Wildlife preserves and similar facilities often provide educational opportunities and allow students to observe living things in their native environment.

More resources for science teachers:

http://sciencepage.org/
teachers.htm

http://www.nbii.gov/
education/

http://www.biologycorner.
com/

Professional scientists and state/national government employees

Research scientists and other professionals may be a good resource to teach students more about certain subjects. This is especially true when they can present demonstrations or invite students to their labs, etc. In some cases an agency such as the Department of Natural Resources, Environmental Protection Agency, or state Extension Service may also be a resource.

Addressing Common Misconceptions about Science

There are many common misconceptions about science. The following are a few scientific misconceptions that are or have been common in the past:

- The Earth is the center of the solar system

- The Earth is the largest object in the solar system

- Rain comes from the holes in the clouds

- Acquired characteristics can be inherited

- The eye receives upright images

- Energy is a thing

- Heat is not energy

Some strategies to uncover and dispel misconceptions include:

1. Planning appropriate activities, so that the students will see for themselves where there are misconceptions.

2. Web search is a very useful tool to dispel misconceptions. Students need to be guided in how to look for answers on the Web, and if necessary, the teacher should explain scientific literature to help the students understand it.

3. Science journals are a great source of information. Recent research is highly beneficial for the senior science students.

4. Critical thinking and reasoning are two important skills that the students should be encouraged to use to discover facts—for example, that heat is a form of energy. Here, the students have to be challenged to use their critical

thinking skills to reason that heat can cause change—for example, causing water to boil—and, thus, it is not a thing but a form of energy, since only energy can cause change.

SKILL 8.6 Materials, equipment, texts, and technology in science

Using Equipment

In addition to the resources noted above in Skill 8.5, the teaching of science also involves the use of laboratory materials and equipment. There are often state requirements regarding the use and maintenance of science labs. Check the Department of Education for your state for safety procedures. You will want to know what your state expects of you, not only for any qualifying test, but also for performance in the classroom and for the welfare of your students.

Some general guidelines for using common equipment are discussed below.

Common science equipment

GRADUATED CYLINDERS are used for precise measurements. They should always be placed on a flat surface. The surface of the liquid will form a meniscus (lens-shaped curve). The measurement is read at the bottom of this curve.

A BURET is used to dispense precisely measured volumes of liquid. A STOPCOCK is used to control the volume of liquid being dispensed at a time.

LIGHT MICROSCOPES are commonly used in laboratory experiments. Several procedures should be followed to properly care for this equipment:

1. Clean all lenses with lens paper only

2. Carry microscopes with two hands: one on the arm and one on the base

3. Always begin focusing on low power; then switch to high power

4. Store microscopes with the low power objective down

5. Always use a coverslip when viewing wet mount slides

6. Bring the objective down to its lowest position; then focus by moving it up to avoid breaking the slide or scratching the lens

Wet mount slides should be made by placing a drop of water on the specimen and then putting a glass coverslip on top of the drop of water. Dropping

GRADUATED CYLINDERS: used for precise measurements

BURET: used to dispense precisely measured volumes of liquid

STOPCOCK: used to control the volume of liquid being dispensed at a time

LIGHT MICROSCOPES: this is a device used to magnify a very small area, thus making it able to be studied

the coverslip at a forty-five degree angle will help in avoiding air bubbles. Total magnification is determined by multiplying the ocular (usually 10X) and the objective (usually 10X on low, 40X on high).

Hot plates should be used whenever possible to avoid the risk of burns or fire. If BUNSEN BURNERS are used, the following precautions should be followed:

1. Know the location of fire extinguishers and safety blankets and train students in their use; long hair and long sleeves should be secured and out of the way

2. Turn the gas all the way on and make a spark with the striker; the preferred method to light burners is to use strikers rather than matches

3. Adjust the air valve at the bottom of the Bunsen burner until the flame shows an inner cone

4. Adjust the flow of gas to the desired flame height by using the adjustment valve

5. Do not touch the barrel of the burner (it is hot)

BUNSEN BURNERS: a common piece of laboratory equipment that produces a single open gas flame

Dissections

Animals that are not obtained from recognized sources should not be used. Decaying animals or those of unknown origin may harbor pathogens and/or parasites. Specimens should be rinsed before handling. Latex gloves are desirable. If gloves are not available, students with sores or scratches should be excused from the activity. Formaldehyde is a carcinogen and should be avoided or disposed of according to district regulations. Students objecting to dissections for moral reasons should be given an alternative assignment.

Live specimens

No dissections may be performed on living mammalian vertebrates or birds. Lower order life and invertebrates may be used.

Biological experiments may be done with all animals except mammalian vertebrates or birds. No physiological harm may result to the animal.

Biological experiments may be done with all animals except mammalian vertebrates or birds. No physiological harm may result to the animal. All animals housed and cared for in the school must be handled in a safe and humane manner. Animals are not to remain on school premises during extended vacations unless adequate care is provided. Many state laws stipulate that any instructor who intentionally refuses to comply with the laws may be suspended or dismissed.

Microbiology

Pathogenic organisms must never be used for experimentation. Students should adhere to the following rules at all times when working with microorganisms to avoid accidental contamination:

- Treat all microorganisms as if they were pathogenic

- Maintain sterile conditions at all times

COMPETENCY 9
SCIENCE ASSESSMENT

SKILL 9.1 Analysis of student work in guiding science instruction

See Skill 6.1

SKILL 9.2 Formal and informal assessment of science knowledge

See Skills 18.2 and 18.3

DOMAIN IV
SOCIAL STUDIES

PERSONALIZED STUDY PLAN

COMPETENCY 10
SOCIAL STUDIES CURRICULUM

Geography

GEOGRAPHY involves studying location and how living things and Earth's features are distributed throughout the Earth. It includes where animals, people, and plants live and the effects of their relationship with Earth's physical features. Geographers also explore the locations of Earth's features, how they got there, and why they are so important.

Another way to describe where people live is by the geography and topography around them. The vast majority of people on the planet live in areas that are very hospitable. Yes, people live in the Himalayas and in the Sahara, but the populations in those areas are small indeed when compared to the plains of China, India, Europe, and the United States. People naturally want to live where they will not have to work really hard just to survive, and world population patterns reflect this.

> **GEOGRAPHY:** the study of location and how living things and Earth's features are distributed throughout the Earth

The six themes of geography
The six major themes in geography are:

- Place
- Spatial organization
- Human-environmental interaction
- Movement
- Regions
- Locations

The theme of PLACE is central to geography. All places have characteristics that give them meaning and character and distinguish them from other places on Earth. Geographers describe places by their physical and human characteristics. Physical characteristics include such elements as animal life. Human characteristics of the landscape can be noted in architecture, patterns of livelihood, land use and ownership, town planning, and communication and transportation networks. Languages, as well as religious and political ideologies, help shape the character of a place. Studied together, the physical and human characteristics of places provide clues to help students understand the nature of places on the Earth.

> **PLACE:** the physical location of where something is on Earth

SPATIAL ORGANIZATION: how things are grouped in a given space

HUMAN-ENVIRONMENTAL INTERACTION: how humans adapt to, modify, and depend on the environment

MOVEMENT: how humans interact with one another through trade, communications, emigration, and other forms of interaction

REGION: an area that has some kind of unifying characteristic, such as a common language, a common government, etc.

PARALLELS OF LATITUDE: measure distances north and south of the line called the Equator

MERIDIANS OF LONGITUDE: measure distances east and west of the line called the Prime Meridian

SPATIAL ORGANIZATION is a description of how things are grouped in a given space. In geographical terms, this can describe people, places, and environments anywhere and everywhere on Earth. The most basic form of spatial organization for people is where they live. The vast majority of people live near other people, in villages and towns and cities and settlements. These people live near others in order to take advantage of the goods and services that naturally arise from cooperation. These villages and towns and cities and settlements are, to varying degrees, near bodies of water.

The theme of HUMAN-ENVIRONMENTAL INTERACTION has three main concepts: humans adapt to the environment (wearing warm clothing in a cold climate, for instance) humans modify the environment (planting trees to block a prevailing wind, for example) and humans depend on the environment (for food, water and raw materials).

MOVEMENT is the geography theme that addresses how humans interact with one another through trade, communications, emigration, and other forms of interaction.

A REGION is an area that has some kind of unifying characteristic, such as a common language, a common government, etc. There are three main types of regions. *Formal* regions are areas defined by actual political boundaries, such as a city, county, or state. *Functional* regions are defined by a common function, such as the area covered by a telephone service. *Vernacular* regions are less formally defined areas that are formed by people's perception, e.g., "the Middle East," and "the South."

Location is a major theme in geography, including relative and absolute location. A relative location refers to the surrounding geography, e.g., "on the banks of the Mississippi River." Absolute location refers to a specific point, such as 41 degrees North latitude, 90 degrees West longitude, or 123 Main Street.

Every point on Earth has a specific location that is determined by an imaginary grid of lines denoting latitude and longitude. PARALLELS OF LATITUDE measure distances north and south of the line called the Equator. MERIDIANS OF LONGITUDE measure distances east and west of the line called the Prime Meridian. Geographers use latitude and longitude to pinpoint a place's absolute, or exact, location.

To know the absolute location of a place is only part of the story. It is also important to know how that place is related to other places—in other words, to know that place's relative location. Relative location deals with the interaction that occurs between and among places. It refers to the many ways—by land, by water, even by technology—that places are connected.

Different Types of Geography

PHYSICAL GEOGRAPHY is concerned with the locations of such Earth features as climate, water, and land; how these relate to and affect each other and human activities; and what forces shaped and changed them. All three of these Earth features affect the lives of all humans having a direct influence on what is made and produced, where it occurs, how it occurs, and what makes it possible. The combination of the different climate conditions and types of landforms and other surface features work together all around the Earth to give the many varied cultures their unique characteristics and distinctions.

CULTURAL GEOGRAPHY studies the location, characteristics, and influence of the physical environment on different cultures around the Earth. Also included in these studies are comparisons and influences of the many varied cultures. Ease of travel and up-to-the-minute, state-of-the-art communication techniques ease the difficulties of understanding cultural differences making it easier to come in contact with them.

Locations on the Earth

PHYSICAL LOCATIONS of the Earth's surface features include the four major hemispheres and the parts of the Earth's continents in them. POLITICAL LOCATIONS are the political divisions, if any, within each continent. Both physical and political locations are precisely determined in two ways:

- Surveying is done to determine boundary lines and distance from other features.

- Exact locations are precisely determined by imaginary lines of latitude (parallels) and longitude (meridians). The intersection of these lines at right angles forms a grid, making it possible to pinpoint an exact location of any place using any two grid coordinates.

The hemispheres

The Eastern Hemisphere, located between the North and South Poles and between the Prime Meridian (0 degrees longitude) east to the International Date Line at 180 degrees longitude, consists of most of Europe, all of Australia, most of Africa, and all of Asia, except for a tiny piece of the easternmost part of Russia that extends east of 180 degrees longitude.

The Western Hemisphere, located between the North and South Poles and between the Prime Meridian (0 degrees longitude) west to the International Date Line at 180 degrees longitude, consists of all of North and South America, a tiny part of the easternmost part of Russia that extends east of 180 degrees longitude, and a part of Europe that extends west of the Prime Meridian (0 degrees longitude).

PHYSICAL GEOGRAPHY: concerned with the locations of such earth features as climate, water, and land

CULTURAL GEOGRAPHY: studies the location, characteristics, and influence of the physical environment on different cultures around the Earth

PHYSICAL LOCATIONS: the four major hemispheres and the parts of the Earth's continents in them

POLITICAL LOCATIONS: the political divisions, if any, within each continent

The Northern Hemisphere, located between the North Pole and the Equator, contains all of the continents of Europe and North America and parts of South America, Africa, and most of Asia.

The Southern Hemisphere, located between the South Pole and the Equator, contains all of Australia, a small part of Asia, about one-third of Africa, most of South America, and all of Antarctica.

The continents

Of the seven continents, only one contains just one entire country and is the only island continent, Australia. Its political divisions consist of six states and one territory:

- Western Australia
- South Australia
- Tasmania
- Victoria
- New South Wales
- Queensland
- Northern Territory

Africa is made up of fifty-four separate countries, the major ones being:

- Egypt
- Nigeria
- South Africa
- Zaire
- Kenya
- Algeria
- Morocco
- The large island of Madagascar

Asia consists of forty-nine separate countries, some of which include:

- China
- Japan
- India
- Turkey
- Israel
- Iraq
- Iran
- Indonesia
- Jordan
- Vietnam
- Thailand
- The Philippines

Europe's forty-three separate nations include:

- France
- Russia
- Malta
- Denmark
- Hungary
- Greece
- Bosnia
- Herzegovina

North America consists of Canada and the United States of America and the island nations of the West Indies and the "land bridge" of Middle America, including Cuba, Jamaica, Mexico, Panama, and others.

Thirteen separate nations together occupy the continent of South America, among them such nations as:

- Brazil

- Paraguay

- Ecuador

- Suriname

The continent of Antarctica has no political boundaries or divisions but is the location of a number of science and research stations managed by nations, such as Russia, Japan, France, Australia, and India.

Physical features of the Earth's surface

The Earth's surface is made up of 70 percent water and 30 percent land. Physical features of the land surface include mountains, hills, plateaus, valleys, and plains. Other minor landforms include deserts, deltas, canyons, mesas, basins, foothills, marshes and swamps. Earth's water features include oceans, seas, lakes, rivers, and canals.

Land features

MOUNTAINS are landforms with rather steep slopes at least 2,000 feet or more above sea level. Mountains are found in groups called mountain chains or mountain ranges. At least one range can be found on six of the Earth's seven continents. North America has the Appalachian and Rocky Mountains; South America the Andes; Asia the Himalayas; Australia the Great Dividing Range; Europe the Alps; and Africa the Atlas, Ahaggar, and Drakensburg Mountains.

MOUNTAINS: landforms with steep slopes at least 2,000 feet or more above sea level

HILLS are elevated landforms rising to an elevation of about 500 to 2,000 feet. They are found everywhere on Earth including Antarctica where they are covered by ice.

HILLS: elevated landforms rising to an elevation of about 500 to 2,000 feet

PLATEAUS are elevated landforms usually level on top. Depending on location, they range from being an area that is very cold to one that is cool and healthful. Some plateaus are dry because they are surrounded by mountains that keep out any moisture. Some examples include the Kenya Plateau in East Africa, which is very cool. The plateau extending north from the Himalayas is extremely dry while those in Antarctica and Greenland are covered with ice and snow.

PLATEAUS: elevated landforms usually level on top

PLAINS are described as areas of flat or slightly rolling land, usually lower than the landforms next to them. Sometimes called lowlands (and sometimes located along seacoasts), they support the majority of the world's people. Some are found inland, and many have been formed by large rivers. This resulted in extremely fertile soil for successful cultivation of crops and numerous large settlements of

PLAINS: areas of flat or slightly rolling land, usually lower than the landforms next to them

people. In North America, the vast plains areas extend from the Gulf of Mexico north to the Arctic Ocean and between the Appalachian and Rocky Mountains. In Europe, rich plains extend east from Great Britain into central Europe on into the Siberian region of Russia. Plains in river valleys are found in China (the Yangtze River valley), India (the Ganges River valley), and Southeast Asia (the Mekong River valley).

VALLEYS: land areas found between hills and mountains

VALLEYS are land areas found between hills and mountains. Some have gentle slopes containing trees and plants; others have steep walls and are referred to as canyons. One example is Arizona's Grand Canyon of the Colorado River.

DESERTS: large dry areas of land receiving ten inches or less of rainfall each year

DESERTS are large dry areas of land receiving ten inches or less of rainfall each year. Among the better-known deserts are Africa's large Sahara Desert, the Arabian Desert on the Arabian Peninsula, and the desert outback covering roughly one third of Australia.

DELTAS: lowlands formed by soil and sediment deposited at the mouths of rivers

DELTAS are areas of lowlands formed by soil and sediment deposited at the mouths of rivers. The soil is generally very fertile and most fertile river deltas are important crop-growing areas. One well-known example is the delta of Egypt's Nile River, known for its production of cotton.

MESAS: the flat tops of hills or mountains usually with steep sides

MESAS are the flat tops of hills or mountains usually with steep sides. Sometimes plateaus are also called mesas.

BASINS: low areas drained by rivers or low spots in mountains

BASINS are considered to be low areas drained by rivers or low spots in mountains.

FOOTHILLS: a low series of hills found between a plain and a mountain range

FOOTHILLS are generally considered a low series of hills found between a plain and a mountain range.

MARSHES AND SWAMPS: wet lowlands providing growth of such plants as rushes and reeds

MARSHES AND SWAMPS are wet lowlands providing growth of such plants as rushes and reeds.

Water features

OCEANS: the largest bodies of water on the planet

OCEANS are the largest bodies of water on the planet. The four oceans of the Earth are the Atlantic Ocean, one-half the size of the Pacific and separating North and South America from Africa and Europe; the Pacific Ocean, covering almost one-third of the entire surface of the Earth and separating North and South America from Asia and Australia; the Indian Ocean, touching Africa, Asia, and Australia; and the ice-filled Arctic Ocean, extending from North America and Europe to the North Pole. The waters of the Atlantic, Pacific, and Indian Oceans also touch the shores of Antarctica.

SEAS are smaller than oceans and are surrounded by land. Some examples include the Mediterranean Sea found between Europe, Asia, and Africa; and the Caribbean Sea, touching the West Indies, South and Central America. A lake is a body of water surrounded by land. The Great Lakes in North America are a good example.

RIVERS, considered a nation's lifeblood, usually begin as very small streams, formed by melting snow and rainfall, flowing from higher to lower land, emptying into a larger body of water, usually a sea or an ocean. Examples of important rivers for the people and countries affected by and/or dependent on them include the Nile, Niger, and Zaire Rivers of Africa; the Rhine, Danube, and Thames Rivers of Europe; the Yangtze, Ganges, Mekong, Hwang He, and Irrawaddy Rivers of Asia; the Murray-Darling in Australia; and the Orinoco in South America. River systems are made up of large rivers and numerous smaller rivers or tributaries flowing into them. Examples include the vast Amazon River system in South America and the Mississippi River system in the United States.

CANALS are human-made water passages constructed to connect two larger bodies of water. Famous examples include the Panama Canal across Panama's isthmus connecting the Atlantic and Pacific Oceans and the Suez Canal in the Middle East between Africa and the Arabian Peninsula connecting the Red and Mediterranean Seas.

Weather

Weather is the condition of the air, which includes the day-to-day atmospheric conditions including temperature, air pressure, wind and moisture or precipitation, which includes rain, snow, hail, or sleet.

CLIMATE is average weather or daily weather conditions for a specific region or location over a long or extended period of time. Studying the climate of an area includes gathering information on the area's monthly and yearly temperatures and its monthly and yearly amounts of precipitation. In addition, a characteristic of an area's climate is the length of its growing season. Four reasons for the different climate regions on the Earth are differences in:

- Latitude

- The amount of moisture

- Temperatures in land and water

- The Earth's land surface

SEAS: smaller than oceans and surrounded by land

RIVERS: usually begin as very small streams, formed by melting snow and rainfall, flowing from higher to lower land, emptying into a larger body of water, usually a sea or an ocean

CANALS: human-made water passages constructed to connect two larger bodies of water

CLIMATE: average weather or daily weather conditions for a specific region or location over a long or extended period of time

There are many different climates throughout the Earth. It is most unusual if a country contains just one kind of climate. Regions of climates are divided according to latitudes:

- 0–23 1/2 degrees are the "low latitudes"

- 23 1/2–66 1/2 degrees are the "middle latitudes"

- 66 1/2 degrees–the Poles are the "high latitudes"

The low latitudes are comprised of the rainforest, savanna, and desert climates. The tropical rainforest climate is found in equatorial lowlands and is hot and wet. There is sun, extreme heat, and rain—everyday. Although daily temperatures rarely rise above 90 degrees F, the daily humidity is always high, leaving everything sticky and damp. North and south of the tropical rainforests are the tropical grasslands called savannas or the "land of two seasons"—a winter dry season and a summer wet season. Further north and south of the tropical grasslands or savannas are the deserts. These areas are the hottest and driest parts of the Earth receiving less than 10 inches of rain a year. These areas have extreme temperatures between night and day. After the sun sets, the land cools quickly dropping the temperature as much as 50 degrees F.

The middle latitudes contain the Mediterranean, humid-subtropical, humid-continental, marine, steppe, and desert climates. Lands containing the Mediterranean climate are considered "sunny" lands found in six areas of the world: lands bordering the Mediterranean Sea, a small portion of southwestern Africa, areas in southern and southwestern Australia, a small part of the Ukraine near the Black Sea, central Chile, and Southern California. Summers are hot and dry with mild winters. The growing season usually lasts all year and what little rain falls are during the winter months. What is rather unusual is that the Mediterranean climate is located between 30 and 40 degrees north and south latitude on the western coasts of countries.

SUBTROPICAL CLIMATE: found north and south of the tropics and is moist

The humid SUBTROPICAL CLIMATE is found north and south of the tropics and is moist indeed. The areas having this type of climate are found on the eastern side of their continents and include Japan, mainland China, Australia, Africa, South America, and the United States—the southeastern coasts of these areas. An interesting feature of their locations is that warm ocean currents are found there. The winds that blow across these currents bring in warm moist air all year round. Long, warm summers; short, mild winters; and a long growing season allow for different crops to be grown several times a year. All contribute to the productivity of this climate type, which supports more people than any of the other climates.

Sample Test Questions and Rationale

(Average)

1. Which of the following is not one of the six major themes in geography?

   A. Regions

   B. Religion

   C. Place

   D. Movement

   Answer: B. Religion

   The six major themes in geography are: place, spatial organization, human-environmental interaction, movement, regions, and locations.

(Average)

2. The Northern Hemisphere contains all of which of the following?

   A. Europe

   B. South America

   C. Africa

   D. Asia

   Answer: A. Europe

   The Northern Hemisphere, located between the North Pole and the Equator, contains all of the continents of Europe and North America and parts of South America, Africa, and most of Asia.

(Easy)

3. Which of the following mountain ranges is located in Asia?

   A. Appalachian

   B. Atlas

   C. Himalayas

   D. Great Dividing Range

   Answer: C. Himalayas

   Mountains are landforms with rather steep slopes at least 2,000 feet or more above sea level. Mountains are found in groups called mountain chains or mountain ranges. At least one range can be found on six of the earth's seven continents. North America has the Appalachian and Rocky Mountains; South America the Andes; Asia the Himalayas; Australia the Great Dividing Range; Europe the Alps; and Africa the Atlas, Ahaggar, and Drakensburg Mountains.

SKILL History
10.2

History is the study of human civilizations. It can take many forms, including a focus on cultures, time periods, geography, economic elements, or social issues. Specialized fields of historical study include the following:

FIELDS OF HISTORICAL STUDY	
Archaeology	The study of prehistoric and historic human cultures through the recovery, documentation and analysis of material remains and environmental data.
Art History	The study of changes in social context through art.
Big History	The study of history on a large scale across long time frames (since the Big Bang and up to the future) through a multi-disciplinary approach.
Chronology	The science of localizing historical events in time.
Cultural History	The study of culture in the past.
Diplomatic History	The study of international relations in the past.
Economic History	The study of economies in the past.
Military History	The study of warfare and wars in history and what is sometimes considered to be a sub-branch of military history, Naval History.
Paleography	The study of ancient texts.
Political History	The study of politics in the past.
Psychohistory	The study of the psychological motivations underpinning historical events.
Historiography of Science	The study of the structure and development of science.
Social History	The approach to the study of history that views a period of time through the eyes of everyday people and is focused on emerging trends.
World History	The study of history from a global perspective.

PERIODIZATION: the practice of dividing history into a number of discrete periods or blocks of time

Historical Periods and Epochs

The practice of dividing history into a number of discrete periods or blocks of time is called PERIODIZATION. Because history is continuous, all systems of periodization are arbitrary to some extent. However, dividing time into segments facilitates understanding of changes that occur over time and helps identify similarities of events, knowledge, and experience within the defined period. Further, some divisions of time into these periods apply only under specific circumstances.

Divisions of time may be determined by date, cultural advances or changes, historical events, the influence of particular individuals or groups, or geography. Speaking of the World War II era defines a particular period of time in which key historical, political, social, and economic events occurred. Speaking of the Jacksonian Era, however, has meaning only in terms of American history. Defining the Romantic Period makes sense only in Europe, and countries under their direct influence.

Problems with terminology and periodization

Many of the divisions of time that are commonly used are open to some controversy and discussion. The use of B.C. and A.D. dating, for example, has clear reference only in societies that account time according to the Christian calendar. Similarly, speaking about "the year of the pig" has greatest meaning in China.

An example of the kind of questions that can be raised about designations of time periods can be seen in the use of "Victorian." Is it possible to speak of a Victorian era beyond England? Is literature written in the style of the English poets and writers "Victorian" if it is written beyond the borders of England?

Some designations also carry both positive and negative connotations. "Victorian" is an example of potential negative connotations, as well. The term is often used to refer to class conflict, sexual repression, and heavy industry. These might be negative connotations. In contrast, the term "Renaissance" is generally read with positive connotations.

Sometimes, several designations can be applied to the same period. The period known as the "Elizabethan Period" in English history is also called "the English Renaissance." In some cases, the differences in designation refer primarily to the specific aspect of history that is being considered. For example, one designation may be applied to a specific period of time when one is analyzing cultural history, while a different designation is applied to the same period of time when considering military history.

Many of the divisions of time that are commonly used are open to some controversy and discussion.

Some designations also carry both positive and negative connotations.

Sample Test Questions and Rationale

(Average)

1. **Which of the following is a weakness of "periodization"?**

   A. It is arbitrary

   B. Facilitates understanding

   C. Identifies similarities

   D. Categorizes knowledge

   Answer: A. It is arbitrary

   The practice of dividing history into a number of discrete periods or blocks of time is called "periodization." Because history is continuous, all systems of periodization are arbitrary to some extent. However, dividing time into segments facilitates understanding of changes that occur over time and helps identify similarities of events, knowledge, and experience within the defined period. Further, some divisions of time into these periods apply only under specific circumstances.

(Easy)

2. **Archaeology is the study of which of the following?**

   A. Norms, values, standards

   B. Material remains of humans

   C. Genetic characteristics

   D. The historical development of language

   Answer: B. Study of material remains of humans

   There are four areas of anthropology:

   1. Archaeology—study of material remains of humans

   2. Social-cultural—norms, values, standards

   3. Biological—genetic characteristics

   4. Linguistics—the historical development of language

SKILL 10.3 Government, civics, and economics

Government and Civics

> **CITIZENSHIP:** in a democracy this bestows on an individual certain rights, foremost being the right to participate in one's own government

Citizenship

CITIZENSHIP in a democracy bestows on an individual certain rights, foremost being the right to participate in one's own government. Along with these rights come responsibilities, including the responsibility of a citizen to participate.

> *The most basic form of participation is the vote.*

The most basic form of participation is the vote. Those who have reached the age of 18 in the United States are eligible to vote in public elections. With this right comes the responsibility to be informed before voting and not to sell or otherwise give away one's vote. Citizens are also eligible to run for public office. These rights are called public sovereignty. Along with the right to run for office comes the responsibility to represent the electors as fairly as possible and to perform the duties expected of a government representative.

Freedoms

In the United States, citizens are guaranteed the right to free speech: i.e., the right to express an opinion on public issues. In turn, citizens have the responsibility to allow others to speak freely. At the community level, this might mean speaking at a city council hearing while allowing others with different or opposing viewpoints to have their say without interruption or comment.

In the United States, citizens are guaranteed the right to free speech.

The U.S. Constitution also guarantees freedom of religion. This means that the government may not impose an official religion on its citizens, and that people are free to practice their religion. Citizens are also responsible for allowing those of other religions to practice freely without obstruction. Occasionally, religious issues will be put before the public at the state level in the form of ballot measures or initiatives. To what extent it should be acceptable for religious beliefs to be expressed in a public setting, such as a public school, is an issue that has been debated recently.

In making decisions on matters like these, citizens are expected to take responsibility to become informed of the issues involved and to make their votes based on their own opinions. Being informed of how one's government works and what the effects of new legislation will be is an essential part of being a good citizen.

The U.S. Constitution also guarantees that all citizens be treated equally by the law. In addition, federal and state laws make it a crime to discriminate against citizens based on their sex, race, religion and other factors. To ensure that all people are treated equally, citizens have the responsibility to follow these laws.

Rights and responsibilities

These rights and responsibilities are essentially the same whether one is voting in a local school board race, for the passage of a new state law, or for the President of the United States. Being a good citizen means exercising one's own rights while allowing others to do the same.

A person who lives in a democratic society legally has a comprehensive list of rights guaranteed to him or her by the government. In the United States, this is the Constitution and its Amendments. Among these very important rights are:

A person who lives in a democratic society legally has a comprehensive list of rights guaranteed to him or her by the government.

- The right to speak out in public

- The right to pursue any religion

- The right for a group of people to gather in public for *any* reason that doesn't fall under a national security cloud;

- The right *not* to have soldiers stationed in your home

- The right *not* to be forced to testify against yourself in a court of law

- The right to a speedy and public trial by a jury of your peers

- The right *not* to be the victim of cruel and unusual punishment

- The right to avoid unreasonable search and seizure of your person, your house, and your vehicle

Civil rights and civil liberties

The terms "civil liberties" and "civil rights" are often used interchangeably, but there are some fine distinctions between the two terms. The term CIVIL LIBERTIES is used to imply that the state has a positive role to play in assuring that all its' citizens will have equal protection and justice under the law. The term implies equal opportunities to exercise their privileges of citizenship and to participate fully in the life of the nation, regardless of race, religion, sex, color or creed. The term CIVIL RIGHTS is used more often to refer to rights that may be described as guarantees that are specified as against the state authority implying limitations on the actions of the state to interfere with citizens' liberties. Although the term "civil rights" has thus been identified with the ideal of equality and the term "civil liberties" with the idea of freedom, the two concepts are really inseparable and interactive. EQUALITY implies the proper ordering of liberty in a society so that one individual's freedom does not infringe on the rights of others.

The beginnings of civil liberties and the concept of civil rights in the United States go back to the ideas of the Greeks, the early British struggle for civil rights, and the very philosophies that led people to come to the New World in the first place. Religious freedom, political freedom, and the right to live one's life as one sees fit are basic to the American ideal. These were embodied in the ideas expressed in the Declaration of Independence and the Constitution.

The Bill of Rights

All these ideas found their final expression in the U.S. Constitution's first ten amendments, known as the BILL OF RIGHTS. In 1789, the first Congress passed these first amendments, and by December 1791, three-fourths of the states had ratified them. The Bill of Rights protects certain liberties and basic rights. James Madison, who wrote the amendments, said that the Bill of Rights does not give Americans these rights. People, Madison said, already have these rights. They are natural rights that belong to all human beings. The Bill of Rights simply prevents the governments from taking away these rights.

CIVIL LIBERTIES: implies that the state has a positive role to play in assuring that all its' citizens will have equal protection and justice under the law

CIVIL RIGHTS: rights that guarantee against the state authority, implying limitations on the actions of the state to interfere with citizens' liberties

EQUALITY: implies the proper ordering of liberty in a society so that one individual's freedom does not infringe on the rights of others

Religious freedom, political freedom, and the right to live one's life as one sees fit are basic to the American ideal.

BILL OF RIGHTS: the first ten amendments to the U.S. Constitution

Federal laws

Federal laws are passed by the Congress and can originate in either the House of Representatives or the Senate. The first step in the passing of a law is for the proposed law to be introduced in one of the houses of Congress. When a proposed law is under consideration by Congress, it is called a BILL. A bill can be introduced, or sponsored, by a member of Congress by giving a copy to the clerk or by placing a copy in a special box called a hopper.

Once a bill is introduced, copies are printed and it is assigned to one of several standing committees of the house in which it was introduced. The committee studies the bill and performs research on the issues it would cover. Committees may call experts to testify on the bill and gather public comments. The committee may revise the bill. Finally, the committee votes on whether to release the bill to be voted on by the full body. A committee may also lay aside a bill so that it cannot be voted on. Once a bill is released, it can be debated and amended by the full body before being voted on. If it passes by a simple majority vote, the bill is sent to the other house of Congress, where the process begins again.

When a bill has passed both the House of Representatives and the Senate, it is assigned to a conference committee that is made up of members of both houses. The conference committee resolves differences between the House and Senate versions of a bill, if any, and then sends it back to both houses for final approval. Once a bill receives final approval, it is signed by the Speaker of the House and the Vice President, who is also the President of the Senate, and sent to the President for consideration. The President may either sign the bill or VETO it. If he or she vetoes the bill, the veto may be overruled if two-thirds of both the Senate and the House vote to do so. Once the President signs it, the bill becomes a law.

The executive branch, and its departments enforce federal laws. The Department of Justice, led by the United States Attorney General, is the primary law enforcement department of the federal government. Other investigative and enforcement departments such as the Federal Bureau of Investigation (FBI), and the U.S. Postal Inspectors aid the Justice Department.

The RULE OF LAW is the ideal that the law applies not only to the governed, but to the government as well. This core value gives authority to the justice system, which grants citizens protection from the government by requiring that any accusation of a crime be proved by the government before a person is punished. This is called DUE PROCESS and ensures that any accused person will have an opportunity to confront his accusers and provide a defense. Due process follows from the core value of a right to liberty. The government cannot take away a citizen's liberty without reason or without proof. The correlating ideal is also a core value—that

BILL: a proposed law that is under consideration by Congress

Once a bill is released, it can be debated and amended by the full body before being voted on.

VETO: the process by which the President stops a bill from becoming law

RULE OF LAW: the ideal that the law applies not only to the governed, but to the government as well

DUE PROCESS: ensures that any accused person will have an opportunity to confront his accusers and provide a defense

someone who does harm another or break a law will receive justice under the democratic system. The ideal of justice holds that a punishment will fit the crime and that any citizen can appeal to the judicial system if he or she feels he or she has been wronged.

Duties of a citizen

Citizens' duties also vary from nation to nation. Duties demanded by law (also considered civic responsibilities) include paying taxes, obeying laws, and defending the country. Although some governments require jury duty, in the United States this would be a duty not required by law along with voting, doing volunteer work to help others, and becoming aware of public problems.

Almost all representative democracies in the world guarantee similar rights to their citizens, and expect them to take similar responsibilities to respect the rights of others. As a citizen of the world, one is expected to respect the rights of other nations, and the people of those nations, in the same way.

Citizenship is granted one of two ways: either by birth or by naturalization. Some Americans hold dual citizenship.

Almost all representative democracies in the world guarantee similar rights to their citizens, and expect them to take similar responsibilities to respect the rights of others.

Economics

ECONOMICS: the study of how a society allocates its scarce resources to satisfy what are basically unlimited and competing wants

ECONOMICS is the study of how a society allocates its scarce resources to satisfy what are basically unlimited and competing wants. A fundamental fact of economics is that resources are scarce and that wants are infinite. The fact that scarce resources have to satisfy unlimited wants means that choices have to be made. If society uses its resources to produce good A then it doesn't have those resources to produce good B. More of good A means less of good B. This trade-off is referred to as the opportunity cost, or the value, of the sacrificed alternative.

The Three Questions

Economic systems refer to the arrangements a society has devised to answer what are known as the Three Questions:

- What goods to produce?

- How to produce the goods?

- For Whom are the goods being produced? (i.e., how is the allocation of the output determined?)

Different economic systems answer these questions in different ways. These are the different "isms" that exist that define the method of resource and output allocation, such as capitalism, socialism, and communism.

Capitalism

Capitalism operates with a market economy. A market economy answers these questions in terms of demand and supply and the use of markets. DEMAND is based on consumer preferences and satisfaction and refers to the quantities of a good or service that buyers are willing and able to buy at different prices during a given period of time. SUPPLY is based on costs of production and refers to the quantities that sellers are willing and able to sell at different prices during a given period of time. The determination of market equilibrium price is where the buying decisions of buyers coincide with the selling decision of sellers.

Capitalism and the Three Questions

Consumers vote for the products they want with their dollar spending. Goods acquiring enough dollar votes are profitable, signaling to the producers that society wants their scarce resources used in this way. This is how the "What" question is answered. The producer then hires inputs in accordance with the goods consumers want, looking for the most efficient or lowest cost method of production. The lower the firm's costs for any given level of revenue, the higher the firm's profits. This is the way in which the "How" question is answered in a market economy. The "For Whom" question is answered in the marketplace by the determination of the equilibrium price.

Price serves to ration the good to those who can and will transact at the market price. Those who can't or won't are excluded from the market. This mechanism results in MARKET EFFICIENCY or obtaining the most output from the available inputs that are consistent with the preferences of consumers. Society's scarce resources are being used the way society wants them to be used.

> **DEMAND:** the quantities of a good or service that buyers are willing and able to buy at different prices during a given period of time

> **SUPPLY:** the quantities that sellers are willing and able to sell at different prices during a given period of time

> Consumers vote for the products they want with their dollar spending.

> **MARKET EFFICIENCY:** obtaining the most output from the available inputs that are consistent with the preferences of consumers

Sample Test Questions and Rationale

(Easy)

1. **Which of the following are U.S. citizens guaranteed?**

   A. Employment

   B. Post-secondary education

   C. Driver's license

   D. Free speech

Answer: D. Free speech

In the United States, citizens are guaranteed the right to free speech: i.e., the right to express an opinion on public issues. In turn, citizens have the responsibility to allow others to speak freely. At the community level, this might mean speaking at a city council hearing while allowing others with different or opposing viewpoints to have their say without interruption or comment.

Sample Test Questions and Rationale

(Easy)

2. **Voting is the most basic form of participation in the United States. Which of the following is not a prerequisite to vote in the United States?**

   A. Reached the age of 18

   B. No felony convictions

   C. Registered to vote

   D. Valid driver's license

Answer: D. Valid driver's license

The most basic form of participation is the vote. Those who have reached the age of 18 in the United States are eligible to vote in public elections. With this right comes the responsibility to be informed before voting, and not to sell or otherwise give away one's vote. Citizens are also eligible to run for public office. These rights are called public sovereignty. Along with the right to run for office comes the responsibility to represent the electors as fairly as possible and to perform the duties expected of a government representative.

(Average)

3. **Freedom of religion means all of the following EXCEPT:**

   A. Government may not impose an official religion

   B. Citizens are free to practice their religion

   C. Citizens can obstruct those of other religions

   D. Government supports each religion

Answer: C. Citizens can obstruct those of other religions

The U.S. Constitution guarantees freedom of religion. This means that the government may not impose an official religion on its citizens, and that people are free to practice their religion. Citizens are also responsible for allowing those of other religions to practice freely without obstruction. Occasionally, religious issues will be put before the public at the state level in the form of ballot measures or initiatives. To what extent it should be acceptable for religious beliefs to be expressed in a public setting, such as a public school, is an issue that has been debated recently.

Sample Test Questions and Rationale

(Average)

4. **Which of the following is NOT protected by the U.S. Constitution?**

   A. The right to speak out in public

   B. The right to hate speech

   C. The right to pursue any religion

   D. The right to avoid unreasonable search and seizure

Answer: B. The right to hate speech

A person who lives in a democratic society legally has a comprehensive list of rights guaranteed to him or her by the government. In the United States, this is the Constitution and its Amendments. Among these very important rights are:

- The right to speak out in public

- The right to pursue any religion

- The right for a group of people to gather in public for any reason that doesn't fall under a national security cloud

- The right not to have soldiers stationed in your home

- The right not to be forced to testify against yourself in a court of law

- The right to a speedy and public trial by a jury of your peers

- The right not to be the victim of cruel and unusual punishment

- The right to avoid unreasonable search and seizure of your person, your house, and your vehicle

---

SKILL **Anthropology and sociology**
10.4

Anthropology

ANTHROPOLOGY is the scientific study of human culture and humanity and the relationship between humans and their culture. Anthropologist Eric Wolf defined it as "the most scientific of the humanities, and the most humanistic of the sciences."

Anthropologists study different groups; how groups relate to other cultures; patterns of behavior; and similarities and differences among cultures. Research is

> **ANTHROPOLOGY:** the scientific study of human culture and humanity and the relationship between humans and their culture

two-fold: cross-cultural and comparative. The major method of study is referred to as PARTICIPANT OBSERVATION. An anthropologist studies and learns about the people by living among them and participating with them in their daily lives.

PARTICIPANT OBSERVATION: when an anthropologist studies and learns about the people by living among them and participating with them in their daily lives

Areas of anthropology

There are four areas of anthropology:

1. Archaeology—study of material remains of humans

2. Social-cultural—norms, values, standards

3. Biological—genetic characteristics

4. Linguistics—the historical development of language

Archaeology

ARCHAEOLOGY: the scientific study of past human cultures by studying the remains they left behind including pottery, bones, buildings, tools, and artwork

ARCHAEOLOGY is the scientific study of past human cultures by studying the remains they left behind including pottery, bones, buildings, tools, and artwork. Archaeologists locate and examine any evidence to help explain the way people lived in past times. They use special equipment and techniques to gather the evidence, keeping detailed records of their findings. Research may result in destruction of the remains being studied.

The first step is to locate an archaeological site using various methods. Next, surveying the site takes place starting with a detailed description of the site with notes, maps, photographs, and the collection of artifacts from the surface. Excavating follows either by digging for buried objects or by diving and working in submersible decompression chambers, when underwater. Archaeologists record and preserve the evidence for eventual classification, then date and evaluate their find.

Sociology

SOCIOLOGY: the study of human society through the individuals, groups, and institutions that make up human society

SOCIOLOGY is the study of human society through the individuals, groups, and institutions that make up human society. Sociology includes every feature of human social conditions. It deals with the predominant behaviors, attitudes, and types of relationships within a society as defined by a group of people with a similar cultural background living in a specific geographical area.

Areas and methods of sociology

Sociology is divided into five major areas of study.

FIVE AREAS OF SOCIOLOGY	
Population Studies	General social patterns of groups of people living in a certain geographical area
Social Behaviors	Changes in attitudes, morale, leadership, conformity, and others
Social Institutions	Organized groups of people performing specific functions within a society such as churches, schools, hospitals, business organizations, and governments
Cultural Influences	Customs, knowledge, arts, religious beliefs, and language
Social Change	Wars, revolutions, inventions, fashions, and other events or activities

Sociologists use three major methods to test and verify theories:

- Surveys

- Controlled experiments

- Field observations

Important figures in sociology

Some important figures and contributions in the field of sociology:

Auguste Comte was the French philosopher who coined the term "sociology" and developed the theory called POSITIVISM which states that social behavior and events can be scientifically measured. Positivism denies metaphysical experience and relies on sensory information for evaluating human experience. Comte is generally regarded as the first Western sociologist.

POSITIVISM: a theory that states that social behavior and events can be scientifically measured

Emile Durkheim is considered the father of sociology because he influenced universities to consider sociology as a discipline. He was influenced by Comte and positivism, and Durkheim essentially viewed the world as influenced by large factors such as group attitudes and cultural norms versus simply being influenced by individuals. Sociologists determine the "social facts." Durkheim is especially famous for his work on the social causes of rates of suicide. He brought into this the word anomie, which means individuals affected by changes in society such as wide unemployment or groups feeling alienated from society at large.

Karl Marx and Friedrich Engels saw the world as a socio-economic struggle between classes. The main thesis in their book *The Communist Manifesto* is that work is a social activity and that the working class will ultimately have a revolution.

Herbert Spencer related the biology of Darwin's *Origin of Species* to sociology by viewing the development of society the same way. He coined the phrase:

"the survival of the fittest." He saw connections between the physical and social parts of life. Despite his being a rival of Darwin, he is credited with Social Darwinism, in which competition drives society.

Max Weber saw the religions of the East and West as a cause for different social directions—with Protestantism spurring capitalism. He said that he had observed that the state views itself as having legitimate causes for violence. The violence is demonstrated in military and police actions as well as citizens using violence to protect themselves or their property. His views were objective; he did not defend the reasons for the pursuit of violence.

SKILL 10.5 Historical analysis and interpretation

Independent Thinking and Social Sciences

An important task teachers face in the social science classroom is aiding students in becoming mindful readers and independent/analytical thinkers.

An important task teachers face in the social science classroom is aiding students in becoming mindful readers and independent/analytical thinkers. Teachers must guide students in their learning how to formulate independent thoughts and not just accepting what is written in textbooks and on websites as the sole truth.

Historic events and social issues cannot be considered only in isolation. People and their actions are connected in many ways, and events are linked through cause and effect over time. Identifying and analyzing these social and historic links is a primary goal of the social sciences. The methods used to analyze social phenomena borrow from several of the social sciences. Interviews, statistical evaluation, observation and experimentation are just some of the ways that people's opinions and motivations can be measured. From these opinions, larger social beliefs and movements can be interpreted, and events, issues and social problems can be placed in context to provide a fuller view of their importance.

Using multiple perspectives

Analyzing an event or issue from multiple perspectives involves seeking out sources that advocate or express those perspectives and comparing them with one another.

Analyzing an event or issue from multiple perspectives involves seeking out sources that advocate or express those perspectives and comparing them with one another. Listening to the speeches of Martin Luther King, Jr., provides insight into the perspective of one group of people concerning the issue of civil rights in the U.S. in the 1950s and 1960s. Public statements of George Wallace (an American governor initially opposed to integration) provide another perspective from the same time period. Looking at the legislation that was proposed at the time and how it came into effect offers a window into the thinking of the day.

Using themes

One way to analyze historical events, patterns, and relationships is to focus on historical themes. There are many themes repeating throughout human history, and they can be used to make comparisons between different historical times as well as between nations and peoples. While new themes are always being explored, a few of the widely recognized historical themes are as follows:

Politics and political institutions can provide information of prevailing opinions and beliefs of a group of people and how they change over time. For example, in some regions and states, one political party has maintained influence and control for many years. In other areas, there have been gradual shifts over the last thirty years to a different political party, or pockets of ideological change. Exploring these patterns can reveal the popular social ideals that developed in a given state or region and how they impact historical perspectives and writings.

Race and ethnicity is another historical theme that runs through the history of our nation. For example, in the state of Washington, there are thirty recognized American Indian tribes and seven other tribes not officially recognized but of distinct cultural difference. Various tribes have occupied the state for over 10,000 years. Significant numbers of Caucasian and Hispanic settlers did not come to Washington until after the 1850s, less than 200 years ago. Therefore, the ethnicity of the people of the state of Washington (like many other states in the U.S.) contributes to a range of differences and similarities in their experiences as citizens. Researching the history of how peoples of different races treated one another reflects on many other social aspects of a society, and can be a fruitful line of historical interpretation.

Researching the history of how peoples of different races treated one another reflects on many other social aspects of a society, and can be a fruitful line of historical interpretation.

Sample Test Questions and Rationale

(Rigorous)

1. **In order to fully understand an era which of the following is not recommended?**

   A. Analyze an event from multiple perspectives

   B. Gather basic factual information from the era

   C. Comprehend an issue beyond a basic level

   D. Evaluate the era based on current social mores

   Answer: D. Evaluate the era based on current social mores

   Analyzing an event or issue from multiple perspectives involves seeking out sources that advocate or express those perspectives and comparing them with one another. Listening to the speeches of Martin Luther King, Jr., provides insight into the perspective of one group of people concerning the issue of civil rights in the U.S. in the 1950s and 1960s. Public statements of George Wallace (an American governor initially opposed to integration) provide another perspective from the same time period. Looking at the legislation that was proposed at the time and how it came into effect offers a window into the thinking of the day.

(Average)

2. **Teachers of social studies want to create what in order maximize student learning?**

   A. Reliance on primary sources

   B. Independent thought

   C. A focus on the textbook

   D. Ignore cultural competency

   Answer: B. Independent thought

   An important task teachers face in the social science classroom is aiding students in becoming mindful readers and independent/analytical thinkers. Teachers must guide students in their learning how to formulate independent thoughts and not just accepting what is written in textbooks and on websites as the sole truth.

COMPETENCY 11
SOCIAL STUDIES INSTRUCTION

SKILL Teaching methods for social studies
11.1

Approaches to Studying History

History is filled with wonderful facts, intriguing stories, and innumerous combinations of perspectives and interpretations on just about every major event. These problems and issues encountered in the past have affected history in immeasurable ways. It is nearly impossible to consider all of the thoughts, values, ideas and perspectives involved.

When studying a time period of United States history, students and teachers should decide on broad key questions that relate to major impacts, the nature of social change, urbanization, cultural effects and so on when entering into an historical analysis. These questions can serve as a foundation to the study, providing a focus for students as they explore the related perspectives.

When studying a time period of United States history, students and teachers should decide on broad key questions that relate to major impacts, the nature of social change, urbanization, cultural effects, and so on when entering into an historical analysis.

Using primary sources

From here, students can explore one or more of these key questions by creating subtopics beneath them as they consider the major elements such as time period, cultural impacts, various viewpoints, previous and concurrent events and so on. This is a great place in which to introduce PRIMARY RESOURCES in the field of social science.

PRIMARY RESOURCES: a source that is first-hand evidence about a certain time period in history

Diaries, field trips, field trips to historic sites and museums, historical documents, photos, artifacts, and other records of the past provide students with alternative voices and accounts of events. Primary sources, first-hand accounts of events, provide the richest and least "processed" information. For example, a letter from a freed slave would provide more valuable information about attitudes toward African Americans in the North in 1860 than a textbook entry.

THINGS TO CONSIDER WHEN ANALYZING HISTORICAL RESOURCES	
The Author	Who is the author? What motivated this author? Why did they create this resource? Is he or she representing a group?
The Time Frame	When was this resource produced? How has it reached us? Was it contemporary at the time of production?
The Location	Where was this document produced?
The Type of Document	Is it a letter, a poem, a report, a song, a study?
The Audience	Who was intended to see this piece?

Judging thinking skills

When engaging in higher-order thinking students should develop their skills through enthusiastic experiences where they can:

- Examine a situation

- Raise questions

- Compare differing ideas, interests, perspectives, actions, and institutions represented in these sources

- Elaborate upon what they read and see to develop interpretations, explanations, or solutions to the questions they have raised

- Analyze historical fiction, nonfiction, and historical illustrations

- Distinguish between fact and fiction

- Consider multiple perspectives

- Explain causes in analyzing historical actions

- Challenge arguments of historical inevitability

- Hypothesize on the influence of the past

Teachers must also create an open and engaging learning environment where students can examine data. Use of libraries, historical collections, museums, newspapers, collections, students' families and artifacts, professional and community resources, historians, local colleges, and more allow students to see history for themselves—the first step in truly teaching them how to analyze history.

Methods in Teaching Geography and Other Social Sciences

Interdisciplinary approaches are very useful and appropriate in teaching social studies. Making a map of an area of study, doing a play that depicts the culture of the region, tallying information about the population of the area, and linking historical events to current sociological and political aspects all offer good strategies for teaching social studies content. Project-based approaches that incorporate the following can be quite effective:

Interdisciplinary approaches are very useful and appropriate in teaching social studies.

- Cooperative learning

- Research methods

- Discovery and inquiry-based lessons

- Audio-visual resources

Immersion in the culture and geography of an area can take many forms; this method is most productive when the students are part of the process of determining what the activities will be in the unit of study, particularly in the intermediate grades.

Using literature to support learning in the social sciences

American Indian literature

The foundation of American Indian writing is found in storytelling, oratory, and autobiographical and historical accounts of tribal village life; reverence for the environment; and the postulation that the Earth with all of its beauty was given in trust, to be cared for and passed on to future generations.

Early American Indian writings that would interest young adults are:

- *Geronimo: His Own Story*—Apache edited by S.M. Barrett

- *Native American Myths and Legends* by C.F. Taylor

- *When Legends Die* by Hal Barland

African American literature

African American literature covers three distinct periods: pre-Civil War, post-Civil War and Reconstruction, and post-Civil War through the present. Some featured resources include:

- Harriet Beecher Stowe's *Uncle Tom's Cabin*

- Ernest Gaines' *The Autobiography of Miss Jane Pittman*

- Maya Angelou's *I Know Why the Caged Bird Sings*

- Alex Haley's popular *Roots*

The Colonial period

Some good examples of works from the colonial period include *The Mayflower Compact* and Thomas Paine's *Common Sense*. Benjamin Franklin's essays from *Poor Richard's Almanac* were popular during his day and are good as well.

American folklore

Folktales with characters such as Washington Irving's Ichabod Crane and Rip Van Winkle create a unique American folklore, with characters marked by their environment and the superstitions of the New Englander. The poetry of Fireside Poets such as James Russell Lowell, Oliver Wendell Holmes, Henry Wadsworth Longfellow, and John Greenleaf Whittier was recited by American families and read in the long New England winters.

SKILL 11.2 Materials, equipment, texts, and technology in social studies

There are many resources available for the teaching of social science concepts. The resources used should be appropriate to the learning objectives specified. The teacher wants to use different kinds of resources in order to make the subject matter more interesting to the student and to appeal to different learning styles. First of all, a good textbook is required. This gives the student something that they can refer to and something to study from. The use of audiovisual aids is also beneficial in the classroom environment. Most people are visual learners and will retain information better when it is in visual form. Audiovisual presentations, like movies, give them concepts in pictures that they will easily retain.

> The teacher wants to use different kinds of resources in order to make the subject matter more interesting to the student and to appeal to different learning styles.

Technology and the Internet

The Internet has made many forms of mapping, archival and historical documents, and other social science data accessible to everyone. Well-conceived searches can unearth much relevant data as well teaching tools. The social studies teacher may utilize various websites for instruction; as always when using the Internet, she or he needs to evaluate online information for accuracy and suitability.

> When doing historical research in particular, students and teachers need to be careful not to rely exclusively on electronic and digital information.

When doing historical research in particular, students and teachers need to be careful not to rely exclusively on electronic and digital information. Traveling to a site of interest or conducting interviews with appropriate subjects may be crucial in not only gathering rich data but also in developing good research skills. While many historical societies, special collections, and other sources have digitized some of their holdings, they often have much more data than can be accessed online.

Maps, Charts, and Other Geographic Tools

See also Skill 10.1

Maps

All classrooms should be equipped with an adequate number and styles of maps and other tools relevant to geography and the social sciences. Again, while the Internet may provide useful resources, there is nothing like putting one's finger on an actual map or globe. This hands-on feature is particularly relevant to elementary students. Further, the best maps will be available locally, as will knowledge and information about the development of the area.

All classrooms should be equipped with an adequate number and styles of maps and other tools relevant to geography and the social sciences.

Projections

The process of putting the features of the Earth onto a flat surface is called PROJECTION. All maps are really map projections. There are many different types. Each one deals in a different way with the problem of distortion. Map projections are made in a number of ways. Some are done using complicated mathematics. However, the basic ideas behind map projections can be understood by looking at the three most common types:

PROJECTION: the process of putting the features of the Earth onto a flat surface

- CYLINDRICAL PROJECTIONS: These are done by taking a cylinder of paper and wrapping it around a globe. A light is used to project the globe's features onto the paper. Distortion is minimal where the paper touches the globe. For example, suppose that the paper was wrapped so that it touched the globe at the equator, the map from this projection would have just a little distortion near the equator. However, in moving north or south of the equator, the distortion would increase as you moved further away from the equator. The best-known and most widely used cylindrical projection is the Mercator Projection. It was first developed in 1569 by Gerardus Mercator, a Flemish cartographer.

CYLINDRICAL PROJECTIONS: projections done by taking a cylinder of paper and wrapping it around a globe

- CONICAL PROJECTIONS: The name for these maps come from the fact that the projection is made onto a cone of paper. The cone is made so that it touches a globe at the base of the cone only. It can also be made so that it cuts through part of the globe in two different places. Again, there is the least distortion where the paper touches the globe. If the cone touches at two different points, there is some distortion at both of them. Conical projections are most often used to map areas in the middle latitudes. Maps of the United States are most often conical projections. This is because most of the country lies within these latitudes.

CONICAL PROJECTIONS: these come from the projections made onto a cone of paper

- FLAT-PLANE PROJECTIONS: These are made with a flat piece of paper. It touches the globe at one point only. Areas near this point show little

FLAT-PLANE PROJECTIONS: projections made with a flat piece of paper that touches the globe at one point only

distortion. Flat-plane projections are often used to show the areas of the north and south poles. One such flat projection is called a Gnomonic Projection. On this kind of map all meridians appear as straight lines. Gnomonic projections are useful because any straight line drawn between points on it forms a Great-Circle Route.

GREAT-CIRCLE ROUTES can best be described by thinking of a globe and when using the globe the shortest route between two points on it can be found by simply stretching a string from one point to the other. However, if the string was extended in reality, so that it took into effect the globe's curvature, it would then make a great-circle. A great-circle is any circle that cuts a sphere, such as the globe, into two equal parts. Because of distortion, most maps do not show great-circle routes as straight lines; Gnomonic projections, however, do show the shortest distance between the two places as a straight line, because of this they are and valuable for navigation. They are called Great-Circle Sailing Maps.

> **GREAT-CIRCLE ROUTES:** routes produced by using a string to measure the distance between two points on a globe

Parts of a map

To properly analyze a given map one must be familiar with the various parts and symbols that most modern maps use. For the most part this is standardized, with different maps using similar parts and symbols. These can include:

PARTS OF A MAP	
The Title	All maps should have a title, just like all books should. The title tells you what information is to be found on the map.
The Legend	Most maps have a legend. A legend tells the reader about the various symbols that are used on that particular map and what the symbols represent (also called a map key).
The Grid	A grid is a series of lines that are used to find exact places and locations on the map. There are several different kinds of grid systems in use, however, most maps do use the longitude and latitude system known as the Geographic Grid System.
Directions	Most maps have some directional system to show which way the map is being presented. Often on a map, a small compass will be present, with arrows showing the four basic directions: north, south, east, and west.

Table continued on next page

The Scale	This is used to show the relationship between a unit of measurement on the map versus the real world measure on the Earth. Maps are drawn to many different scales. Some maps show a lot of detail for a small area. Others show a greater span of distance. Whichever is being used, one should always be aware of just what scale is being used. For instance, the scale might be something like 1 inch = 10 miles for a small area or for a map showing the whole world it might have a scale in which 1 inch = 1,000 miles. The point is that one must look at the map key in order to see what units of measurements the map is using.

Maps have four main properties. They are:

1. The size of the areas shown on the map

2. The shapes of the areas

3. Consistent scales

4. Straight line directions.

A map can be drawn so that it is correct in one or more of these properties. No map can be correct in all of them.

Equal areas

One property which maps can have is that of equal areas. In an equal area MAP, the meridians and parallels are drawn so that the areas shown have the same proportions as they do on the Earth. For example, Greenland is about 1/18th the size of South America, thus it will be shown as 1/18th the size on an equal area map. The Mercator projection is an example of a map that does not have equal areas. In it, Greenland appears to be about the same size of South America. This is because the distortion is very bad at the poles and Greenland lies near the North Pole.

Conformal map

A second map property is conformal, or correct shapes. There are no maps that can show very large areas of the Earth in their exact shapes. Only globes can really do that, however conformal maps are as close as possible to true shapes. The United States is often shown by a Lambert Conformal Conic Projection Map.

Consistent scales

Many maps attempt to use the same scale on all parts of the map. Generally, this is easier when maps show a relatively small part of the Earth's surface. For example, a map of Florida might be a consistent scale map. Generally maps showing large areas are not consistent-scale maps. This is because of distortion. Often such maps will have two scales noted in the key. One scale, for example, might be accurate to measure distances between points along the Equator. Another might be then used to measure distances between the North Pole and the South Pole.

Elevation and relief maps

Maps showing physical features often try to show information about the elevation or relief of the land. ELEVATION is the distance above or below the sea level. The elevation is usually shown with colors, for instance, all areas on a map which are at a certain level will be shown in the same color.

Relief Maps show the shape of the land surface: flat, rugged, or steep. Relief maps usually give more detail than simply showing the overall elevation of the land's surface. Relief is also sometimes shown with colors, but another way to show relief is by using contour lines. These lines connect all points of a land surface which are the same height surrounding the particular area of land.

Thematic maps

These are used to show more specific information, often on a single theme, or topic. Thematic maps show the distribution or amount of something over a certain given area in topics of interest such as population density, climate, economic information, cultural, political information, etc.

Photographs and globes

Photographs and globes are useful as well, but as they are limited in what kind of information that they can show, they are rarely used. Unless, as in the case of a photograph, it is of a particular political figure or a time that one wishes to visualize.

Although maps have advantages over globes and photographs, they do have a major disadvantage. This problem must be considered as well. The major problem of all maps comes about because most maps are flat and the Earth is a sphere. It is impossible to reproduce exactly on a flat surface an object shaped like a sphere. In order to put the Earth's features onto a map they must be stretched in some way. This stretching is called DISTORTION.

Graphs

Most often, the graphs that are used are known as bar graphs and line graphs. Graphs themselves are most useful when one wishes to demonstrate the sequential increase or decrease of a variable or to show specific correlations between two or more variables in a given circumstance.

Most common is the BAR GRAPH because it has an easy to see and understand way of visually showing the difference in a given set of variables. However it is limited in that it cannot really show the actual proportional increase, or decrease, of each given variable to each other. (In order to show a decrease, a bar graph must show

ELEVATION: the distance above or below the sea level

Photographs and globes are useful as well, but as they are limited in what kind of information that they can show, they are rarely used.

DISTORTION: stretching that occurs when Earth's features are put onto a map

Graphs themselves are most useful when one wishes to demonstrate the sequential increase or decrease of a variable or to show specific correlations between two or more variables in a given circumstance.

the "bar" under the starting line, thus removing the ability to really show how the various different variables would relate to each other).

Thus in order to accomplish this, one must use a LINE GRAPH. Line graphs can be of two types: a linear or non-linear graph. A LINEAR LINE GRAPH uses a series of straight lines; a NONLINEAR LINE GRAPH USES a curved line. Though the lines can be either straight or curved, all of the lines are called curves.

A line graph uses a number line or axis. The numbers are generally placed in order, equal distances from one another; the number line is used to represent a number, degree, or some such other variable at an appropriate point on the line. Two lines are used, intersecting at a specific point. They are referred to as the X-axis and the Y-axis. The Y-axis is a vertical line and the X-axis is a horizontal line. Together they form a COORDINATE SYSTEM. The difference between a point on the line of the X-axis and the Y-axis is called the SLOPE of the line, or the change in the value on the vertical axis divided by the change in the value on the horizontal axis. The Y-axis number is called the rise and the X-axis number is called the run, thus the equation for slope is:

$$SLOPE = \frac{RISE - (Change\ in\ value\ on\ the\ vertical\ axis)}{RUN - (Change\ in\ value\ on\ the\ horizontal\ axis)}$$

The slope tells the amount of increase or decrease of a given specific variable. When using two or more variables, one can plot the amount of difference between them in any given situation. This makes presenting information on a line graph more involved. It also makes it more informative than a bar graph. Knowledge of the term slope and what it is and how it is measured helps us to describe verbally the pictures we are seeing visually. For example, if a curve is said to have a slope of "zero," you should picture a flat line. If a curve has a slope of "one," you should picture a rising line that makes a 45-degree angle with the horizontal and vertical axis lines.

The preceding examples are of linear (straight line) curves. With non-linear curves (the ones that really do curve), the slope of the curve is constantly changing; so as a result, we must then understand that the slope of the non-linear curved line will be at a specific point. How is this done? The slope of a non-linear curve is determined by the slope of a straight line that intersects the curve at that specific point. In all graphs, an upward sloping line represents a direct relationship between the two variables. A downward slope represents an inverse relationship between the two variables. In reading any graph, one must always be very careful to understand what is being measured, what can be deduced and what cannot be deduced from the given graph.

BAR GRAPH: uses bars of different lengths that are proportional to the information they represent

LINE GRAPH: uses lines, both straight and/or curved, to represent data

LINEAR LINE GRAPH: uses a series of straight lines

NONLINEAR LINE GRAPH: uses a curved line

COORDINATE SYSTEM: the system of graphing that utilizes points plotted relative to an X-axis and a Y-axis.

SLOPE: the difference between a point on the line of the X-axis and the Y-axis

In reading any graph, one must always be very careful to understand what is being measured, what can be deduced and what cannot be deduced from the given graph.

Charts

To use charts correctly, one should remember the reasons one uses graphs. The general ideas are similar. It is usually a question as to which, a graph or chart, is more capable of adequately portraying the information one wants to illustrate. One can see the difference between them and realize that in many ways graphs and charts are interrelated. One of the most common types is the pie chart because it is easy to read and understand, even for the lay person. Pie charts are used often, especially when one is trying to illustrate the differences in percentages among various items or when one is demonstrating the divisions of a whole.

COMPETENCY 12
SOCIAL STUDIES ASSESSMENT

SKILL 12.1 Analysis of student work in guiding social studies instruction

Since cooperative and project-based learning is often utilized in social studies instruction, it is helpful for teachers to provide rubrics for students to guide them in their explorations. The rubric details different points in the project development process, thus allowing for stage-wise progression on the project. This helps students judge if they are on track or not prior to completion of the project.

See also Skill 6.1

SKILL 12.2 Formal and informal assessment of social studies knowledge

See Skills 18.2 and 18.3

DOMAIN V
ARTS AND PHYSICAL EDUCATION

PERSONALIZED STUDY PLAN

COMPETENCY 13
ARTS AND PHYSICAL EDUCATION CURRICULUM

Basic Concepts in Visual Arts

Students should have an early introduction to the principles of visual art and should become familiar with the basic level of the following terms:

BASIC ART TERMS	
Abstract	An image that reduces a subject to its essential visual elements, such as lines, shapes, and colors.
Background	Portions or areas of composition that are behind the primary or dominant subject matter or design areas.
Balance	The arrangement of one or more elements in a work of art so that they appear symmetrical or asymmetrical in design and proportion.
Contrast	Juxtaposing one or more elements in opposition, to show their differences.
Emphasis	Making one or more elements in a work of art stand out in such a way as to appear more important or significant.
Sketch	An image-development strategy; a preliminary drawing.
Texture	The way something feels by representation of the tactile character of surfaces.
Unity	The arrangement of one or more of the elements used to create a coherence of parts and a feeling of completeness or wholeness.

Various Forms of Visual Arts

It is vital that students learn to identify characteristics of visual arts that include materials, techniques, and processes necessary to establish a connection between art and daily life. Early ages should begin to experience art in a variety of forms. It is important to reach many areas at an early age to establish a strong artistic foundation for young students.

Introduction to visual arts

Students should be introduced to the recognition of simple patterns found in the art environment, as well as varied art materials such as clay, paint, crayons, print-making ink, chalk, and mosaic objects. Each of these materials should be introduced and explained for use in daily lessons with young children. More elaborate and involved exposure is appropriate for older elementary students, including the addition of other media such as stone and wood carving, digital photography and video, oil pastels, and stained glass, to name a few.

The major mediums, which are defined by the materials utilized and the activities involved, are:

- Drawing and Painting
- Sculpture
- Printmaking
- Ceramics
- Architecture
- Photography and Filmmaking
- Fiber and Fabric
- Glass
- Jewelry Making and Metal Work

Art Genres by Historical Periods

HISTORICAL PERIODS OF ART AND THEIR DEFINING CHARACTERISTICS	
Ancient Greek Art (circa 800-323 B.C.)	Dominant genres from this period were vase paintings, both black-figure and red-figure, and classical sculpture.
Roman Art (circa 480 B.C.- 476 A.D.)	Major genres from the Romans include frescoes (murals done in fresh plaster to affix the paint), classical sculpture, funerary art, state propaganda art, and relief work on cameos.
Middle Ages Art (circa 300-1400 A.D.)	Significant genres during the Middle Ages include Byzantine mosaics, illuminated manuscripts, ivory relief, altarpieces, cathedral sculpture, and fresco paintings in various styles.
Renaissance Art (1400-1630 A.D.)	Important genres from the Renaissance included Florentine fresco painting (mostly religious), High Renaissance painting and sculpture, Northern oil painting, Flemish miniature painting, and Northern printmaking.
Baroque Art (1630-1700 A.D.)	Pivotal genres during the Baroque era include Mannerism, Italian Baroque painting and sculpture, Spanish Baroque, Flemish Baroque, and Dutch portraiture. Genre paintings in still-life and landscape appear prominently in this period.

Table continued on next page

Eighteenth Century Art (1700-1800 A.D.)	Predominant genres of the century include Rococo painting, portraiture, social satire, Romantic painting, and Neoclassic painting and sculpture.
Nineteenth Century Art (1800-1900 A.D.)	Important genres include Romantic painting, academic painting and sculpture, landscape painting of many varieties, realistic painting of many varieties, impressionism, and many varieties of post-impressionism.
Twentieth Century Art (1900-2000 A.D.)	Major genres of the twentieth century include symbolism, art nouveau, fauvism, expressionism, cubism (both analytical and synthetic), futurism, non-objective art, abstract art, surrealism, social realism, constructivism in sculpture, Pop and Op art, and conceptual art.

SKILL 13.2 Music

Basic Components of Music

Melody, harmony, rhythm, timbre, dynamics and texture are some of the basic components of music.

MELODY is the tune, a specific arrangement of sounds in a pleasing pattern. Melody is often seen as the horizontal aspect of music, because melodic notes on a page travel along horizontally.

HARMONY refers to the vertical aspect of music, or the musical chords related to a melody. So, when looking at a piece of music, the harmony notes are the ones lined up below each note of the melody, providing a more complex, fuller sound to a piece of music.

RHYTHM refers to the duration of musical notes. Rhythms are patterns of long and short music note durations. A clear way to describe rhythm to young students is through percussion instruments. A teacher creates a rhythmic pattern of long and short drum beats and asks the students to repeat the rhythm.

TIMBRE is the quality of a sound. If a clarinet and a trumpet play the same exact note, they will still have a different timbre, or unique quality of sound. You can also describe different timbres using the same instrument. You may have two singers, but one has a harsh timbre and the other has a warm or soothing timbre to their voice. Timbre is subjective and lends itself to a number of creative exercises for early childhood students to describe what they hear in terms of the timbre of the sound.

MELODY: the tune, a specific arrangement of sounds in a pleasing pattern

HARMONY: refers to the vertical aspect of music, or the musical chords related to a melody

RHYTHM: refers to the duration of musical notes

TIMBRE: the quality of a sound

DYNAMICS: refer to the loudness or softness of music

DYNAMICS refer to the loudness or softness of music. Early Childhood students should develop a basic understanding of music vocabulary for dynamics. Piano describes soft music. Forte describes loud music. Pianissimo is very soft music. Double Forte refers to very loud music. Mezzo piano is kind of soft, while mezzo forte is kind of loud. These definitions can be organized on a continuum of soft to loud, with music examples for each.

TEXTURE: in music usually refers to the number of separate components making up the whole of a piece

TEXTURE in music usually refers to the number of separate components making up the whole of a piece. A monophonic texture is a single melody line, such as a voice singing a tune. Polyphonic texture denotes two or more music lines playing at the same time. A single melodic line with harmonic accompaniment is called homophonic texture.

Types of Musical Instruments

Instruments are categorized by the mechanism that creates its sound. Musical instruments can be divided into four basic categories.

- String
- Percussion
- Brass
- Wind

String instruments

STRING INSTRUMENTS: all make their sounds through strings

STRING INSTRUMENTS all make their sounds through strings. The sound of the instrument depends on the thickness and length of the strings. The slower a string vibrates, the lower the resulting pitch. Also, the way the strings are manipulated varies among string instruments. Some strings are plucked (e.g., guitar) while others use a bow to cause the strings to vibrate (e.g., violin). Some are even connected to keys (e.g., piano). Other common string instruments include the viola, double bass, cello, and piano.

Wind instruments

WIND INSTRUMENTS: these instruments make their sounds by wind vibrating in a pipe or tube

The sound of WIND INSTRUMENTS is caused by wind vibrating in a pipe or tube. Air blows into one end of the instrument, and in many wind instruments, air passes over a reed, which causes the air to vibrate. The pitch depends on the air's frequency as it passes through the tube, and the frequency depends on the tube's length or size. Larger tubes create deeper sounds in a wind instrument. The pitch is also controlled by holes or values. As fingers cover the holes or press the valve, the pitch changes for the notes the musician intends. Other common wind instruments include pipe organ, oboe, clarinet and saxophone.

Brass instruments

BRASS INSTRUMENTS are similar to wind instruments since music from brass instruments also results from air passing through an air chamber. They are called brass instruments, however, because they are made from metal or brass. Pitch on a brass instrument is controlled by the size or length of the air chamber. Many brass instruments are twisted or coiled which lengthens the air chamber without making the instrument unmanageably long. Like wind instruments, larger air chambers create deeper sounds, and the pitch can be controlled by valves on the instrument. In addition, some brass instruments also control the pitch by the musician's mouth position on the mouthpiece. Common brass instruments include the French horn, trumpet, trombone and tuba.

> **BRASS INSTRUMENTS:** these instruments make their sounds by air passing through an air chamber made from metal or brass

Percussion instruments

To play a PERCUSSION INSTRUMENT, the musician hits or shakes the instrument. The sound is created from sound vibrations as a result of shaking or striking the instrument. Many materials, such as metal or wood, are used to create percussion instruments, and different thicknesses or sizes of the material help control the sound. Thicker or heavier materials like drum membranes make deeper sounds, while thinner, metal materials (e.g., triangle) make higher-pitched sounds. Other common percussion instruments include the cymbals, tambourine, bells, xylophone and wood block.

> **PERCUSSION INSTRUMENT:** these instruments make their sound from vibrations as a result of shaking or striking the instrument

---

**SKILL Physical education
13.3**

Concept of Spatial Awareness Applied to Physical Education Activities

SPATIAL AWARENESS is the ability to make decisions about an object's positional changes in space (i.e., awareness of three-dimensional space position changes).

Developing spatial awareness requires two sequential phases:

- Identifying the location of objects in relation to one's own body in space

- Locating more than one object in relation to each object and independent of one's own body

Plan activities using different size balls, boxes, or hoops and have children move towards and away; under and over; in front of and behind; and inside, outside, and beside the objects.

> **SPATIAL AWARENESS:** the ability to make decisions about an object's positional changes in space (i.e., awareness of three-dimensional space position changes)

Concepts of Space, Direction, and Speed Related to Movement Concepts

Research shows that the concepts of space, direction, and speed are interrelated with movement concepts. Such concepts and their understanding are extremely important for students, as they need to relate movement skills to direction in order to move with confidence and avoid collisions.

A student or player in motion must take the elements of space, direction, speed, and vision into consideration in order to perform and understand a sport. A player must decide how to handle their space as well as numerous other factors that arise on the field.

For a player, the concepts are all interlinked. He or she has to understand how to maintain or change pathways with speed. This ability allows him to change motion and perform well in space (or the area that the players occupy on the field).

COMPETENCY 14
ARTS AND PHYSICAL EDUCATION INSTRUCTION

SKILL 14.1 Teaching methods for art and music

Education experts agree that the arts curriculum content for elementary students should emphasize the experimental and discovery aspects of the arts, rather than a perfect result. Elementary students are developing their sense of self and how they fit into society, and their curriculum should allow for an open creative process with little judgment. Students should feel safe as they use dance, drama, music, or visual arts in expressing themselves, without the threat of criticism. Countless research projects provide anecdotal evidence of young students blossoming through the arts and becoming more social or increasing their cognitive skills or motor skills.

Techniques for the Visual Arts

Some of the areas that can be modeled by the teacher include the following:

- Experimentation through works of art using a variety of mediums such as drawing, painting, sculpture, ceramics, printmaking and video

- Producing a collection of art works (portfolio) and using a variety of mediums, topics, themes and subject matter

- Conveying meaning by choosing specific art works

- Creating and evaluating different art works and mediums

- Reflection on various works

Some examples include:

- Mixing paint in ranges of shades and tints

- Including in the portfolio works that display at least two mediums

- Trying to include at least ten works of art in each portfolio

- Including early sketches, research and development of each project with each entry

- Painting a picture using tempera or watercolor recalling a specific experience or memory

- Creating an "art sample" book, with various examples of texture, shape, color, and line

- Using a color wheel

The major art forms that young students should experience include the following:

- Painting by using tempera or watercolors

- Sculpture, typically using clay or play-dough

- Architecture by building or structuring design using 3D materials such as cardboard and poster board to create a desired effect

- Ceramics by using hollow clay sculpture and pots made from clay and fired in a kiln

- Metalworking by engraving or cutting designs or letters into metal with a sharp tool

- Printmaking with sponges or other materials

Fundamental Music Techniques

Rhythm

Some of the most basic music techniques include learning about rhythm, tempo, melody, and harmony. Rhythm refers to the pattern of regular or irregular pulses in music that result from the melodic beats of the music. When rhythm is measured and divided into parts of equal time value, it is called METER.

> **METER:** when rhythm is measured and divided into parts of equal time value

Simple techniques to teach and practice rhythm include clapping hands and tapping feet to the beat of the music. Teachers can also incorporate the use of percussion instruments to examine rhythmic patterns, which also increases students' awareness of rhythm. As a result of exercises such as these, students learn the basics of conducting music, and through conducting, students learn to appreciate and develop musical awareness.

Tempo

> **TEMPO:** the speed of a given musical piece

Understanding rhythm also introduces students to the concept of TEMPO, or the speed of a given musical piece. Practicing with well-known songs with a strong musical beat such as "Happy Birthday" helps students become aware of patterns and speed.

The ability to repeat melodies and rhythms of varying lengths and read musical notation are early signs of creative development. Older students expand their skills by learning to play an instrument or singing. The motor skills and listening techniques required to play an instrument or to learn a vocal piece of music are important indicators of creative development.

Using music in the classroom

The use of music vocabulary taught in the classroom and the ability to describe music using this vocabulary is another barometer of creative development in music. Students show musical development by using words such as legato, staccato, forte, and piano to describe music. They can also classify a musical work, such as a symphony, and name typical instruments used in performing that work, such as the violin, viola, cello, and bass. These are all signs that students are developing their knowledge and skills in the arts.

> *Students can explore creating moods with music, analyzing stories, and creating musical compositions that reflect or enhance moods.*

Students can explore creating moods with music, analyzing stories, and creating musical compositions that reflect or enhance moods. Their daily routines can include exploration, interpretation, and understanding of musical sound. Immersing them in musical conversations as we sing, speak rhythmically, and walk in step stimulates their awareness of the beauty and structure of musical sound.

As students acquire the skills and knowledge that music brings to their lives, they go through stages similar to the development of language skills. Singing, chanting, and moving—exposing them in play to many different sound sources, including a variety of styles of music and reinforcing rhythm through patting, tapping, and moving—will enhance their awareness of musical sound. Involvement in music is thought to teach basic skills such as:

- Concentration

- Counting

- Listening

- Promoting understanding of language

Students can take music courses, which typically take the form of an overview course on the history of music or a music appreciation course that focuses on listening to music and learning about different musical styles.

A musical performance (a concert or a recital) may take place indoors in a hall or theater or outdoors in a field and may either require the audience to remain very quiet or encourage them to sing or dance along with the music. Although music cannot contain emotions in and of itself, it is sometimes designed to elicit the emotion of the listener/listeners. Music created for movies is a good example of its use to manipulate emotions.

Although music cannot contain emotions in and of itself, it is sometimes designed to elicit the emotion of the listener/listeners.

Performance analysis works through and for the ear. The greatest analysts are those with the keenest ears; their insights reveal how a piece of music should be heard, which in turn implies how it should be played. Analysis consists of "putting oneself in the composer's shoes" and explaining what s/he was experiencing as s/he was writing.

Live Performance, Gallery Tours, and Aesthetic Appreciation

A live performance or firsthand view of the arts is invaluable when it comes to promoting children's aesthetic appreciation of the arts. The best resources for teachers are local performing arts venues, art museums, symphonies, operas and dance companies. All of these venues have outreach programs geared toward elementary school students. In fact, many of the venues provide programs where artists visit the school and offer hands-on lessons for kids, as well as a live performance. Kindling an appreciation of the arts in students is a priority for most arts organizations, as these students will become their future patrons.

A live performance or first hand view of the arts is invaluable when it comes to promoting children's aesthetic appreciation of the arts.

Two excellent online resources for arts appreciation are:

http://www.metmuseum.org/

Sample Test Questions and Rationale

(Average)

1. Some areas that should be mastered by students and can be modeled by teachers include all of the following EXCEPT:

   A. Create and evaluate art works

   B. Mixing paints in different shades and tints

   C. Producing a portfolio

   D. Selling created works of art

   Answer: D. Selling created works of art

   All of the above except selling works of art are areas that should be mastered by students and can be modeled by the teacher.

(Average)

2. Skills necessary for character development include all of the following EXCEPT:

   A. Expression of feelings both verbally and nonverbally

   B. Assuming roles of the leader

   C. Recognition of appropriate dialogue

   D. Use of movement and voice to represent a feeling or action

   Answer: B. Assuming the roles of the leader

   Skills necessary for character development include assuming roles of *both* the leader and the follower.

SKILL 14.2 Interdisciplinary approaches to teaching the arts

The arts provide essential opportunities to explore connections among all disciplines. Content areas are unique, but they share common themes and terms and ideas. Skills developed in the arts enhance learning across content areas. Conversely, increased knowledge in curriculum content areas enhance the depth of knowledge and experience in the arts. Further, the concrete, sensory nature of the arts is very compatible with childhood development.

Skills developed in the arts enhance learning across content areas. Conversely, increased knowledge in curriculum content areas enhance the depth of knowledge and experience in the arts

Charles Fowler effectively argues in his book *Strong Arts, Strong Schools: the Promising Potential and Shortsighted Disregard of the Arts in American Schooling* that the best schools have the best arts programs. He explains that we need to utilize every possible way to represent and interpret our world, and that means combining content areas, not isolating them. Science, math, literature, history, or the arts by themselves only convey a part of the subject. Fowler believes that integrating these programs to provide students with a more complete picture is crucial.

Examples of Art Enhancing Other Disciplines

Fowler uses the Grand Canyon as an example. A teacher can discuss mathematically the dimensions of the Grand Canyon or the science behind how it was formed, but this lesson is taken a step further by providing examples of artistic renderings of the Grand Canyon or asking students to write a poem describing the canyon. This integration provides a more three dimensional understanding of the subject.

Using African cultural history as another example, a teacher begins with a short history lesson on select African cultures. Geography may also come into play in the lesson, as the teacher chooses a specific region, such as Senegal-Gambia in West Africa, to describe to the children what an area of Africa looks like. This may be expanded to a music lesson on African musical styles and how they influenced Western music, such as gospel, jazz, spirituals, hip hop, and rap. The teacher can introduce various African instruments and discuss what the instruments are made of and how they are played. Students will learn several drum techniques and experiment with creating their own unique drum beats. Again, at the end of this lesson students have experienced Africa through an integrated teaching approach, and they come away with a more complete understanding.

Lynn Hallie Najem provides further evidence of the importance of integrating the arts into standard curriculum in her research article "Sure It's Fun, But Why Bother With It During the School Day? The Benefits of Using Drama with Primary Students." In her research, she found that integrating the arts into primary school curriculum had a very positive effect on the self-esteem of students and opened them up to learning in all subject areas.

Works of art should most often be interpreted through a wide variety of rich art and literature experience. Students will be able to react to art experiences by understanding the definitions of the basic principles of art, such as line, color, value, space, texture, shape, and form. Early childhood students are most greatly affected by these experiences. An excellent resource is the author Eric Carle. His books are age-appropriate for young children and include a wide variety of shape, color, line, and media for young students to explore.

Once students have been introduced to a wide range of materials, they are able to better relate and explain the elements they have observed through artwork and generously illustrated literature. Literature is the most common form of exposure for young students, but video and other types of media also provide rich art experiences.

A teacher can discuss mathematically the dimensions of the Grand Canyon or the science behind how it was formed, but this lesson is taken a step further by providing examples of artistic renderings of the Grand Canyon or asking students to write a poem describing the canyon.

Read the text of this article:

http://www.madison.k12.wi.us/

Students will be able to react to art experiences by understanding the definitions of the basic principles of art, such as line, color, value, space, texture, shape, and form.

SKILL
14.3 **Materials, equipment, texts, and technology in the arts**

Basic Supplies and Equipment in Visual Arts

Visual arts require students to have the opportunity to produce original pieces of artwork. All students will require models of the projects that are expected to be made. Providing them with the model allows the students to understand the final product and be able to work with the end in mind. This process does not hamper creativity but instead provides specific criteria for the students in order to ensure their success.

The materials and equipment varies depending on the age of the students. In the younger grades, materials and supplies might include:

- Paints
- Crayons
- Markers
- Chalk/pastels
- Pencils
- Glue
- Scissors
- Construction paper

As students develop more motor skills, materials may become more complex and might include additional items such as:

- Clay and pottery wheels
- Weaving looms
- Cloth
- Stained glass

Basic Equipment Needed for Music Education

Students of all ages benefit from instruction in music education. Music instruction requires a specific training and knowledge in order to provide competent instruction to students. A well-developed curriculum is essential to ensure the students are receiving information and instruction that will be beneficial to them throughout their lives.

Students of all ages benefit from instruction in music education. Music instruction requires a specific training and knowledge in order to provide competent instruction to students.

Some equipment that is needed for music education might include:

- Piano
- CD/tape player
- Music (CDs, paper copies of songs, etc.)

- Instruments for the students to explore and interact with (i.e., bells, drums, recorders, etc.)

- Desks/bleachers

Computer and Online Resources

Computer-assisted programs provide students with opportunities to evaluate music. Programs are designed to present two performances of one or more musical pieces so the students can work with the teacher to compare and contrast the pieces. The Internet allows students to collect musical information for evaluation and provide information about studied or performed compositions. Knowledge of these resources and tools enable teachers to provide the richest education in music.

Further, many arts organizations provide many resources via the Internet. Their websites can be explored by both teachers and students for many purposes in learning about the arts.

Examples of specific resources

For example, the "Explore and Learn" section of the Metropolitan Museum of Art online has a vast collection of images, video and printed material. The "Timeline of Art History" allows students to explore history through images at the Museum of Art.

"Arts Edge" on the Kennedy Center website provides a wealth of information for teachers. The "Look.Listen.Learn" section highlights various arts forms through audio, video, images, printed material and interactive exercises.

Link to Kennedy Center website:

http://artsedge.kennedy-center.org/

SKILL 14.4 Teaching methods for physical education

Activities, Games, and Sports

Different purposes and varying developmental, age, and ability levels

The activities, games, and sports in a physical education program vary according to the developmental and chronological age of the students and their ability levels. In addition, one of the main skills involved in teaching physical education at the elementary and middle school level is to instill a sense of fair play in the students along with helping them keep active to develop a healthy lifestyle.

The activities, games, and sports in a physical education program vary according to the developmental and chronological age of the students and their ability levels.

For all the activities used in the program, it is important for teachers to be mindful of any special needs children in the class. They may or may not be able to do the same types of activities as the rest of the students, so accommodations must be included in the program to teach them how they can be healthy and active as well as develop a repertoire of physical skills.

Therefore, different strategies and activities must be used with different grade levels. The curriculum is spiral in nature so that children learn very basic skills in the primary grades and then expand on these skills to incorporate other and more complex skills in the higher grades.

All levels

At all ages, students should be taught to warm up before beginning exercises and to cool down afterward.

Most physical education programs encompass varying levels of instruction in the areas of health, individual sports and skills, and team sports, skills, and activities. At all ages, students should be taught to warm up before beginning exercises and to cool down afterward. In developing activities to help strengthen students' nonlocomotor skills, young children can begin by imitating the actions of animals, such as the swaying trunk of an elephant.

Upper elementary and middle school levels

At the upper elementary and middle school levels, students will demonstrate rules, skills, and terminology associated with individual physical activities. These activities include:

- Dance
- Rhythm
- Track & field
- Wrestling
- Tennis

It is within individual activities such as these where locomotor skills are important in the physical education curriculum. Strategies that practice flexibility, agility, and basic physical skill drills are important. For example, obstacle courses are effective at all age levels but must include objects that the students are able to jump or climb over with ease. These can be taller for older students. Another example includes kicking a ball. Also, throwing a ball and catching it are important skills for students. These activities usually start off with each student with a soccer ball that they learn to control with their feet and keep inside a designated space.

Competitive activities

As students progress in development with flexibility and locomotor skills, competitive activities can be included. Usually around grade 3 or 4, students begin with organized team or group activities.

Some games and activities to use at this level include:

- Stop and start games (in which students learn how to follow directions and follow a designed path)

- Tag and dodge ball games (where there is a safe personal space for the students and at the same time they learn how to avoid others so as to be safe)

- Flag football

- Basketball

- Volleyball

- Soccer

- Ultimate Frisbee

- Floor hockey

- Other large group games

With these games, the rules, skills, and terms associated with the game are covered, as well as elements of group activities including:

- Sportsmanship

- Healthy competition

- Social skills

- The emphasis on fun, physical activity

Promoting Skill Development and Safe Participation

Using progressive resistance

The practice of progressive resistance has become ingrained in the physical development and training programs of individuals, be it children or adults. Progressive resistance, like all other forms of exercise, should always be performed while following certain principles and safety practices. A considerable amount of controversy and debate exists as to the proper procedures for developing fitness.

Progressive resistance, like all other forms of exercise, should always be performed while following certain principles and safety practices.

As a safety precaution, a health or medical questionnaire should be formulated and completed. This can serve as a screening before enrolling a student into a progressive resistance program. While training, too much weight should not be undertaken by a novice.

Other principles and guidelines that should be followed include:

- A warm-up prior to performing resistance exercises

- A gradual increase in the number of repetitions for the exercise

- Exercising at least two days and resting for a while in order to achieve proper muscle development

- Performing exercises in a controlled manner

- Performing each exercise through a functional range of motion

- Working in conjunction with instructors who provide adequate feedback and guidance

Apart from the aforementioned principles, there are other basic principles of progressive resistance training which include careful monitoring of types of lifts, intensity, volume, and variety of lifts, and taking adequate rest for recovery.

The equipment used for progressive resistance training or exercise includes fit strips, dumbbells or barbells, and other equipment used to develop resistance and endurance.

Object control skills

Object control skills help kids to remain fit and agile. These skills also help students to become better performers. Physical educators will often combine a number of object control skills to enhance a child's reflexes.

Catch and throw is an ideal example of integrating such skills. This type of skill requires a high level of concentration and nimbleness.

Catch and throw is an ideal example of integrating such skills. This type of skill requires a high level of concentration and nimbleness. A combination of object control skills is always at the heart of any physical activity.

Object control skills make all the difference when it comes to imparting a comprehensive physical training program. An ideal combination of these skills keeps students healthy. If a teacher starts a training schedule with simple activities, they are more likely to keep the students interested. Once the interest is developed, teachers should introduce complex activities such as running and catching, pivoting and throwing, running and jumping, etc.

Body Awareness Applied to Physical Education Activities

BODY AWARENESS is a person's understanding of his or her own body parts and their capability of movement. Instructors can assess body awareness by playing and watching a game of "Simon Says" and asking the students to touch different body parts. You can also instruct students to make their bodies into various shapes, from straight to round to twisted, and varying sizes, to fit into different sized spaces.

> **BODY AWARENESS:** a person's understanding of his or her own body parts and their capability of movement

In addition, you can instruct children to touch one part of their body to another and to use various body parts to:

- Stamp their feet
- Twist their neck
- Clap their hands
- Nod their heads
- Wiggle their noses
- Snap their fingers

- Wiggle their toes
- Bend their elbows
- Close their eyes
- Bend their knees
- Shrug their shoulders
- Open their mouths

Locomotor Skills: Sequential Development and Activities

Sequential development for locomotor skills includes the ability to crawl, creep, walk, run, jump, hop, gallop, slide, leap, skip, step-hop.

ACTIVITIES FOR SEQUENTIAL DEVELOPMENT OF LOCOMOTOR SKILLS	
Activities to Develop Walking Skills	Include walking slower and faster in place; walking forward, backward, and sideways with slower and faster paces in straight, curving, and zigzag pathways with various lengths of steps; pausing between steps; and changing the height of the body.
Activities to Develop Running Skills	Include having students pretend they are playing basketball, trying to score a touchdown, trying to catch a bus, finishing a lengthy race, or running on a hot surface.
Activities to Develop Jumping Skills	Include alternating jumping with feet together and feet apart, taking off and landing on the balls of the feet, clicking the heels together while airborne, and landing with a foot forward and a foot backward.
Activities to Develop Galloping Skills	Include having students play a game of Fox and Hound, with the lead foot representing the fox and the back foot the hound trying to catch the fox (alternate the lead foot).
Activities to Develop Sliding Skills	Include having students hold hands in a circle and sliding in one direction, then sliding in the other direction.

Table continued on next page

Activities to Develop Hopping Skills	Include having students hop all the way around a hoop and hopping in and out of a hoop reversing direction. Students can also place ropes in straight lines and hop side-to-side over the rope from one end to the other and change (reverse) the direction.
Activities to Develop Skipping Skills	Include having students combine walking and hopping activities leading up to skipping.
Activities to Develop Step-hopping Skills	Include having students practice stepping and hopping activities while clapping hands to an uneven beat.

Nonlocomotor Skills: Sequential Development and Activities

Sequential development for non-locomotor skills includes the ability to stretch, bend, sit, shake, turn, rock and sway, swing, twist, dodge, and fall.

ACTIVITIES FOR SEQUENTIAL DEVELOPMENT OF NON-LOCOMOTOR SKILLS	
Activities to Develop Stretching	Include lying on the back and stomach and stretching as far as possible; stretching as though one is reaching for a star, picking fruit off a tree, climbing a ladder, shooting a basketball, or placing an item on a high self; waking and yawning
Activities to Develop Bending	Include touching knees and toes then straightening the entire body and straightening the body halfway; bending as though picking up a coin, tying shoes, picking flowers/vegetables, and petting animals of different sizes
Activities to Develop Sitting	Include practicing sitting from standing, kneeling, and lying positions without the use of hands
Activities to Develop Falling Skills	Include first collapsing in one's own space and then pretending to fall like bowling pins, raindrops, snowflakes, a rag doll, or Humpty Dumpty

Manipulative Skill Development: Sequential Development and Activities

Sequential development for manipulative skills includes striking, throwing, kicking, ball rolling, volleying, bouncing, catching, and trapping.

ACTIVITIES FOR SEQUENTIAL DEVELOPMENT OF MANIPULATIVE SKILLS	
Activities to Develop Striking	Begin with the striking of stationary objects by a participant in a stationary position. Next, the person remains still while trying to strike a moving object. Then, both the object and the participant are in motion as the participant attempts to strike the moving object.
Activities to Develop Throwing	Include throwing yarn/foam balls against a wall, then at a big target, and finally at targets decreasing in size.
Activities to Develop Kicking	Include alternating feet to kick balloons/beach balls, then kicking them under and over ropes. Change the type of ball as proficiency develops.
Activities to Develop Ball Rolling	Include rolling different size balls to a wall, then to targets decreasing in size.
Activities to Develop Volleying	Include using a large balloon and, first, hitting it with both hands, then one hand (alternating hands), and then using different parts of the body. Change the object as students progress (balloon, to beach ball, to foam ball, etc.)
Activities to Develop Bouncing	Include starting with large balls and, first, using both hands to bounce and then using one hand (alternate hands).
Activities to Develop Catching	Include using various objects (balloons, beanbags, balls, etc.) to catch and, first, catching the object the participant has thrown him/herself, then catching objects someone else threw, and finally increasing the distance between the catcher and the thrower.
Activities to Develop Trapping	Include trapping slow and fast rolling balls; trapping balls (or other objects such as beanbags) that are lightly thrown at waist, chest, and stomach levels; trapping different size balls.

Rhythmic Awareness

Instilling RHYTHMIC AWARENESS among students is another vital aspect of fitness that physical educators must not overlook. One of the basic elements of rhythm is to understand the fundamental movement models. Students should be trained in responding to different verbal commands.

Instructors also have a big role to play. They have to demonstrate how to use suitable terms related to rhythm, movement, and position. For the students, they will have to carry out locomotor movements rhythmically as well as such movements as 45-degree turns, etc. At the next level, teachers should encourage students to integrate movement patterns with music (i.e., dance aerobics).

> **RHYTHMIC AWARENESS:** this skill involves understanding fundamental movement models, usually by responding to verbal commands or music

Sample Test Questions and Rationale

(Average)

1. Calisthenics develops all of the following health and skill-related components of fitness except:

   A. Muscle strength

   B. Body composition

   C. Power

   D. Agility

   Answer: C. Power

   Calisthenics is a sport that actually helps to keep a body fit by combining gymnastic and aerobic activities. Calisthenics develop muscle strength and agility and improves body composition. However, calisthenics do not develop power because they do not involve resistance training or explosiveness.

(Average)

2. Adding more reps to a weightlifting set applies which exercise principle?

   A. Anaerobic

   B. Progression

   C. Overload

   D. Specificity

   Answer: B. Progression

   Adding more repetitions (reps) to sets when weightlifting, is an example of progression. Adding reps can result in overload, but the guiding principle is progression.

(Rigorous)

3. Which is not a benefit of cooling down?

   A. Preventing dizziness

   B. Redistributing circulation

   C. Removing lactic acid

   D. Removing myoglobin

   Answer: D. Removing myoglobin

   Cooling down helps the body to regain blood circulation and to remove lactic acid. It also prevents dizziness, which may occur after extensive exercises. The only thing that cooling down does not support is removing myoglobin. However, it can help myoglobin get a strong hold in the muscles.

(Average)

4. What is the proper sequential order of development for the acquisition of nonlocomotor skills?

   A. Stretch, sit, bend, turn, swing, twist, shake, rock & sway, dodge; fall

   B. Bend, stretch, turn, twist, swing, sit, rock & sway, shake, dodge; fall

   C. Stretch, bend, sit, shake, turn, rock & sway, swing, twist, dodge; fall

   D. Bend, stretch, sit, turn, twist, swing, sway, rock & sway, dodge; fall

   Answer: C. Stretch, bend, sit, shake, turn, rock & sway, swing, twist, dodge; fall

   Each skill in the progression builds on the previous skills.

Sample Test Questions and Rationale (cont.)

(Average)

5. Playing "Simon Says" and having students touch different body parts applies which movement concept?

    A. Spatial awareness

    B. Effort awareness

    C. Body awareness

    D. Motion awareness

Answer: C. Body awareness

Body Awareness is a method that integrates European traditions of movement and biomedical knowledge with the East Asian traditions of movement (e.g., Tai chi and Zen meditation).

SKILL 14.5 Materials, equipment, texts, and technology in physical education

Basic equipment for a range of games and sports activities is required to teach physical education both indoors and outdoors. These include:

- Balls of all sorts
- Bats and sticks
- Nets
- Goal posts and bases
- Balance beams and parallel bars
- Workout equipment
- Weights
- Trampolines
- Mats

Other equipment includes tools for performance assessment such as pedometers and other body monitors, audio-visual equipment (for both videotaped performance feedback and demonstration purposes), and cones and targets.

Further, the physical educator may choose to supplement his or her teaching with the use of instructional devices. Examples of instructional devices may include technology such as DVDs, computer programs, or interactive white boards.

COMPETENCY 15
ARTS AND PHYSICAL EDUCATION ASSESSMENT

SKILL 15.1 Analysis of student work in guiding arts instruction

Teachers must be able to make judgments regarding the quality of art using their prior knowledge of the concepts and principles that are standards for effective art

Teachers must be able to make judgments regarding the quality of art using their prior knowledge of the concepts and principles that are standards for effective art. Each teacher must develop a system that can be used for judging art and that will provide a framework for students to follow. Clearly explained expectations help guide students in their art lessons. Early childhood students often need very clear standards to follow.

Not only is it important for young students to make connections between the vocabulary of art, but the pictures or examples are always helpful too. For example, when instructing a young pupil to use scissors and glue in a project, the words "glue" and "scissors" should be clearly defined, with a picture of each object next to the instructions. Once the tasks are clearly explained and labeled, it is important to develop a testing system to evaluate how accurately each student meets the standards.

The most appropriate evaluation tool for young students is typically a rubric designed by the teacher. Evaluation using rubrics is very simple; the teacher just checks off each standard met by the students, with little or no effort. By monitoring each student while he or she is working, teachers are able to identify the skills mastered with ease.

See also Skill 6.1

SKILL 15.2 Formal and informal assessment of arts knowledge

See also Skills 18.2 and 18.3

SKILL 15.3 Analysis of student work in guiding physical education instruction

Techniques for Assessing Rhythmic Skills

There are some proven techniques with which one can assess rhythmic skills. Students are often asked to demonstrate a known vocabulary of basic movement concepts. Physical education teachers should make sure to evaluate whether the students are responding to the verbal commands or not. This particular exercise gives the teachers a proper idea of their students' performances.

Sometimes, the students have to perform locomotor movements at different levels while going in different directions. This will give the physical educator teacher a better understanding of a student's proficiency. Performing dance routines are another framework for assessing rhythmic skills.

See also Skill 6.1

SKILL 15.4 Formal and informal assessment of physical education knowledge and ability

See Skills 18.2 and 18.3

DOMAIN VI

GENERAL INFORMATION ABOUT CURRICULUM, INSTRUCTION, AND ASSESSMENT

PERSONALIZED STUDY PLAN

COMPETENCY 16
CURRICULUM

SKILL **State and national standards**
16.1

State and Local Responsibilities

In the United States, education is primarily a state and local responsibility. Business, churches, and communities can establish schools. However, regardless of who establishes a school, there are state standards that all schools must use in developing the curriculum for each subject and grade level. The state government is the primary legal decision-making authority and funder of public school districts.

All student activities should be aligned with the state standards. They should include after-school activities to provide the students with opportunities for physical education or interactive events during the school day such as field trips to points of interest. At regular intervals, the administration must collect and analyze student performance data. This information should then be used in modifying the curriculum to maximize student learning and attainment of the educational objectives.

All student activities should be aligned with the state standards.

The Role of the Federal Government

The federal government is able to make policy decisions and directives only for programs to which it provides funding (such programs include Title 1, Reading First, etc.). The federal legislation commonly referred to as No Child Left Behind (NCLB) is intended to improve student proficiency. The NCLB addresses accountability of school personnel for student achievement with the expectation that every child will demonstrate proficiency in reading, math, and science as indicated by Adequate Yearly Progress (AYP). For example, all students should know how to read by grade three. NCLB operates largely on the principle that rewards and punishments will increase motivational levels of teachers, principals, and students. Growth targets are incremental; however, when they are not met, punishment may include staff being transferred to other schools in the district.

The federal government is able to make policy decisions and directives only for programs to which it provides funding

Students with special needs, such as those with a physical or mental disability or an emotional problem, generally require specific educational planning. Based on the unique needs of the child, such programs are documented in the child's Individualized Education Program (IEP), as dictated by the federal Individuals with Disabilities Education Act (IDEA).

Federal, State, and Local Interaction

The federal government passes laws that govern education but leaves the interpretation of these laws to the state to ensure compliance.

Currently in the United States, education policy comes from the three levels of government—federal, state and local school boards. The federal government passes laws that govern education but leaves the interpretation of these laws to the state to ensure compliance. There is much funding that is passed on to states from the federal government, who then pass it on to local schools. There is talk in 2010 of implementing national standards, but at this time there are no national standards that exist for the United States.

Each state is responsible for creating their own standards students are to master and are held accountable to. These standards are the guide for teachers to know what content all students at specific grade levels are expected to master within that state; they are the basis upon which local curriculums are designed. The states have some form of assessment that is given to the students to assess how many students have mastered these standards. Schools are measured by their students' performance on these assessments.

Localities develop their own curriculums. These curriculums are based on the state standards for their area. They are designed to provide the teacher with a clear map or path to meet the standards designated by the states. Localities use their curriculums to ensure students are learning the information that is necessary for them to succeed in school and life. Curriculums change on an ongoing basis depending on the new advances in society or research into teaching methods.

It is through the combination of the local curriculum, state standards, and national laws that school systems function and succeed in the United States. Tax dollars and other funding sources are often based on the manner in which students demonstrate mastery of these standards. The standards are designed to prepare students to be life-long learners who are successful in life.

Curriculum Development

CURRICULUM DEVELOPMENT today must consider many factors including:

- Alignment
- Scope
- Sequence
- Design

First, curriculum must be aligned to state standards, state and local assessments, and district and school goals. CURRICULUM ALIGNMENT simply means that there is reflection in the curriculum of these elements. In other words, what students learn should reflect state requirements. Usually, this also means that what students' learn is tested on state assessments. If the district wanted all students to learn how to live in a multi-cultural society, curriculum would address that theme in a variety of ways; this would be an example of alignment to district and school goals.

Second, CURRICULUM SCOPE is the "horizontal" aspect of curriculum. For example, if a topic of study in a biology class is invertebrate animals, the scope would define everything that must be taught for students to adequately understand this concept.

While on the other hand, CURRICULUM SEQUENCE is the outline of what should be taught before and after a particular subject. So, for example, a sequence in math might suggest that students should learn addition and subtraction before multiplication and division. Likewise, basic math topics, like those just described, should be taught before decimals and fractions. A sequence would put all of these elements into an appropriate order.

CURRICULUM DESIGN considers the progression from the beginning of a unit of study to the end of the same unit of study. First, curriculum should be designed with the end in mind. What do you want students to know and be able to do when finished? How would they prove that they know the material or have the skill? If that information has been defined, it is much easier to design a curriculum. Too often, curricula is designed only considering forward steps in a process without concern for what students should be getting out of the curriculum.

CURRICULUM DEVELOPMENT: the process of developing and maintaining the standards of what students should learn in public schools

CURRICULUM ALIGNMENT: the curriculum aligns to state or local standards

CURRICULUM SCOPE: the "horizontal" aspect of curriculum, and includes everything that must be taught for students to adequately understand a given concept

CURRICULUM SEQUENCE: the outline of what should be taught before and after a particular subject

CURRICULUM DESIGN: considers the progression from the beginning of a unit of study to the end of the same unit of study

As a teacher implements a curriculum, the teacher should be familiar with these three main components:

MAIN COMPONENTS OF CURRICULUM	
The Philosophy or Principal Aims	In other words, what the curriculum wants students to get out of it.
The Knowledge Base	If teachers are not deeply familiar with what they are teaching to students, they will be very ineffective at getting students to learn it.
The Plan, Scope, and Sequence	What would students have learned prior? Where will they go next?

SKILL Implementing curricula
16.3

Strategies for Modifying Curricula Based on Learner Characteristics

The effective teacher will seek to connect all students to the subject matter using multiple techniques.

The effective teacher will seek to connect all students to the subject matter using multiple techniques. The goal should be that each student, through their own abilities, will relate to one or more techniques and excel in the learning process. While all students need to have exposure to the same curriculum, not all students need to have the curriculum taught in the same way. Differentiation is the term used to describe the variations of curriculum and instruction that can be provided to an entire class of students.

PRIMARY WAYS OF DIFFERENTIATION	
Content	The specifics of what is learned. This does not mean that whole units or concepts should be modified. However, within certain topics, specifics can be modified.
Process	The route to learning the content. This means that not everyone has to learn the content in exactly the same method.
Product	The result of the learning. Usually, a product is the end result or assessment of learning. For example, not all students are going to demonstrate complete learning on a quiz; likewise, not all students will demonstrate complete learning on a written paper.

The following are two keys to successful differentiation:

- Knowing what is essential in the curriculum. Although certain things can be modified, other things must remain intact in a specific order.

Disrupting central components of a curriculum can actually damage a student's ability to learn something successfully.

- Knowing the needs of the students. While this can take quite some time to figure out, it is very important that teachers pay attention to the interests, tendencies, and abilities of their students so that they understand how each of their students will best learn.

Many students will need certain concepts explained in greater depth; others may pick up on concepts rather quickly. For this reason, teachers will want to adapt the curriculum in a way that allows students with the opportunity to learn at their own pace, while also keeping the class together as a community. While this can be difficult, the more creative a teacher is with the ways in which students can demonstrate mastery, the more fun the experience will be for students and teachers. Furthermore, teachers will reach students more successfully as they tailor lesson plans, activities, groupings, and other elements of curriculum to each student's need.

Strategies for Integrating Curricula and Incorporating Interdisciplinary Themes

Keeping in mind what is understood about the students' abilities and interests, the teacher needs to design a course of study that presents units of instruction in an orderly sequence. The instruction should be planned so as to advance all students toward the next level of instruction, although exit behaviors need not be identical because of the inevitability of individual differences.

Studies have shown students learn best when what is taught in lecture and textbook reading is presented more than once in a variety of formats. In some instances, students themselves may be asked to reinforce what they have learned by completing some original production—for example:

- By drawing pictures to explain some scientific process

- By writing a monologue or dialogue to express what some historical figure might have said on some occasion

- By devising a board game to challenge the players' mathematical skills

- By acting out (and perhaps filming) episodes from a classroom reading selection

Students usually enjoy having their work displayed or presented to an audience of peers. Thus, their productions may supplement and personalize the learning experiences that the teacher has planned for them.

Teachers should combine instructional activities so as to reinforce information by providing students with relevant learning experiences throughout instructional activities.

The effective teacher takes care to select appropriate activities and classroom situations in which learning is optimized. The classroom teacher should manipulate instructional activities and classroom conditions in a manner that enhances group and individual learning opportunities. For example, the classroom teacher can organize group learning activities in which students are placed in a situation in which cooperation, sharing ideas, and discussion occurs. Cooperative learning activities can assist students in learning to share personal and cultural ideas and values in a classroom learning environment.

The effective teacher plans his or her learning activities so as to introduce them in a meaningful instructional sequence. Teachers should combine instructional activities so as to reinforce information by providing students with relevant learning experiences throughout instructional activities.

Curricular Materials and Resources

In considering suitable learning materials for the classroom, the teacher must have a thorough understanding of the state-mandated competency-based curriculum. According to state requirements, certain objectives must be met in each subject taught at every designated level of instruction. It is necessary that the teacher become well acquainted with the curriculum for which he or she is assigned. The teacher must also be aware that it is unlawful to require students to study from textbooks or materials other than those approved by the State Department of Education.

In choosing materials, teachers should keep in mind that not only do students learn at different rates, but they bring a variety of cognitive styles to the learning process.

Learning materials

Keeping in mind the state requirements concerning the objectives and materials, the teacher must determine the abilities of the incoming students assigned to his or her class or supervision. It is essential to be aware of their ENTRY BEHAVIOR— that is, their current level of achievement in the relevant areas. The next step is to take a broad overview of students who are expected to learn before they are passed on to the next grade or level of instruction. Finally, the teacher must design a course of study that will enable students to reach the necessary level of achievement, as displayed in their final assessments, or EXIT BEHAVIORS. Textbooks and learning materials must be chosen to fit into this context.

ENTRY BEHAVIOR:
a student's level of achievement in the relevant areas when entering a new class/course/lesson

EXIT BEHAVIOR:
a student's level of achievement in the relevant areas after completing a class/course/lesson

COGNITIVE STYLE:
a student's method of accepting, processing, and retaining information

Once students' abilities are determined, the teacher will select the learning materials for the class. In choosing materials, teachers should also keep in mind that not only do students learn at different rates, but they bring a variety of cognitive styles to the learning process. Prior experiences influence the individual's COGNITIVE STYLE, or method of accepting, processing, and retaining information.

Most teachers choose to use textbooks that are suitable to the age and developmental level of specific student populations. Textbooks reflect the values and assumptions of the society that produces them, while they also represent the knowledge and skills considered to be essential in becoming an educated adult. Finally, textbooks are useful to the school bureaucracy and the community, for they make public and accessible the private world of the classroom.

Aside from textbooks, a wide variety of materials are available to today's teachers. Computers are now commonplace, and DVDs bring alive the content of a reference book in text, motion, and sound. Hand-held calculators eliminate the need for drill and practice in number facts, while they also support a problem solving and process approach to mathematics. Textbook publishers often provide films, recordings, and software to accompany the text, as well as maps, graphics, and colorful posters to help students visualize what is being taught. Another way to stay current in the field is by attending workshops or conferences. Teachers will be enthusiastically welcomed on those occasions when educational publishers are asked to display their latest productions and revised editions of materials.

Media centers

In addition, yesterday's libraries are today's media centers. Teachers can usually have opaque projectors delivered to the classroom to project print or pictorial images (including student work) onto a screen for classroom viewing. Some teachers have chosen to replace chalkboards with projectors that reproduce the print or images present on the plastic sheets known as transparencies, which the teacher can write on during a presentation or have machine-printed in advance. In either case, the transparency can easily be stored for later use. In an art or photography class, or any class in which it is helpful to display visual materials, slides can easily be projected onto a wall or a screen. Cameras are inexpensive enough to enable students to photograph and display their own work, as well as keep a record of their achievements in teacher files or student portfolios.

Many schools now have advanced technological tools that make graphic displays even more powerful. Interactive whiteboards (also known as smart boards) and computer projectors that allow for PowerPoint presentations offer teachers many options.

COMPETENCY 17
INSTRUCTION

SKILL 17.1 Learning theories

Learning theories serve as the foundation for methods of teaching, materials for learning, and activities that are age and developmentally appropriate for learning. Major theories of learning include behaviorism, cognitive development, and phenomenology or humanistic psychology.

Behaviorism

BEHAVIORISM represents traditional psychology that emphasizes conditioning the behavior of the learner and altering the environment to obtain specific responses. As the oldest theories of learning, behaviorism focuses specifically on stimulus response and reinforcement for learning. The work of Thorndike led to the development of connectionism theories from which come the laws of learning. These are:

BEHAVIORISM: represents traditional psychology that emphasizes conditioning the behavior of the learner and altering the environment to obtain specific responses

LAWS OF LEARNING	
Law of Readiness	When the conduction is ready to conduct, satisfaction is obtained and, if readiness is not present, it results in dissatisfaction.
Law of Exercise	A connection is strengthened based on the proportion to the number of times it occurs, its duration and intensity.
Law of Effect	Responses accompanied by satisfaction strengthens the connection, while responses accompanied by dissatisfaction weakens the connection.

These laws also influenced the curriculum contributions of Ralph Tyler, Hilda Taba, and Jerome Brunner who discarded the view of specific stimuli and responses to endorse broader views of learning. For example, Taba recognized that practice alone does not transfer learning; therefore, rote learning and memorization should not be emphasized. Jerome Bruner, on the other hand, contributed the notion that learning is better transferred when students learn structure rather than by rote memorization.

Classical conditioning

CLASSICAL CONDITIONING theories emphasized the elicited response aspect of learning through adequate stimuli. Pavlov and Watson taught a dog who learned to salivate at the sound of a bell. This was accomplished by presenting food simultaneously with a stimulus, the bell. Their experiment gave the notion that the learner could be conditioned for learning or training.

Operant conditioning

OPERANT CONDITIONING is a behavioral theory promoted by B. Frederick Skinner. It emphasizes learning by following behavior with either positive or negative reinforcers. This theory uses "reinforcers" to increase desirable behavior and "punishments" to decrease unwanted behavior. Positive reinforcers give desirable stimuli, and negative reinforcers take away unpleasant stimuli. In contrast, positive punishment gives unpleasant stimuli, and negative punishment removes desirable stimuli.

Behavioral theories

Behavioral theories gave birth to behavior-modification approaches to discipline and learning. Albert Bandura's theory of OBSERVATIONAL LEARNING AND MODELING focuses on children learning through modeling the behaviors of others. HIERARCHICAL LEARNING THEORIES by Robert Gagne organize types of learning into a classical, hierarchical model of intellectual skills, information, cognitive strategies, motor skills, and attitudes learned through positive experiences.

Cognitive Development

COGNITIVE DEVELOPMENT THEORIES focus on human growth and development in terms of cognitive, social, psychological, and physical development. These theories suggest that schools should not focus solely on children's cognitive development. The DEVELOPMENTAL THEORY of Jean Piaget proposes that growth and development occur in stages. Piaget identified four stages of development, including:

PIAGET'S FOUR STAGES OF DEVELOPMENT	
Sensory-Motor Stage (birth to age two)	The child manipulates the physical surroundings
Pre-Operational Stage (ages 2-7)	Complex learning takes place through experiences

Table continued on next page

CLASSICAL CONDITIONING: emphasizes the elicited response aspect of learning through adequate stimuli

OPERANT CONDITIONING: emphasizes learning by following behavior with either positive or negative reinforcers

OBSERVATIONAL LEARNING AND MODELING: focuses on children learning through modeling the behaviors of others

HIERARCHICAL LEARNING THEORIES: organizes types of learning into a classical, hierarchical model of intellectual skills, information, cognitive strategies, motor skills, and attitudes learned through positive experiences

COGNITIVE DEVELOPMENT THEORIES: focus on human growth and development in terms of cognitive, social, psychological, and physical development

DEVELOPMENTAL THEORY: proposes that growth and development occur in stages

Concrete operational stage (age 7-11)	the child organizes information in logical forms using concrete objects
Formal operational stage (age 11 and above)	the child can perform formal and abstract operations

Brain-Based Learning and Multiple Intelligence Theory

Two of the most prominent learning theories in education today are Brain-Based Learning Theory and the Multiple Intelligence Theory. Recent brain research suggests that increased knowledge about the way the brain retains information will enable educators to design the most effective learning environments. As a result, researchers have developed twelve principles that relate knowledge about the brain to teaching practices. These twelve principles of Brain-Based Learning Theory are:

- The brain is a complex adaptive system

- The brain is social

- The search for meaning is innate

- We use patterns to learn more effectively

- Emotions are crucial to developing patterns

- Each brain perceives and creates parts and whole simultaneously

- Learning involves focused and peripheral attention

- Learning involves conscious and unconscious processes

- We have at least two ways of organizing memory

- Learning is developmental

- Complex learning is enhanced by challenge (and inhibited by threat)

- Every brain is unique

—(Caine & Caine, 1994, *Mind/Brain Learning Principles*)

Educators can use these principles to help design methods and environments in their classrooms to maximize student learning.

The Multiple Intelligence Theory, developed by Howard Gardner, suggests that students learn in (at least) seven different ways. These include:

- Visually/spatially
- Musically
- Verbally
- Logically/mathematically
- Bodily/kinesthetically
- Intrapersonally
- Interpersonally

Constructivism

Another learning theory is that of constructivism. The theory of CONSTRUCTIVIST LEARNING allows students to construct learning opportunities. For constructivist teachers, the belief is that students create their own reality of knowledge and how to process and observe the world around them. Students are constantly constructing new ideas, which serve as frameworks for learning and teaching. Researchers have shown that the constructivist model is comprised of the following four components:

- Learner creates knowledge
- Learner constructs and makes meaningful new knowledge to existing knowledge
- Learner shapes and constructs knowledge by life experiences and social interactions
- In constructivist learning communities, the student, teacher, and classmates establish knowledge cooperatively on a daily basis

> **CONSTRUCTIVIST LEARNING:** allows students to construct learning opportunities

SKILL 17.2 Instructional strategies

Ideally, teachers serve as the initiators and guides to learning, with students gradually taking more responsibility for learning as a lifelong skill and desire. Learning progresses in stages from initial acquisition, when the student requires a lot of teacher guidance and instruction, to adaptation, where the student is able to apply what he or she has learned to new situations outside of the classroom. As students progress through the stages of learning, the teacher gradually decreases the amount of direct instruction and guidance. The teacher is slowly encouraging the student to function more independently.

> *Ideally, teachers serve as the initiators and guides to learning, with students gradually taking more responsibility for learning as a lifelong skill and desire.*

The ultimate goal of the learning process is to teach students how to become independent and apply their knowledge. A summary of these states and their features appears here:

STATE	TEACHER ACTIVITY	EMPHASIS
Initial Acquisition	Provide rationale guidance Demonstration Modeling Shaping Cueing	Errorless learning Backward Chaining (working from the final product backward through the steps) Forward Chaining (proceeding through the steps to a final product)
Advanced Acquisition	Feedback Error correction Specific directions	Criterion evaluation Reinforcement and reward for accuracy
Proficiency	Positive reinforcement Progress monitoring Teach self-management Increased teacher expectations	Increase speed or performance to the automatic level with accuracy Set goals Self-management
Maintenance	Withdraw direct reinforcement Retention and memory Overlearning Intermittent schedule of reinforcement	Maintain high level of performance Mnemonic techniques Social and intrinsic reinforcement
Generalization	Corrective feedback	Perform skill in different times and places
Adaptation	Stress independent problem-solving	Independent problem-solving methods No direct guidance or direct instruction

Major Methods of Instruction

Direct instruction

DIRECT INSTRUCTION:
a teaching method that emphasizes well-developed and carefully planned lessons with small learning increments

Siegfried Engelmann and Dr. Wesley Becker, and several other researchers proposed the direct instruction method. DIRECT INSTRUCTION (DI) is a teaching method that emphasizes well-developed and carefully planned lessons with small learning increments. DI assumes that the use of clear instruction eliminates misinterpretations and will therefore improve outcomes. Their approach is being used by thousands of schools. It recommends that the popular valuing of teacher creativity and autonomy be replaced by a willingness to follow certain carefully prescribed instructional practices. At the same time, it encourages the retention of hard work, dedication, and commitment to students. It demands that teachers adopt and internalize the belief that all students, if properly taught, can and will learn.

Discovery learning

Beginning at birth, DISCOVERY LEARNING is a normal part of the growing-up experience. This naturally occurring phenomenon can be used to improve the outcomes within classrooms. Discovery learning, in the classroom, is based upon inquiry, and it has been a factor in many of the advances mankind has made through the years. For example, Rousseau constantly questioned his world, particularly the philosophies and theories that were commonly accepted. Dewey, himself a great discoverer, wrote, "There is an intimate and necessary relation between the processes of actual experience and education." Piaget, Bruner, and Papert have all recommended this teaching method as well. In discovery learning, students solve problems by using their own experiences and their prior knowledge to determine what truths can be learned. Bruner wrote "Emphasis on discovery in learning has precisely the effect on the learner of leading him to a constructionist, to organize what he is encountering in a manner not only designed to discover regularity and relatedness, but also to avoid the kind of information drift that fails to keep account of the uses to which information might have to be put."

> **DISCOVERY LEARNING:** this is when students solve problems by using their own experiences and their prior knowledge to determine what truths can be learned.

Whole group discussion

WHOLE GROUP DISCUSSION can be used in a variety of settings, but the most common is in the discussion of an assignment. Since learning is peer-based with this strategy, students gain a different perspective on the topic, as well as learn to respect the ideas of others. One obstacle that can occur with this teaching method is that the same students tend to participate over and over while the same students also do not participate time after time. However, with proper teacher guidance during this activity, whole group discussions are highly valuable.

> **WHOLE GROUP DISCUSSION:** this is when students discuss a topic, usually, an assignment as a group. Students gain a different perspective on the topic, as well as learn to respect the ideas of others.

Case method learning

Providing an opportunity for students to apply what they learn in the classroom to real-life experiences has proven to be an effective way of both disseminating and integrating knowledge. CASE METHOD LEARNING is an instructional strategy that engages students in active discussion about issues and the problems inherent in practical application. It can highlight fundamental dilemmas or critical issues and provide a format for role-playing ambiguous or controversial scenarios.

> **CASE METHOD LEARNING:** a strategy that engages students in active discussion about issues and the problems inherent in practical application

Obviously, a successful class discussion involves planning on the part of the instructor and preparation on the part of the students. Instructors should communicate this commitment to the students on the first day of class by clearly articulating course expectations. Just as the instructor carefully plans the learning experience, the students must comprehend the assigned reading and show up for class on time, ready to learn.

Concept mapping

CONCEPT MAPPING:
a strategy that maps out concepts, themes, and other facets of the main topic of a lesson

CONCEPT MAPPING is a common tool used by teachers in various disciplines. Many different kinds of maps have been developed. They are useful devices, but each teacher must determine which is appropriate for use in his or her own classroom. Following is a common one used in writing courses:

Concept Mapping

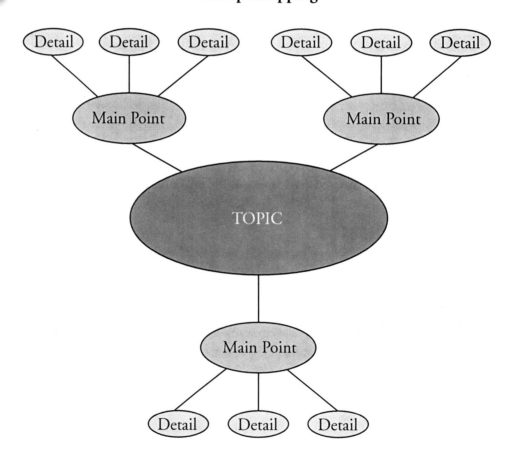

Inquiry

All learning begins with the learner. What children know and what they want to learn are not just constraints on what can be taught; they are the very foundation for learning. Dewey's description of the four primary interests of the child are still appropriate starting points. The following are these starting points:

- The child's instinctive desire to find things out

- In conversation, the propensity children have to communicate

- In construction, their delight in making things

- In their gifts of artistic expression

Questioning

Questioning is a teaching strategy as old as Socrates. The most important factor for the teacher to remember is that questioning must be deliberative and carefully planned. This is an important tool for leading students into critical thinking. Bloom's Taxonomy provides a hierarchy for increasing the critical thinking levels of question posed.

Play

So many useful games are available that the most difficult task is choosing which will fit into your classroom. Some are electronic, some are board games, and some are designed to be played by a child individually. Even in those cases, a review of the results by the entire classroom can be used to provide a useful learning experience.

Learning centers

In a flexible classroom where students have some time when they can choose which activity they will complete, learning centers are extremely important. They take out-of-class time for creating them, collecting the items that will make them up, and then setting up the center. In some classes, the students might participate in creating a learning center.

Small group work

In today's diverse classrooms, small group work is vital. Children can be grouped according to their level of development or the small groups themselves can be diverse, giving the students who are struggling an opportunity to learn from a student who is already proficient. The better-prepared student will learn from becoming a source for the weaker student, and the weaker student may be more likely to accept help from another student sometimes than from the teacher.

Revisiting

Revisiting should occur during a unit, at the end of a unit, and at the end of a semester. In other words, giving students more than one opportunity to grasp principles and skills and to integrate them is practical teaching theory.

Reflection

Teaching can move along so rapidly sometimes that students fail to incorporate what they've learned and to think about it in terms of what they bring to the topic in the first place. Providing time for reflection and guiding students in developing tools for it is a wise teaching method.

Projects

Seeing a unit as a project is also very useful. It opens the door naturally to a multitask approach to learning. For example, not only can students learn about birds, they can have an opportunity to observe them, they can try their hand at drawing them, and they can learn to differentiate one from the other. It's easy to see how a lifetime interest in bird watching can take root in such a project, which is more effective than in simply reading about the topic and talking about it.

Cooperative Learning Strategies

Cooperative learning situations, as practiced in today's classrooms, grew out of searches conducted by several groups in the early 1970s. Cooperative learning situations can range from very formal applications such as Student Teams-Achievement Divisions (STAD) and Cooperative Integrated Reading and Composition (CIRC) to less formal groupings known variously as "group investigation," "learning together," "discovery groups." COOPERATIVE LEARNING as a general term is now firmly recognized and established as a teaching and learning technique in American schools.

Since cooperative learning techniques are so widely diffused in the schools, it is necessary to orient students in the skills cooperative learning groups use to operate smoothly, and thereby enhance learning. Students who cannot interact constructively with other students will not be able to take advantage of the learning opportunities provided by the cooperative learning situations and will furthermore deprive their fellow students of the opportunity for cooperative learning.

> **COOPERATIVE LEARNING:** a classroom technique whereby students work with each other to discover the main points of a lesson.

Cooperative skills

These skills form the hierarchy of cooperation in which students first learn to work together as a group, so they may then proceed to levels at which they may engage in simulated conflict situations. This cooperative setting allows different points of view to be constructively entertained.

To teach cooperative skills, the teacher should:

- Ensure that students see the need for the skill
- Ensure that students understand what the skill is and when it should be used

- Set up practice situations and encourage mastery of the skill

- Ensure that students have the time and the needed procedures for discussing (and receiving feedback on) how well they are using the skill

- Ensure that students persevere in practicing the skill until the skill seems a natural action

A further goal of cooperative learning techniques is to establish and enhance mutual respect for other students. Cooperative learning can promote positive social goals when used effectively as a teaching and learning tool. When the teacher promotes interaction of students among ethnic and social groups, students tend to respond positively by forming friendships and having enhanced respect for other sociological groups. Thus, the teacher who effectively manages cooperative learning groups has not only promoted cognitive learning, but has also promoted desirable behaviors in terms of mutual respect for all students.

A further goal of cooperative learning techniques is to establish and enhance mutual respect for other students.

SKILL 17.3 Classroom management

The dynamics of classroom management generally correspond to the leadership styles of individual teachers. An autocratic leadership style yields a punitive, harsh, and critical classroom environment. A laissez-faire leadership style, on the other hand, yields a permissive classroom environment where disorder and anarchy dominate. The democratic leadership style is more characteristic of today's school reform in which a participatory classroom is expected. This style yields a classroom that is firm but friendly, encouraging and stimulating, and caring and guiding. Most of all, fairness prevails as a way of resolving conflicts.

Regardless of the discipline model endorsed by the school, the effectively managed classroom follows basic principles generated by research. Various disciplinary models exist for the prevention and correction of misbehavior, any of which may produce good results based on the teacher's leadership/management style and philosophy. General knowledge of classroom management techniques can prevent behavioral problems and may prove much more effective than many leading models.

General knowledge of classroom management techniques can prevent behavioral problems and may prove much more effective than many leading models.

Management Basics

Current educational research suggests simple yet fundamental strategies for effective classroom management. These include:

- Beginning class on time

- Setting up classroom procedures and routines

- Keeping desk and storage spaces clean and organized from the very beginning of the school year

Making smooth transitions from one activity to another, or from one class to another in a quick and orderly manner, is also important. This practice cuts down on idle time that generally encourages misbehavior. Making eye contact, being polite to students, and reinforcing positive interaction with and among the students all engender a healthy learning atmosphere.

"With-it-ness" is another component of good classroom management. This technique is often compared to "teachers having eyes behind their backs". Even though they appear to be doing something else, these teachers are always monitoring student behavior, especially when students are not paying attention. It also implies having a general sense of what is going on in the classroom at all times, giving verbal and nonverbal encouragement, and stopping misbehavior in a firm and consistent manner as soon as it occurs without the use of threats, and conveying consistent purpose and expectations. Careful instructional planning and pace of teaching may also reduce opportunities for problems in the classroom.

Planning for Behavior Management

Classroom management plans should be in place when the school year begins and should be proactive.

Classroom management plans should be in place when the school year begins and should be proactive. A proactive approach involves:

- Deciding what behaviors will be expected of the class as a whole

- Anticipating possible problems

- Teaching the behaviors early in the school year

- Implementing behavior management techniques that focus on positive procedures that can be used at home as well as at school

It is important to involve the students in the development of the classroom rules. The benefits include:

- It lets the students understand the rationale for the rules

- It allows the students to assume responsibility for the rules because they had a part in developing them. When students get involved in helping establish the rules, they will be more likely to assume responsibility for following them

Once the rules are established, enforcement and reinforcement for following the rules should begin right away.

Once the rules are established, enforcement and reinforcement for following the rules should begin right away.

Consequences and rewards

Consequences should be introduced when the rules are introduced, clearly stated, and understood by all of the students. The severity of the consequence should match the severity of the offense and must be enforceable. The teacher must apply the consequence consistently and fairly, so the students will know what to expect when they choose to break a rule.

Like consequences, students should understand what rewards to expect for following the rules. The teacher should never promise a reward that cannot be delivered, and follow through with the reward as soon as possible. Consistency and fairness is also necessary for rewards to be effective. Students will become frustrated and give up if they see that rewards and consequences are not delivered timely and fairly.

About four to six classroom rules should be posted where students can easily see and read them. These rules should be stated positively and describe specific behaviors so they are easy to understand. Certain rules may also be tailored to meet target goals and IEP requirements of individual students. (For example, a new student who has had problems with leaving the classroom may need an individual behavior contract to assist him or her with adjusting to the class rule about remaining in the assigned area.) As the students demonstrate the behaviors, the teacher should provide reinforcement and corrective feedback.

Maintaining the rules

Periodic refresher practice can be done as needed; for example, it can be conducted after a long holiday or if students begin to "slack off." A copy of the classroom plan should be readily available for substitute use, and the classroom aide should also be familiar with the plan and procedures.

The teacher should clarify and model the expected behavior for the students. In addition to the classroom management plan, a management plan should be developed for special situations, (i.e., fire drills) and transitions (i.e., going to and from the cafeteria). Periodic review of the rules, as well as modeling and practice, may be conducted as needed, such as after an extended school holiday.

Procedures that use social humiliation, withholding of basic needs, pain, or extreme discomfort should never be used in a behavior management plan. Emergency intervention procedures used when the student is a danger to himself or others are not considered behavior management procedures. Throughout the

Procedures that use social humiliation, withholding of basic needs, pain, or extreme discomfort should never be used in a behavior management plan.

year, the teacher should periodically review the types of interventions being used and assess their effectiveness and make revisions as needed.

SKILL Student motivation
17.4

Extrinsic vs. Intrinsic Motivation

EXTRINSIC MOTIVATION is motivation that comes from the expectation of rewards or punishments. The rewards and punishments can be varied. For example, in social situations, most human beings are extrinsically motivated to behave in common, socially accepted ways. The punishment for NOT doing so might be embarrassment or ridicule. The reward for doing so might be the acceptance of peers. In the classroom, rewards might be grades, candy, or special privileges. Punishments might be phone calls to parents, detention, suspension, or poor grades.

INTRINSIC MOTIVATION is motivation that comes from within. For example, while some children only read if given extrinsic rewards (e.g., winning an award for the most pages read), other children read because they enjoy it.

In learning, we of course want all students to be intrinsically motivated. We would want students to not care about grades or prizes as much as we might want them to do their work, listen attentively, and read just because they want to learn. And while all teachers should work tirelessly to ensure that they develop intrinsic motivation as much as possible within their students, everyone knows that for certain students and subjects, extrinsic motivators must be used.

Encouraging intrinsic motivation

The best way to encourage intrinsic motivation is to engage students in the learning. Engagement happens most when students work with material that is of greatest interest to them and if they feel there is a useful application for such material. For example, teachers will notice intrinsic motivation in reading when students have found books that they relate to.

When teachers believe that certain students just will not read, often (though not always), those students have not found books that they like. Considering that hundreds of thousands of books are out there, most likely, each student can find at least one book that interests him or her.

While teachers may want to encourage students to learn for the sake of the learning itself, they must contend with students who have been trained to "win at all

EXTRINSIC MOTIVATION: motivation that comes from the expectation of rewards or punishments

INTRINSIC MOTIVATION: motivation that comes from within

While all teachers should work tirelessly to ensure that they develop intrinsic motivation as much as possible within their students, everyone knows that for certain students and subjects, extrinsic motivators must be used.

costs." Teachers can therefore use many strategies—NOT to eradicate the very act of cheating, for example—but to encourage students to explore topics that are of interest to them or to create more meaningful, authentic assessments. AUTHENTIC ASSESSMENTS are those in which students have to use new learning in a real-world, deeply meaningful way.

The potential dangers of extrinsic motivation

Finally, it must be noted that punishment as an extrinsic motivator, while necessary at some times, often creates greater problems in the future. Students who feel like they are constantly punished into better behavior or to do better academically lose interest in pleasing teachers, acting appropriately, or learning. It is always better, whenever possible, for teachers to work at engaging students first, and then punishing if all options have been exhausted.

> **AUTHENTIC ASSESSMENTS:** those in which students have to use new learning in a real-world, deeply meaningful way

Factors and Situations that Tend to Promote or Diminish Student Motivation

A teacher's voice and speech

Teachers need to be aware that much of what they say and do can be motivating and may have a positive effect on students' achievement. Studies have been conducted to determine the impact of teacher behavior on student performance. Surprisingly, a teacher's voice can really make an impression on students. Teachers' voices have several dimensions—volume, pitch, rate, etc. A recent study on the effects of speech rate indicates that, although both boys and girls prefer to listen at the rate of about 200 words per minute, boys tend to prefer slower rates overall than girls. This same study indicates that a slower rate of speech directly affects processing ability and comprehension.

> *Teachers need to be aware that much of what they say and do can be motivating and may have a positive effect on students' achievement.*

Other speech factors such as communication of ideas, communication of emotion, distinctness and pronunciation, quality variation and phrasing, correlate with teaching criterion scores. These scores show that "good" teachers ("good" meaning teachers who positively impact and motivate students) use more variety in speech than do "less effective" teachers. A teacher's speech skills can be strong motivating elements. A teacher's body language has an even greater effect on student achievement and ability to set and focus on goals.

Teacher smiles provide support and give feedback about the teacher's affective state. A deadpan expression can actually be a detriment to the student's progress. Teacher frowns are perceived by students to mean displeasure, disapproval, and even anger. Studies also show that teacher posture and movement are indicators of the teacher's enthusiasm and energy, which emphatically influence student learning, attitudes, motivation, and focus on goals. Teachers have a greater efficacy on student motivation than any person other than parents.

Direct Engagement as a Motivator

Research substantiates that cooperative group projects decrease student behavior problems and increase student on-task behavior

Teachers can enhance student motivation by planning and directing interactive, "hands-on" learning experiences. Research substantiates that cooperative group projects decrease student behavior problems and increase student on-task behavior. Students who are directly involved with learning activities are more motivated to complete a task to the best of their ability.

Students generally do not realize their own abilities and frequently lack self-confidence. Teachers can instill positive self-concepts in children and thereby enhance their innate abilities by providing certain types of feedback. Such feedback includes attributing students' successes to their effort and specifying what the student did that produced the success. Qualitative comments influence attitudes more than quantitative feedback such as grades.

Enhancing student motivation

Despite a teacher's best efforts to provide important and appropriate instruction, there may be times when a teacher is required to teach a concept, skill, or topic that students perceive as trivial and irrelevant. These tasks can be effectively presented if the teacher exhibits a sense of enthusiasm and excitement about the content. Teachers can help spark the students' interest by providing anecdotes and interesting digressions. Research indicates that as teachers become significantly more enthusiastic, students exhibit increased on-task behavior.

Teachers must avoid teaching tasks that fit their own interests and goals and design activities that address the students' concerns. In order to do this, it is necessary to find out about students and to have a sense of their interests and goals. Teachers can do this by conducting student surveys and simply by questioning and listening to students. Once this information is obtained the teacher can link students' interests with classroom tasks.

Meeting student needs

It has been established that student choice increases student originality, intrinsic motivation, and higher mental processes.

Teachers are learning the value of giving assignments that meet the individual abilities and needs of students. After instruction, discussion, questioning, and practice have been provided, rather than assigning one task to all students, teachers are asking students to generate tasks that will show their knowledge of the information presented. Students are given choices and thereby have the opportunity to demonstrate more effectively the skills, concepts, or topics that they as individuals have learned. It has been established that student choice increases student originality, intrinsic motivation, and higher mental processes.

Child development, growth, and stress

Developmental theories and milestones provide a background against which teachers are better able to determine if a child or adolescent is developmentally delayed or needs assistance in reaching his or her full potential. However, the uniqueness of each individual should also be perceived and valued when assessing a particular child's developmental status. Any given child's developmental path is not as tidy and consistent as theory and therefore does not always fit into ordered patterns. This is an important concept when reviewing theories, stages and developmental milestones. Stage theories and lists of developmental milestones are markers to guide the observer, not absolute standards within which all children will neatly fit.

Basic Milestones in Physical, Motor, and Language Development

The majority of changes in physical and motor growth and the development of language occur prior to five years of age. The primary exception to this is the transition at preadolescence (approximately ages 9-12) into puberty. Hormonal shifts and ongoing physical growth become acute at preadolescence and bring children into adolescence and physical maturity.

The majority of changes in physical and motor growth and the development of language occur prior to five years of age.

Language development in elementary school proceeds primarily in terms of the development of vocabulary and increased sophistication in the use of words and concepts.

The key physical and motor developmental milestones for school-age children and adolescents are noted below.

PHYSICAL AND MOTOR DEVELOPMENTAL MILESTONES BY AGE GROUP	
Ages 6-8	Growth slows but remains steady Body proportions change, with legs getting longer Less body fat and more muscle develops, with an increase in overall strength Fine motor skills are enhanced, though muscle coordination is still uneven This results in the ability to write in cursive in addition to the ability to print Permanent teeth come in, sometimes causing crowding if the mouth has not developed enough
Ages 9-12	Significant body changes as puberty approaches: weight gain, pubic and body hair, increased sweating, oily skin, genital development Some children experience joint pain as a result of growth spurts Girls generally develop sooner: their hips widen, breasts start to emerge, menstruation begins Boys enter preadolescence later and their growth changes last longer

The following websites provide detailed information about developmental milestones and changes:
- *www.ces.ncsu.edu/depts/ fcs/human.html, www. littleab.com/ABcare/ develoment.html*
- *www.education.com/ reference/ontrack/.*

Physical, Genetic, Environmental, and Cultural Effects on Development

The differences in children and their rate of development are influenced by the experiences they have and the environment or culture in which they live. Basic differences in caregiver style and availability, the quality of physical nutrition, and the presence or lack of trauma and violence in the environment all impact children's development. Socioeconomic status, gender, language acquisition, basic cognitive ability, and heredity are other factors that influence children's development, behavior and their perspective on the world, as do ethnicity and race. Religion does not generally affect developmental growth, except to the extent that religious practices set the student apart from peers and therefore impact social development in the context of the larger world (outside of the religious group).

The Impact of Stress on School Performance and Students' Well-being

Students' academic performance and behavior is impacted by a range of external factors as well as the students' developmental growth path.

Students' academic performance and behavior is impacted by a range of external factors as well as the students' developmental growth path. In subsequent sections of this study guide, we will address some of the issues affecting students at school as well as in their lives outside the school. These include, among others:

- Exceptional educational needs
- Stereotyping and prejudice
- Bullying
- Violence
- Substance abuse
- Mental health problems and family issues

STRESSORS: any factor, circumstance, or event that causes stress

These circumstances, characteristics and events can all be considered STRESSORS on students.

Development as stress

The normal challenges of developmental change can also function as stressors in a child's life. As children grow, experience hormonal shifts, increase their skill base, and gradually shift from a focus on family to peers and then to the larger world, they may experience the stress that often accompanies change. Some children seem to move easily from one stage to another; others feel each developmental shift acutely. Some experience generalized anxiety, revert to earlier levels of functioning for a short time, or become clingy and demanding. They may avoid opportunities for new friends, skill development, or extracurricular activities.

It is important for teachers to have an awareness of the range of reactions to developmental change. These responses can be the primary factor underlying difficulties in peer relationships or academic performance. Considering the role of development in each child's experience is crucial to addressing student needs and concerns effectively.

Impact on school performance

Stressors can negatively impact academic achievement by making it difficult for the student to focus on learning. When a student is homeless, for example, it may be difficult for him or her to pay attention in class because of lack of sleep, worry about what is happening with a parent, or concerns about where dinner is coming from and other pressing life issues. Similarly, if a child is being abused at home, he or she may have difficulties with attention and focus.

Some stressors, such as medical conditions, may prevent a child from participating in some school activities or require homebound instruction. While accommodations need to be made for alternative programming, the inability to be "part of the group" still may impair peer relationships and affect skill development and motivation.

Stressors can also have a less direct impact. A challenging home life may make it hard for a student to complete homework assignments or study effectively. Chronic stress and traumatic events also contribute to:

- A lack of self-confidence
- Poor motivation
- Inadequate social skills
- Anxiety
- Depression
- Other mental health problems

These difficulties may interfere with a student's ability to participate effectively in the school environment. They can also disrupt the student's efforts to study and do homework.

Individuality and resiliency

Individuals respond in different ways to the same or similar stressors, and the impact of such stressors needs to be assessed for each student. Mitigating factors in the way a student deals with stress include:

- Coping skills
- Personality traits
- Prior experience with stress and trauma
- The degree of social isolation created by the stressful event(s)

- The quality of attachment to and presence of significant adults in the student's life

- The amount and kind of support the student receives in relation to the stressor

RESILIENCY is the ability to thrive in spite of difficult circumstances. Research suggests that several of the most important factors in building resiliency are the presence of a caring, competent adult in the child's life, an attitude of hope and interest in life, and good problem solving skills. Helping students identify or find an important adult upon whom they can rely, teaching problem solving and coping skills, and discussing ways to think about what life brings to us are all good strategies for helping students become more resilient. This, in turn, enhances their well-being as well as their capacity for academic and vocational achievement.

> **RESILIENCY:** the ability to thrive in spite of difficult circumstances

SKILL 17.6 Students with special needs

> Teachers need to be aware of characteristics of students with special educational needs in order to provide equitable educational experiences for all students.

As noted in the previous skill, stress is only one of many factors that impact on students' ability to function well in school and achieve at their highest potential. Various issues related to cultural and language differences, discrimination, and cognitive limitations, among others, affect how students perform. Teachers need to be aware of characteristics of students with special educational needs in order to provide equitable educational experiences for all students.

Inclusion of students with special educational needs into the general education classroom is not only essential for advanced academic achievement but also for socio-cultural development. Researchers continue to show that personalized learning environments increase the learning effect for students, decrease drop-out rates among marginalized students, and decrease unproductive student behavior that can result from constant cultural misunderstandings or miscues between students.

Needs of Specific Populations

Although every student has special needs because he or she is an individual, there are some students who, by virtue of birth or life circumstance, belong to a group with specific needs. Again, as noted previously, not all children and adolescents who belong to a certain group will necessarily fit a description or profile of group characteristics, because each student is an individual. For example, a particular girl may express a learning style more commonly associated with boys.

Some Common Classes of Special Needs Students

However, for the purpose of alerting teachers to issues their students may face, these factors may be of concern to selected populations.

Migrant worker families:

- Chronic disruption in living circumstances and education, resulting in significant gaps in learning

- Social isolation

- Inadequate nutrition and medical care

- Bias due to stereotyping

- Stress due to the problems noted above as well as economic hardship

Immigrant families and those for whom English is a second language:

- Loss of homeland and extended family

- Difficulties with learning, socialization and peer group acceptance due to language limitations

- Bias due to stereotyping

- Post-traumatic stress due to precipitating events that prompted immigration and/or losses associated with relocation

Homeless families:

- Multiple losses and traumas, and related post-traumatic stress

- Disruption in living circumstances and education, resulting in significant gaps in learning

- Inadequate nutrition, sleep and medical care

- Underlying anxiety due to chaotic and/or unpredictable environment

- Absenteeism for various reasons

Families displaced due to catastrophic events (such as hurricanes):

- Multiple losses and traumas, and related post-traumatic stress

- Disruption in living circumstances and education

- Lack of social network and extended family support

- Sudden change in economic circumstances

Families living in poverty:

- Chronic stress due to economic hardship and challenging life circumstances
- Inadequate resources for special events at school (field trips, testing, dances, sporting events, etc.)
- Inadequate nutrition and medical care
- Absenteeism due to the need to attend to pressing family matters

Gifted and talented students:

- Boredom, which may lead to behavior problems
- Need for special services and/or creative programming
- Bias due to stereotyping

Learning support and special education students:

- Increased need for appropriate attention and support from faculty and staff
- Specific accommodations during standardized testing situations
- Need for evaluation, special services and/or creative programming
- Bias due to stereotyping

Emotional support students:

- Presence of significant mental health issues
- Increased need for appropriate attention from faculty and staff, including consultation with other professionals, evaluation, referral, and follow-up
- Specific accommodations during standardized testing situations
- Need for special services and/or creative programming
- Bias due to stereotyping

Sensory-impaired students:

- Specific accommodations for various classroom activities, as well as during standardized testing situations
- Increased need for consultation with other professionals, and, at times, need for evaluation, referral, and follow-up
- Need for special services and/or creative programming
- Bias due to stereotyping

Characteristics of Students with Cognitive Impairment

Students with cognitive impairments are one group of students with what are often called "exceptional" educational needs. Other students, as noted above, are those with social or emotional problems, sensory impairment, medical conditions, or learning disabilities. There are many different categories and diagnoses that may be utilized to describe these students. Though not detailed here, schoolteachers need to familiarize themselves with the needs of these students.

Traditionally, "special education" referred to students with cognitive impairment or "mental retardation." Cognitive impairments exist on a continuum, and different students will need varying degrees of support and special programming. The basic characteristics of students with cognitive impairment fall into four categories linked largely to IQ scores.

Cognitive impairments exist on a continuum, and different students will need varying degrees of support and special programming.

IQ CATEGORY AND CORRESPONDING IMPAIRMENTS	
Mild (IQ of 50–55 to 70)	Delays in most areas (communication, motor, academic) Often not distinguished from normal children until of school age Can acquire both academic and vocational skills; can become self-supporting
Moderate (IQ of 35–40 to 50–55)	Only fair motor development; clumsy Poor social awareness Can be taught to communicate Can profit from training in social and vocational skills; needs supervision, but can perform semiskilled labor as an adult
Severe (IQ of 20–25 to 35–40)	Poor motor development Minimal speech and communication Minimal ability to profit from training in health and self-help skills; may contribute to self-maintenance under constant supervision as an adult
Profound (IQ below 20–25)	Gross retardation, both mental and sensor-motor Little or no development of basic communication skills Dependency on others to maintain basic life functions Lifetime of complete supervision (institution, home, nursing home)

Characteristics of Students with Learning Disabilities

Characteristics that students with a learning disability may display in the class-rooms include:

CHARACTERISTICS OF LEARNING DISABILITIES	
Hyperactivity	A rate of motor activity higher than normal
Perceptual Difficulties	Visual, auditory, and perceptual problems
Perceptual-Motor Impairments	Poor integration of visual and motor systems, often affecting fine motor coordination
Disorders of Memory and Thinking	Memory deficits, trouble with problem-solving, concept formation and association, poor awareness of own metacognitive skills (learning strategies)
Impulsiveness	Act before considering consequences, poor impulse control, often followed by remorselessness
Academic Problems	In reading, math, writing or spelling; significant discrepancies in ability levels

Characteristics of individuals with autism

This exceptionality appears very early in childhood. Six common features of autism are:

COMMON FEATURES OF AUTISM	
Apparent Sensory Deficit	The child may appear not to see, hear or react to a stimulus and then react in an extreme fashion to a seemingly insignificant stimulus.
Severe Affect Isolation	The child does not respond to the usual signs of affection such as smiles and hugs.
Self-Stimulation	Stereotyped behavior takes the form of repeated or ritualistic actions that make no sense to others, such as hand flapping, rocking, staring at objects, or humming the same sounds for hours at a time.
Tantrums and Self-Injurious Behavior (SIB)	Autistic children may bite themselves, pull their hair, bang their heads, or hit themselves. They can throw severe tantrums and direct aggression and destructive behavior toward others.

Table continued on next page

Echolalia (also known as "parrot talk")	The autistic child may repeat what is played on television, for example, or respond to others by repeating what was said to him. Alternatively, he may simply not speak at all.
Severe Deficits in Behavior and Self-care Skills	Autistic children may behave like children much younger than themselves.

SKILL 17.7 Cultural, linguistic, and socioeconomic diversity and their significance for child development and learning

Diversity in the Classroom

Effective teaching and learning for students begins with teachers who can demonstrate sensitivity for diversity in teaching and relationships within school communities. Student portfolios should include work that includes a multicultural perspective. Teachers also need to be responsive to including cultural and diverse resources in their curriculum and instructional practices.

Exposing students to culturally sensitive room decorations or posters that show positive and inclusive messages is one way to demonstrate inclusion of multiple cultures. Teachers should also continuously make cultural connections that are relevant and empowering for all students while communicating academic and behavioral expectations. Cultural sensitivity is communicated beyond the classroom with parents and community members to establish and maintain relationships.

Diversity can be further defined as the following:

- Differences among learners, classroom settings and academic outcomes

- Biological, sociological, ethnicity, socioeconomic status, psychological needs, learning modalities and styles among learners

- Differences in classroom settings that promote learning opportunities such as collaborative, participatory, and individualized learning groupings

- Expected learning outcomes that are theoretical, affective and cognitive for students

Teachers should establish a classroom climate that is culturally respectful and engaging for students. In a culturally sensitive classroom, teachers maintain equity and fairness in student interactions and curriculum implementation. Assessments include cultural responses and perspectives that become further learning

Effective teaching and learning for students begins with teachers who can demonstrate sensitivity for diversity in teaching and relationships within school communities.

Teachers should establish a classroom climate that is culturally respectful and engaging for students.

opportunities for students. Other artifacts that could reflect teacher and student sensitivity to diversity might consist of the following:

- Student portfolios reflecting multicultural/multiethnic perspectives

- Journals and reflections from field trips and guest speakers from diverse cultural backgrounds

- Printed materials and wall displays from multicultural perspectives

- Parent or guardian letters in a variety of languages reflecting cultural diversity

- Projects that include cultural history and diverse inclusions

- Disaggregated student data reflecting cultural groups

- Classroom climate of professionalism that fosters diversity and cultural inclusion

The encouragement of diversity education allows teachers a variety of opportunities to expand their experiences with students, staff, community members and parents from culturally diverse backgrounds. These experiences can be proactively applied to promote cultural diversity inclusion in the classroom. Teachers are able to engage and challenge students to develop and incorporate their own diversity skills in building character and relationships with cultures beyond their own. In changing the thinking patterns of students to become more culturally inclusive in the 21st century, teachers are addressing the globalization of our world.

Classroom Strategies

A positive environment, where open, discussion-oriented, non-threatening communication among all students can occur, is a critical factor in creating an effective learning culture.

A positive environment, where open, discussion-oriented, non-threatening communication among all students can occur, is a critical factor in creating an effective learning culture. The teacher must take the lead and model appropriate actions and speech, while intervening quickly when a student makes a misstep and offends (often inadvertently) another.

Communication issues that the teacher in a diverse classroom should be aware of include:

- Being sensitive to terminology and language patterns that may exclude or demean students. Regularly switch between the use of "he" and "she" in speech and writing. Know and use the current terms that ethnic and cultural groups use to identify themselves (e.g., "Latinos" [favored] vs. "Hispanics").

- Being aware of body language that is intimidating or offensive to some cultures, such as direct eye contact, and adjust accordingly.

- Monitoring your own reactions to students to ensure equal responses to males and females, as well as differently-performing students.

- Don't "protect" students from criticism because of their ethnicity or gender. Likewise, acknowledge and praise all meritorious work without singling out any one student. Both actions can make all students hyper-aware of ethnic and gender differences and cause anxiety or resentment throughout the class.

- Emphasize the importance of discussing and considering different viewpoints and opinions. Demonstrate and express value for all opinions and comments and lead students to do the same.

Gender

When teaching in diverse classrooms, teachers must also expect to be working and communicating with all kinds of students. The first obvious difference among students is gender. Interactions with male students are often different than those with female students. Depending on the lesson, female students are more likely to be interested in working with partners or perhaps even individually. On the other hand, male students may enjoy a more collaborative or hands-on activity. The gender of the teacher may also come into play when working with male and female students. Of course, every student is different and may not fit into a stereotypical role, and getting to know their students' preferences for learning will help teachers to truly enhance learning in the classroom.

The first obvious difference among students is gender. Interactions with male students are often different than those with female students.

Cultural diversity

Most class rosters will consist of students from a variety of cultures, as well. Teachers should get to know their students (of all cultures) so that they may incorporate elements of their cultures into classroom activities and planning. Also, getting to know about a student's background or cultural traditions helps to build a rapport with each student, as well as further educate the teacher about the world in which he or she teaches.

ESL students

For students still learning English, teachers must make every attempt to communicate with that student daily. Whether it's with another student who speaks the same language, word cards, computer programs, drawings or other methods, teachers must find ways to encourage each student's participation. Of course, the teacher must also be sure the appropriate language services begin for the student in a timely manner, as well.

For students still learning English, teachers must make every attempt to communicate with that student daily.

Socioeconomic differences

Teachers must also consider students from various socioeconomic backgrounds. These students are just as likely as anyone else to work well in a classroom; unfortunately, sometimes difficulties occur with these children when it comes to completing homework consistently. These students may need help deriving a homework system or perhaps need more attention on study or test-taking skills. Teachers should encourage these students as much as possible and offer positive reinforcements when they meet or exceed classroom expectations. Teachers should also watch these students carefully for signs of malnutrition, fatigue, or possible learning disorders.

COMPETENCY 18
ASSESSMENT

SKILL 18.1 Basic principles and purposes of assessment

Teachers should use a variety of assessment techniques to determine a student's existing knowledge and skills, as well as their needs.

Assessment is key to providing differentiated and appropriate instruction to all students. Teachers should use a variety of assessment techniques to determine a student's existing knowledge and skills, as well as their needs. Depending on the age of the student and the subject matter under consideration, diagnosis of readiness may be accomplished through:

- Pre-test
- Checklists
- Teacher observation
- Student self-report

Diagnosis serves two related purposes—to identify those students who are not ready for the new instruction and to identify for each student what prerequisite knowledge is lacking.

Student assessment is an integral part of the teaching and learning process.

Student assessment is an integral part of the teaching and learning process. Identifying student, teacher, or program weaknesses is only significant if the information so obtained is used to remedy the concerns. Lesson materials and lesson delivery must be evaluated to determine relevant prerequisite skills and abilities. The teacher must be capable of determining whether a student's difficulties lie with the new information or with a lack of significant prior knowledge. The ultimate goal of any diagnostic or assessment endeavor is improved learning. Thus, instruction is adapted to the needs of the learner based on assessment information.

Principles of Assessment

As is the case with purposes of assessment, a number of lists identify principles of assessment. Linn and Gronlund (1995) identify the following five principles of assessment:

1. Clearly specifying what is to be assessed has priority in the assessment process

2. An assessment procedure should be selected because of its relevance to the characteristics or performance to be measured

3. Comprehensive assessment requires a variety of procedures

4. Proper use of assessment procedures requires an awareness of their limitations

5. Assessment is a means to an end, not an end in itself

Stiggins (1997) introduces seven guiding principles for classroom assessment:

1. Assessments require clear thinking and effective communication

2. Classroom assessment is key

3. Students are assessment users

4. Clear and appropriate targets are essential

5. High-quality assessment is a must

6. Understand personal implications of assessment

7. Assessment as teaching and learning

Purposes of Assessment

A number of different classification systems identify the various purposes for assessment. A compilation of several lists identifies some common purposes, such as the following:

COMMON ASSESSMENT TYPES AND THEIR PURPOSES	
Diagnostic Assessments	Used to determine individual weakness and strengths in specific areas.
Readiness Assessments	Measure prerequisite knowledge and skills.
Interest and Attitude Assessments	Attempt to identify topics of high interest or areas in which students may need extra motivational activities.
Evaluation Assessments	Are generally program or teacher focused and helps to determine progress made.
Placement Assessments	Used for purposes of grouping students or determining appropriate beginning levels in leveled materials.
Formative Assessment	Provides ongoing feedback on student progress and the success of instructional methods and materials.
Summative Assessment	Defines student accomplishment with the intent to determine the degree of student mastery or learning that has taken place.

For most teachers, assessment purposes vary according to the situation. It may be helpful to consult several sources to help formulate an overall assessment plan. Kellough and Roberts (1991) identify the following six purposes for assessment:

1. To evaluate and improve student learning

2. To identify student strengths and weaknesses

3. To assess the effectiveness of a particular instructional strategy

4. To evaluate and improve program effectiveness

5. To evaluate and improve teacher effectiveness

6. To communicate to parents their children's progress

RELIABLE ASSESSMENT: provides accurate and consistent results; there is little error from one time it is given to the next

VALID ASSESSMENT: one which tests what it intends to test

Validity and Reliability

A desirable assessment is both reliable and valid. Without adequate reliability and validity, an assessment provides unusable results. A RELIABLE ASSESSMENT provides accurate and consistent results; there is little error from one time it is given to the next. A VALID ASSESSMENT is one which tests what it intends to test.

Reliability can sometimes be described by a correlation. A perfect positive correlation equals + 1.00 and a perfect negative correlation equals -1.00. The reliability of an assessment tool is generally expressed as a decimal to two places (e.g., 0.85). This decimal number describes the correlation that would be expected between two scores if the same student took the test two times.

Measuring reliability

Actually, we have several ways to estimate the reliability of an instrument. The method that is conceptually the most clear is the TEST-RETEST METHOD. When the same test is administered again to the same students, if the test is perfectly reliable, each student will receive the same score each time. Even as the scores of individual students vary some from one time to the next, it is desirable for the rank order of the students to remain unchanged. Other methods of estimating reliability operate off of the same conceptual framework.

SPLIT-HALF METHODS divide a single test into two parts and compares them. EQUIVALENT FORM METHODS use two versions of the same test and compares results. With some types of assessment, such as essays and observation reports, reliability concerns also deal with the procedures and criteria used for scoring. The inter-rater reliability asks the question—how much will the results vary depending on who is scoring or rating the assessment data?

Types of validity

Three commonly described types of validity are:

1. Content validity

2. Criterion validity

3. Construct validity

CONTENT VALIDITY describes the degree to which the assessment actually measures the skills it was designed to measure, say, arithmetic. Story problems on an arithmetic test will lower its validity as a measure of arithmetic since reading ability will also be reflected in the results. However, note that it remains a valid test of the ability to solve story problems.

CRITERION VALIDITY is so named because of the concern with the test's ability to predict performance on another measure or test. For example, a college admissions test is highly valid if it predicts very accurately those students who will attain high GPAs at that college. The criterion in this case is college GPA.

CONSTRUCT VALIDITY is concerned with describing the usefulness or reality of what is being tested. The recent interest in multiple intelligences, instead of a

TEST-RETEST METHOD: way of testing reliability that involves administering the same test multiple times to the same students, expecting the same students to the get the same score

SPLIT-HALF METHODS: dividing a single test into two parts and comparing them

EQUIVALENT FORM METHODS: using two versions of the same test and comparing results

CONTENT VALIDITY: the degree to which the assessment actually measures the skills it was designed to measure

CRITERION VALIDITY: so named because of the concern with the test's ability to predict performance on another measure or test

CONSTRUCT VALIDITY: concerned with describing the usefulness or reality of what is being tested

single IQ score, is an example of the older construct of intelligence being reexamined as potentially several distinct constructs.

Screening

A student's readiness for a specific subject is not an absolute concept but is determined by the relationship between the subject matter/topic and the student's prior knowledge, interest, motivation, attitude, experience and other similar factors.

Thus, the student's readiness to learn about the water cycle depends on whether the student already knows related concepts such as evaporation, condensation, and filtration. Readiness, then, implies that no "gap" exists between what the student knows and the prerequisite knowledge base for learning. This readiness is judged by SCREENING.

A pretest designed to assess significant and related prerequisite skills and abilities is the most common method of identifying the students' readiness. This assessment should focus, not on the content to be introduced, but on prior knowledge judged to be necessary for understanding the new content. A pretest that focuses on the new content may identify students who do not need the new instruction (who have already mastered the material), but it will not identify students with readiness gaps.

The most common areas of readiness concerns are in the basic academic skill areas. Mastery of the basic skill areas is a prerequisite for almost all subject area learning. Arithmetic skills and some higher-level mathematic skills are generally necessary for science learning or for understanding history and related time concepts.

Reading skills are necessary throughout the school years and beyond. A student with poor reading skills is at a disadvantage when asked to read a textbook chapter independently. Writing skills, especially handwriting, spelling, punctuation, and mechanics, are directly related to success in any writing-based activity. A weakness in any of these basic skill areas may at first glance appear to be a difficulty in understanding the subject area.

> A student's readiness for a specific subject is not an absolute concept but is determined by the relationship between the subject matter/topic and the student's prior knowledge, interest, motivation, attitude, experience and other similar factors.

> **SCREENING:** a method of assessing a student's significant and related prerequisite skills and abilities

> The most common areas of readiness concerns are in the basic academic skill areas.

SKILL 18.2   Standardized assessment tools

It is useful to consider the types of assessment procedures that are available to the classroom teacher. The types of assessment discussed below represent many of the more common types, but the list is not exhaustive.

Types of Tests

FORMAL TESTS are those tests that have been standardized using a large sample population. The process of standardization provides various comparative norms and scales for the assessment instrument.

The term INFORMAL TEST includes all other tests. Most publisher-provided tests and teacher-made tests are informal tests using this definition. Note clearly that an informal test is not necessarily unimportant. A teacher-made final exam, for example, is informal by definition simply because it has not been standardized.

FORMAL TESTS: those tests that have been standardized using a large sample population

INFORMAL TEST: any test that is not a formal test

Other Types of Assessments

Anecdotal records

These are notes recorded by the teacher concerning an area of interest or concern with a particular student. These records should focus on observable behaviors and should be descriptive in nature. They should not include assumptions or speculations regarding effective areas such as motivation or interest. These records are usually compiled over a period of several days to several weeks.

Rating scales and checklists

These assessments are generally self-appraisal instruments completed by the students or observations-based instruments completed by the teacher. The focus of these is frequently on behavior or effective areas such as interest and motivation.

Portfolio assessment

The use of student portfolios for some aspect of assessment has become quite common. The purpose, nature, and policies of portfolio assessment vary greatly from one setting to another. In general, though, a student's portfolio contains samples of work collected over an extended period of time. The nature of the subject, age of the student, and scope of the portfolio, all contribute to the specific mechanics of analyzing, synthesizing, and otherwise evaluating the portfolio contents.

The purpose, nature, and policies of portfolio assessment vary greatly from one setting to another.

In most cases, the student and teacher make joint decisions as to which work samples will go into the student's portfolios. A collection of work compiled over an extended time period allows teacher, student, and parents to view the student's progress from a unique perspective. Qualitative changes over time can be readily apparent from work samples. Such changes are sometimes difficult to establish with strictly quantitative records, such as those typical of the scores recorded in the teacher's grade book.

A collection of work compiled over an extended time period allows teacher, student, and parents to view the student's progress from a unique perspective.

Questioning

One of the most frequently occurring forms of assessment in the classroom is oral questioning by the teacher. As the teacher questions the students, he/she collects a great deal of information about the degree of student learning and potential sources of confusion for the students. While questioning is often viewed as a component of instructional methodology, it is also a powerful assessment tool.

Tests

Tests and similar direct assessment methods represent the most easily identified types of assessment. Thorndike (1997) identifies three types of assessment instruments:

1. Standardized achievement tests

2. Assessment material packaged with curricular materials

3. Teacher-made assessment instruments

    – Pencil and paper test

    – Oral tests

    – Product evaluations

    – Performance tests

    – Effective measures

Kellough and Roberts (1991) take a slightly different perspective. They describe three avenues for assessing student achievement:

• What the learner says

• What the learner does

• What the learner writes

Performance-based assessments

PERFORMANCE-BASED ASSESSMENTS: measure the learning outcomes of individual students in subject content areas

PERFORMANCE-BASED ASSESSMENTS are currently being used in a number of state testing programs to measure the learning outcomes of individual students in subject content areas. Washington State uses performance-based assessments for the WASL (Washington Assessment of Student Learning) in reading, writing, math, and science to measure student-learning performance. Attaching a graduation requirement to passing the required state assessment for the class of 2008 has created high-stakes testing and educational accountability for both students and teachers in meeting the expected skill based requirements for 10th grade students taking the test.

In today's classrooms, performance-based assessments in core subject areas must have established and specific performance criteria that start with pre-testing in the subject area and maintaining of daily or weekly testing to gauge student progress toward learning goals and objectives. To understand a student's learning is to understand how a student processes information. Effective performance assessments will show the gaps or holes in student learning that allows for an intense concentration on providing fillers to bridge non-sequential learning gaps. Typical performance assessments include oral and written student work in the form of research papers, oral presentations, class projects, journals, student portfolio collections of work, and community service projects.

In today's classrooms, performance-based assessments in core subject areas must have established and specific performance criteria that start with pre-testing in the subject area and maintaining of daily or weekly testing to gauge student progress toward learning goals and objectives.

Criterion-referenced assessments

CRITERION-REFERENCED ASSESSMENTS examine specific student learning goals and performance compared to a norm group of student learners. According to Bond (1996) "Educators or policy makers may choose to use a Criterion-referenced test (CRT) when they wish to see how well students have learned the knowledge and skills that they are expected to have mastered." Many school districts and state legislation use CRTs to ascertain whether schools are meeting national and state learning standards. The latest national educational mandate of No Child Left Behind (NCLB) and Adequate Yearly Progress (AYP) use CRTs to measure student learning, school performance, and school improvement goals as structured accountability expectations in school communities. CRTs are generally used in learning environments to reflect the effectiveness of curriculum implementation and learning outcomes.

CRITERION-BASED ASSESSMENTS: used to examine specific student learning goals and performance compared to a norm group of student learners

Norm-referenced assessments

NORM-REFERENCED TESTS (NRT) are used to classify student learners for homogenous groupings based on ability levels or basic skills into a ranking category. In many school communities, NRTs are used to classify students into Advanced Placement (AP), honors, regular, or remedial classes that can significantly impact student future educational opportunities or success. NRTs are also used by national testing companies such as Iowa Test of Basic Skills (Riverside), Florida Achievement Test (McGraw-Hill), and other major test publishers to test a national sample of students that are used to develop norms against standard test-takers. Stiggins (1994) states "Norm-referenced tests (NRT) are designed to highlight achievement differences between and among students to produce a dependable rank order of students across a continuum of achievement from high achievers to low achievers."

NORM-REFERENCED TESTS (NRT): used to classify student learners for homogenous groupings based on ability levels or basic skills into a ranking category

Educators may use the information from NRTs to provide students with academic learning that accelerates student skills from the basic level to higher skill applications and thereby enable students to meet the requirements of state assessments and core subject expectations. NRT ranking ranges from 1–99 with 25 percent of students scoring in the lower ranking of 1-25 and 25 percent of students scoring in the higher ranking of 76–99. Florida uses a variety of NRTs for student assessments that range from Iowa Basic Skills Testing to California Battery Achievement testing to measure student learning in reading and math.

SKILL 18.3 Evaluation of student progress and instructional techniques

Whether a teacher is using criterion-referenced, norm-referenced or performance-based data to inform and impact student learning and achievement, the more important objective is ensuring that teachers know how to effectively use the data to improve and reflect upon existing teaching instructions. The goal of identifying ways for teachers to use the school data is simple, "Is the teacher's instructional practice improving student learning goals and academic success?"

School data can include:

- Demographic profiling

- Cultural and ethnic academic trends

- State and national assessments

- Portfolios

- Academic subject pre-post assessment and weekly assessments

- Projects

- Disciplinary reports

By looking at trends and discrepancies in school data, teachers can ascertain whether they are meeting the goals and objectives of the state, national, and federal mandates for school improvement reform and curriculum implementation.

Assessments can be used to motivate students to learn and shape the learning environment to provide learning stimulation that optimizes student access to learning. Butler and McMunn (2006) have shown that factors that help motivate students to learn are:

1. Involving students in their own assessment

2. Matching assessment strategies to student learning

3. Consider thinking styles and using assessments to adjust the classroom environment in order to enhance student motivation to learn

Teachers can shape the way students learn by creating engaging learning opportunities that promote student achievement.

SKILL 18.4 **Professional development**

The very nature of the teaching profession—the yearly cycle of doing the same thing over and over again—creates the tendency to fossilize, to quit growing, to become complacent. The teachers who are truly successful are those who have built into their own approach a strategy against that tendency. They see themselves as constant learners. They believe that learning never ends. They are careful never to teach their classes the same as they did the last time. They build in a tendency to reflect on what is happening to their students under their care or what happened this year as compared to last year. Some questions successful teachers ask of themselves are:

- What worked the best?

- What didn't work so well?

- What can be changed to improve success rates?

- What about continuing education?

- Would they go for another degree or should they enroll in more classes?

Self-assessment

There are several avenues a teacher might take in order to assess his or her own teaching strengths and weaknesses. Having several students who are unable to understand a concept might be an early indicator of the need for a self-evaluation. In such a case, a teacher might want to go over his or her lesson plans to make sure the topic is being covered thoroughly and in a clear fashion. Brainstorming other ways to tackle the content might also help. Speaking to other teachers, asking how they teach a certain skill, might give new insight to one's own teaching tactics.

Any good teacher will understand that he or she needs to self-evaluate and adjust his or her lessons periodically. Signing up for professional courses or workshops can also help a teacher assess his or her abilities by opening one's eyes to new ways of teaching.

Any good teacher will understand that he or she needs to self-evaluate and adjust his or her lessons periodically.

Workshops and Community Support

Professional development opportunities for teacher performance improvement or enhancement in instructional practices are essential for creating comprehensive learning communities.

The development of student-centered learning communities that foster the academic capacities and learning synthesis for all students should be the fundamental goal of professional development for teachers.

In order to promote the vision, mission, and action plans of school communities, teachers must be given the toolkits to maximize instructional performances. The development of student-centered learning communities that foster the academic capacities and learning synthesis for all students should be the fundamental goal of professional development for teachers.

The level of professional development may include traditional district workshops that enhance instructional expectations for teachers or the more complicated multiple day workshops given by national and state educational organizations. Most workshops on the national and state level provide clock hours that can be used to renew certifications for teachers every five years. Typically, 150 clock hours is the standard certification number needed to provide a five-year certification renewal, so teachers must attend and complete paperwork for a diversity of workshops that range from 1–50 clock hours according to the timeframe of the workshops.

Most districts and schools provide in-service professional development opportunities for teachers during the school year dealing with district objectives and expectations and relevant workshops or classes that can enhance the teaching practices for teachers. Clock hours are provided with each class or workshop and the type of professional development being offered to teachers determines clock hours. Each year, schools are required to report the number of workshops, along with the participants attending the workshops to the superintendent's office for filing. Teachers collecting clock hour forms are required to file the forms to maintain certification eligibility and job eligibility.

Practices for expanding development opportunities

The research by the National Association of Secondary Principals' Breaking Ranks II: Strategies for Leading High School Reform created the following multiple listing of educational practices needed for expanding the professional development opportunities for teachers:

- Interdisciplinary instruction between subject areas

- Identification of individual learning styles to maximize student academic performance

- Training teachers in understanding and applying multiple assessment formats and implementations in curriculum and instruction

- Looking at multiple methods of classroom management strategies

- Providing teachers with national, federal, state and district curriculum expectations and performance outcomes

- Identifying the school communities' action plan of student learning objectives and teacher instructional practices

- Helping teachers understand how to use data to impact student learning goals and objectives

- Teaching teachers on how to disaggregate student data in improving instruction and curriculum implementation for student academic equity and access

- Develop leadership opportunities for teachers to become school and district trainers to promote effective learning communities for student achievement and success

In promoting professional development opportunities for teachers that enhance student achievement, the bottom line is that teachers must be given the time to complete workshops at no or minimal costs. School and district budgets must include financial resources to support and encourage teachers to engage in mandatory and optional professional development opportunities that create a "win-win" learning experience for students.

In promoting professional development opportunities for teachers that enhance student achievement, the bottom line is that teachers must be given the time to complete workshops at no or minimal costs.

SKILL 18.5 Professional relationships with colleagues, families, and other community members

Relationships with Colleagues

Part of being an effective teacher is to not only have students grow educationally but to allow oneself to also continue to grow as a teacher. Working with other members of the school community—peers, supervisors, and other staff—will give the teacher the necessary grounding needed to increase skills and knowledge sets. Identifying possible mentors, teachers should choose fellow teachers who are respected and whom should be emulated. Searching out other teachers who have had an amount of success in the area needing growth is another step. Asking them questions and for advice on brushing up lesson plans or techniques for delivery of instruction can be helpful.

Talk to the supervisor or the principal when you are having difficulties, or when you want to learn more about a topic. They may know of development training seminars, books, journals, or other resources that might be available. Teachers should remember that they are part of a team of professionals, and that their personal success is part of a greater success that everyone hopes to achieve.

Many people may have something to say about the way you handle any given situation or subject. If you are hearing the same critiques from many different sources, then there is probably some truth behind what is being said. Take a step back and examine the criticism. Putting personal feelings aside is important; look at the mechanics of the problem. Work with your supervisor, your mentor, and your colleagues to restructure your lesson plans or your way of interacting with the students.

Even when a piece of feedback seems spurious, a fair response is to thank the person for their thoughts and say that you will take them into consideration. Always give the critic the benefit of the doubt; chances are they have your and your students' best interests at heart. If a discussion becomes heated, everyone will lose sight of the goal— to make the classes the best they can be so that the students meet the standards they need to meet in order to progress, learn, and grow.

Relationships with Parent/Guardians and Families

Research proves that the more families are involved in a child's educational experience, the more that child will succeed academically.

Research proves that the more families are involved in a child's educational experience, the more that child will succeed academically. The problem is that often teachers assume that involvement in education simply means that the parents show up to help at school events or participate in parental activities on campus. With this belief, many teachers devise clever strategies to increase parental involvement at school. However, just because a parent shows up to school and assists with an activity does not mean that the child will learn more. Many parents work all day long and cannot assist in the school. Teachers, therefore, have to think of different ways to encourage parental and family involvement in the educational process.

Quite often, teachers have great success within involving families by just informing families of what is going on in the classroom. Newsletters are particularly effective for this purpose. Parents love to know what is going on in the classroom, and this way, they'll feel included. In newsletters, teachers can provide suggestions on how parents can help with the educational goals of the school. For example, teachers can recommend that parents read with their children for twenty minutes per day. To increase effectiveness, teachers can also provide suggestions on what to do when their children come across difficult words or when they ask a question about comprehension. These suggestions give parents practical strategies to use with their children.

Parents often equate phone calls from teachers with news about misbehaviors of their children. Teachers can change that tone by calling parents with good news. Or they can send positive notes home with students. Thus, when they need to make negative phone calls, teachers will have greater success.

Teachers can also provide very specific suggestions to individual parents. For example, let's say a student needs additional assistance in a particular subject. The teacher can provide tips to parents to encourage and increase deeper understandings in the subject outside of class.

When it is necessary to communicate (whether by phone, letter, email, or in person) with a parent regarding a concern about a student, the teacher should allow a "cooling off" period before making contact with the parent. It is important that the teacher remain professional and objective. The purpose for contacting the parent is to elicit support and additional information that may have a bearing on the student's behavior or performance. The teacher should be careful to not demean the child and not to appear antagonistic or confrontational. Be aware that the parent is likely to be quite uncomfortable with the bad news and will respond best if you take a cooperative, problem solving approach to the issue. It is also a nice courtesy to notify parents of positive occurrences with their children. The teacher's communication with parents should not be limited to negative items.

Parent conferences
The parent-teacher conference is generally for one of three purposes:

1. The teacher may wish to share information with the parents concerning the performance and behavior of the child

2. The teacher may be interested in obtaining information from the parents about the child; such information may help answer questions or concerns that the teacher has

3. The teacher may request parent support or involvement in specific activities or requirements

In many situations, more than one of the purposes may be involved.

Planning the conference
When a conference is scheduled, whether at the request of the teacher or parent, the teacher should allow sufficient time to prepare thoroughly. Collect all relevant information, samples of student work, records of behavior, and other items needed to help the parent understand the circumstances. It is also a good idea to compile a list of questions or concerns you wish to address. Arrange the time and location of the conference to provide privacy and to avoid interruptions.

When a conference is scheduled, whether at the request of the teacher or parent, the teacher should allow sufficient time to prepare thoroughly.

Conducting the conference

Begin the conference by putting the parents as ease. Take the time to establish a comfortable mood, but do not waste time with unnecessary small talk. Begin your discussion with positive comments about the student. Identify strengths and desirable attributes, but do not exaggerate.

The teacher should address issues or areas of concern, being sure to focus on observable behaviors and concrete results or information. It is important to not make judgmental statements about parent or child. Sharing specific work samples, anecdotal records of behavior, etc., that demonstrate clearly the concerns is important as well. The teacher should be a good listener by hearing the parent's comments and explanations. Such background information can be invaluable in understanding the needs and motivations of the child.

Finally, end the conference with an agreed plan of action between parents and teacher (and, when appropriate, the child). Bring the conference to a close politely but firmly and thank the parents for their involvement.

After the conference

A day or two after the conference, it is a good idea to send a follow-up note to the parents. In this note, briefly and concisely reiterate the plan or step agreed to in the conference. Be polite and professional; avoid the temptation to be too informal or chatty. If the issue is a long-term one such as the behavior or on-going work performance of the student, make periodic follow-up contacts to keep the parents informed of the progress.

Community Relationships

The community is a vital link to increasing learning experiences for students. Community resources can supplement the minimized and marginal educational resources of school communities. With state and federal educational funding becoming increasingly subject to legislative budget cuts, school communities welcome the financial support that community resources can provide in terms of discounted prices on high-end supplies (e.g., computers, printers, and technology supplies), along with providing free notebooks, backpacks, and student supplies for low income students who may have difficulty obtaining the basic supplies for school.

Community stores can provide cash rebates and teacher discounts for educators in struggling school districts and compromised school communities. Both professionally and personally, communities can enrich the student learning experiences by including the following support strategies:

- Provide programs that support student learning outcomes and future educational goals

- Create mentoring opportunities that provide adult role models in various industries to students interested in studying in that industry

- Provide financial support for school communities to help low-income or homeless students begin the school year with the basic supplies

- Develop paid internships with local university students to provide tutorial services for identified students in school communities who are having academic and social difficulties processing various subject areas

- Providing parent-teen-community forums to create a public voice of change in communities

- Offer parents without a computer or Internet connection stipends to purchase technology to create equitable opportunities for students to do research and complete requirements

- Stop in classrooms and ask teachers and students what's needed to promote academic progress and growth

Community resources are vital in providing the additional support to students, school communities, and families struggling to remain engaged in declining educational institutions competing for federal funding and limited district funding. The commitment that a community shows to its educational communities is a valuable investment in the future. Community resources that are able to provide additional funding for tutors in marginalized classrooms or help schools reduce classrooms of students needing additional remedial instruction directly impact educational equity and facilitation of teaching and learning for both teachers and students.

The commitment that a community shows to its educational communities is a valuable investment in the future.

SAMPLE TEST

SAMPLE TEST

(Average) (Skill 1.3)

1. When students understand how sentences are built and the words needed for the sentences to "sound" right, they have developed a sense of:

    A. Morphology

    B. Syntax

    C. Semantics

    D. Fluency

(Rigorous) (Skill 1.4)

2. If you have had a cough for a long time, it is said to be:

    A. Chronic

    B. Prescriptive

    C. Contagious

    D. Malicious

(Average) (Skill 1.4)

3. How does adding the prefix *dis-* to the word *continue*, change its meaning?

    A. It now means "to continue later"

    B. It now means "to do again"

    C. It now means "to not continue"

    D. It doesn't change the meaning

(Rigorous) (Skill 1.4)

4. Besides teaching scientific methods and information, what might be a good lesson to teach along with a book about photosynthesis?

    A. The first photograph taken

    B. The root *–photo-* means light

    C. The food chain

    D. The letters /*ph*/ make the "f" sound

Directions: For Questions 5-7, read the following passage and choose the best answer for each question.

You might think that an easy-going, laid back, unstructured summer is good for children. But chances are, due to our lack of routine and structure, children's sleep habits often suffer. Don't let your summer turn into the "dog days of summer" like mine have before. Be sure that your children get enough sleep even during the unstructured months of June, July, and August.

Of course not all children are the same and do not require the same amount of sleep. I was surprised to learn that a 5-year old still needs about 11 hours of sleep a night. That means that if Rachel goes to bed at 8:00 then she should sleep until about 7:00 the next morning. Or if she goes to bed at 9:30 she should sleep until about 8:30 the next morning. If this isn't the case, there are a couple of things that can be done to help a child catch up. Options include taking a nap during the day, putting children to bed at an early hour, never waking a sleeping child, and keeping daily activities limited. Remember, children who are well rested have better temperaments and are much more enjoyable to be around.

(Rigorous) (Skill 1.5)

5. What is MOST LIKELY true based on the above passage?

   A. The author is a parent

   B. The author is a pediatrician

   C. The author is a teacher

   D. The author has twins

(Easy) (Skill 1.5)

6. What will most likely happen if a young child does not get enough sleep?

   A. They won't be able to sleep well at night

   B. They will be fine and make it through the day

   C. They will get sick more easily

   D. They will misbehave and act irrational

(Average) (Skill 1.5)

7. The author was surprised to learn that a 5-year-old still needs about 11 hours of sleep. Does this sentence contain a fact or an opinion?

   A. Fact

   B. Opinion

Directions: For Question 8, read the following passage and choose the best answer.

Many people say that the story *The Ugly Duckling* mirrors Hans Christian Andersen's childhood. He was an odd child and did not fit in well with other children. Hans was often older than other children and because of this felt alienated. He was interested in the stage and visited the playhouse outside of Copenhagen with his father. However, eventually he was sent away to a boarding school. His experience there was dreadful. He lived with the schoolmaster where he was abused. The headmaster had said it was a way to improve his character.

(Rigorous) (Skill 1.5)

8. Which detail supports the main idea, "Hans Christian Andersen had a difficult childhood"?

   A. Hans Christian Andersen's headmaster abused him

   B. Hans' life mirrored that of *The Ugly Duckling*

   C. Hans was often older than other children

   D. Hans enjoyed the theatre as a child

(Rigorous) (Skill 1.5)

9. What are the two basic types of questions?

   A. Easy and hard questions

   B. Verbal and written questions

   C. In the book and in the reader's head

   D. Teacher made and student made

(Easy) (Skill 1.5)

10. Engineers thought it would be difficult to *construct* the Golden Gate Bridge because of the weather conditions and the ocean currents that exist in California.

    What does the word *construct* mean in the sentence above?

    A. Drive across

    B. Close down

    C. Make longer

    D. Build or create

(Easy) (Skill 1.7)

11. A student writes an essay that shows the similarities and differences between a book and a movie of the same title. What type of essay is it?

    A. Classification

    B. Compare and contrast

    C. Cause and effect

    D. Statement support

(Average) (Skill 1.7)

12. In Writer's Workshop students are asked to write a personal narrative. How should their writing be organized?

    A. Statement support

    B. Compare and contrast

    C. Sequence of events

    D. Classification

(Rigorous) (Skill 1.7)

13. Ants have three main parts to their bodies. The first part is the head which contains the jaw, eyes, and antennae. The second part of an ant's body is the trunk. The trunk has six legs attached to it. The third part of an ant's body is the rear. I was surprised to learn that the rear contains a poison sac. This is one way the ant defends itself.

    What type of writing is demonstrated in the passage above?

    A. Descriptive

    B. Narrative

    C. Expository

    D. Persuasive

(Average) (Skill 1.7)

14. What type of writing includes headings, subheadings, and titles?

    A. Persuasive

    B. Descriptive

    C. Narrative

    D. Informative

(Average) (Skill 1.8)

15. Which combination of words produces an irregular contraction?

    A. did + not

    B. you + are

    C. I + will

    D. will + not

(Easy) (Skill 1.8)

16. **What is the plural of the word _rose_?**

    A. Rosis

    B. Rosses

    C. Roses

    D. Rose's

(Rigorous) (Skill 1.8)

17. **Which word needs to be corrected in the sentence below?**

    The presents on the table is wrapped in beautiful wrapping paper.

    A. presents

    B. is

    C. wrapped

    D. beautiful

(Rigorous) (Skill 1.8)

18. **What type of sentence is the sentence below?**

    Jarrett and Austin like to read and write.

    A. Simple

    B. Compound

    C. Complex

    D. Compound/complex

(Rigorous) (Skill 1.8)

19. **What must be done to make this sentence correct?**

    Before the children were allowed to go outside.

    A. Place a comma after before

    B. Change the word *children* to *child*

    C. Change the period to a comma and add an independent clause

    D. Nothing, it is fine the way it is

(Easy) (Skill 1.8)

20. **Which sentence is punctuated incorrectly?**

    A. Tomorrow night we'll have pizza for dinner?

    B. Close the door please.

    C. Go away!

    D. What time does the movie begin?

(Easy) (Skill 1.8)

21. **Which punctuation mark is required, if any, in the sentence?**

    Let's have some chocolate graham crackers and marshmallows for dessert

    A. !

    B. ?

    C. ,

    D. None

(Rigorous) (Skill 1.8)

22. **What type of sentence is the sentence below?**

    Millie and Max seemed tired and bored.

    A. Simple

    B. Compound

    C. Complex

    D. Compound/complex

(Rigorous) (Skill 1.8)

23. **Which word needs to be corrected in the sentence below?**

    The Biggilow family were concerned with the appearance of their home.

    A. family

    B. were

    C. appearance

    D. their

(Rigorous) (Skill 1.10)

24. **How would a letter to the editor be written?**

    A. Using formal language

    B. Using informal/slang language

    C. Using informal language with informal mechanics

    D. Using words from the dialect of its intended audience

(Easy) (Skill 2.1)

25. **How many syllables does the word *chocolate* have?**

    A. 1

    B. 2

    C. 3

    D. 4

(Rigorous) (Skill 2.2)

26. **What is the best strategy to help students alphabetize words?**

    A. Have students write random words in alphabetical order

    B. Have students pick a favorite letter in the alphabet

    C. Have students count the number of letters in their name

    D. Have students alphabetize the class names

(Average) (Skill 2.3)

27. **What pattern in spelling does C-V-C represent?**

    A. Consonant vowel combination

    B. Compare verbs critically

    C. Consonant vowel consonant

    D. Continent vowel component

(Rigorous) (Skill 2.4)

28. **When is the best time for a teacher to introduce vocabulary words to readers?**

    A. Before reading

    B. During reading

    C. After reading

    D. All of the above

(Average) (Skill 2.4)

29. **Context clues refer to:**

   A. Defining new words using the dictionary

   B. Choosing the meaning of words from pre-selected choices

   C. Creating a list of vocabulary from the text

   D. Defining unknown words based on the surrounding text

Directions: For Question 30, read the following passage and choose the best answer.

Time seemed to be passing so slowly. Leslie looked at the clock for at least the hundredth time in the past hour. She turned back and looked the other way. Soon this became uncomfortable too and she turned and laid on her back. This position also didn't feel right so she turned back toward the clock. Twenty minutes had passed. "Umph," Leslie grunted closing her eyes again.

(Average) (Skill 2.5)

30. **From Leslie's actions we can determine that:**

   A. Leslie is laying on the beach somewhere

   B. Leslie is at the doctor's office waiting her turn

   C. Leslie is excited about an upcoming event

   D. Leslie is having a difficult time sleeping

Directions: For Question 31, read the following passage and choose the best answer.

Molly slid into her gorgeous dress. She had imagined this day since she was a young girl living in Hartford, Connecticut. Checking herself in the mirror one last time, she decided that this was as good as it was going to get. Her hair was perfect, just the way she had imagined—the hairdresser had definitely earned her fee this morning. As did the make-up specialist Molly thought to herself as she examined her face in the mirror. Then she heard the anthem of the orchestra. She turned from the mirror and headed toward the aisle.

(Average) (Skill 2.5)

31. **It can be inferred from the passage above that Molly is:**

   A. A runway model

   B. About to get married

   C. Shopping at a store

   D. A Broadway performer

(Rigorous) (Skill 2.5)

32. According to this Venn Diagram, what fits within all three categories?

Sample Venn Diagram

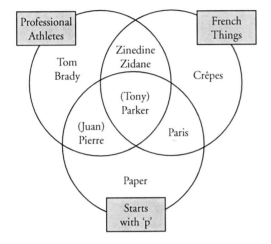

A. Tony Parker

B. Zinedine Zidane

C. Juan Pierre

D. Paris

(Rigorous) (Skill 2.5)

33. **According to the Venn Diagram, what is true about "Paris"?**

A. It starts with "P"

B. It is a French Thing

C. It is the name of a professional athlete

D. It starts with "P", and is a French Thing

(Rigorous) (Skill 2.5)

34. **A student reads the sentence, "The boy saw a worm in the ground," and says "The boy saw a worm in the grass." What might you say to the student as a paraprofessional?**

A. "You said grass. Look at this word and tell me why it can't be grass."

B. "Look at this word again [pointing to ground]. What sound does this word begin with?"

C. "What vowels do you see in this word? [pointing to ground]"

D. "Where is another place you might see a worm?"

(Rigorous) (Skill 2.5)

35. **Before reading a story, what should students use to make predictions?**

A. The first sentence in the book

B. The cover and other illustrations in the story

C. Information from other students

D. The length of a book or story

(Rigorous) (Skill 2.5)

36. **When should a KWL chart be filled out?**

A. After reading only

B. Before and during reading

C. During reading only

D. Before and after reading

(Average) (Skill 2.6)

37. When students just sit down and write about a topic, writing everything that comes to mind, this is called:

   A. Brainstorming

   B. Outlining

   C. Free writing

   D. Drafting

(Rigorous) (Skill 2.6)

38. What is the difference between drafting and revising?

   A. Nothing—they are the same thing

   B. Drafting is the first copy and revising is the final copy

   C. Drafting is the first copy and revising corrects spelling errors, etc.

   D. Drafting is the first copy and revising improves the craft of writing

(Average) (Skill 2.6)

39. What is the purpose of proofreading?

   A. To publish a piece of writing for presentation

   B. To rewrite it in one's neatest handwriting

   C. To spell check it in a word processing program

   D. To check it for spelling, correct punctuation, and grammar

(Average) (Skill 3.2)

40. A student is reading and gets stuck on the word *sure*. All of the following are good ways to help the student decode the word EXCEPT:

   A. Have the student sound it out

   B. Have the student skip the word and come back to it later

   C. Tell the student *is* rhymes with *lure*

   D. Tell the student that *ur* makes the *er* sound

(Average) (Skill 3.3)

41. A teacher has letter tiles and she distributes some to students so they can participate in a making and breaking words activity. This activity is especially helpful in supporting which phase of reading?

   A. Orthographic phase

   B. Analyzing phase

   C. Logographic phase

   D. Emergent reader phase

(Rigorous) (Skill 3.3)

42. When a teacher refers to one-to-one corresponding in reading what is she referring to?

   A. One-to-one reading conferences with students

   B. One-to-one letter sound relationship in spelling

   C. One-to-one reading/pointing of a word to what is on the page

   D. One-to-one matching of students to an appropriate text

(Average) (Skill 3.5)

43. **If a teacher gives students a concept and asks students to formulate questions about that concept during reading and answer those questions after reading, what strategy is the teacher using?**

    A. Preview in context

    B. Predicting

    C. Word mapping

    D. Hierarchical and linear arrays

(Average) (Skill 3.5)

44. **What is the best way to assess student's comprehension of reading material?**

    A. Have students read a page from the text aloud

    B. Have students write definitions of words using the dictionary

    C. Have students write a summary of what they have read

    D. Have students recommend a book to a classmate

(Average) (Skill 3.5)

45. **Which choice shows the best way to check a student's comprehension of a non-fiction reading selection?**

    A. Have the student point out the headings

    B. Have the student identify the main idea

    C. Have the student read all of the captions

    D. Have the student complete a vocabulary quiz

(Rigorous) (Skill 3.6)

46. **Students in a classroom are asked to keep a Writer's Notebook which they write in every day. What is the purpose of this notebook?**

    A. To write down ideas for poems that students might want to write

    B. To keep lists of ideas on certain topics that might be developed later

    C. To draw quick sketches and then write about them in greater detail

    D. All of the above

(Rigorous) (Skill 3.7)

47. **What does "Story Mapping" have children do?**

    A. The students retell the story details

    B. Identify the characters, setting, problem and solution

    C. Identify the main idea and supporting details

    D. Draw a map to show what the characters did

(Easy) (Skill 4.1)

48. **State the number modeled below.**

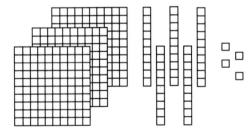

    A. 354

    B. 345

    C. 453

    D. 543

(Average) (Skill 4.1)

49. Which of the numbers is an example of an irrational number?

A. 3

B. $\sqrt{7}$

C. 0.5

D. $\frac{3}{4}$

(Average) (Skill 4.1)

50. Which property is illustrated by the following?

$(5 \times 4) \times 8 = 5 \times (4 \times 8)$

A. Associative property of addition

B. Commutative property of multiplication

C. Inverse property of multiplication

D. Associative property of multiplication

(Average) (Skill 4.1)

51. Emma had a balance of $236 in her savings account. She deposits the $55 she made babysitting this week. How much money will she have in her savings account?

A. $181

B. $55

C. $291

D. $236

(Easy) (Skill 4.1)

52. Solve. $463.7 - 51.672$

A. 412.028

B. 412.172

C. 47.035

D. 412.138

(Rigorous) (Skill 4.2)

53. Find the sixth term in the sequence 3, 7, 11, 15 …

A. 19

B. 23

C. 27

D. 31

(Rigorous) (Skill 4.3)

54. What solid can be made from the following net diagram?

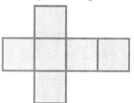

A. Rectangular prism

B. Square

C. Cube

D. Sphere

(Average) (Skill 4.4)

55. Consider the set of test scores from a math test. Find the mean, median, and the mode.

90, 92, 83, 83, 83, 90, 90, 83, 90, 93, 90, 97, 80, 67, 90, 85, 63, 60

A. Mean: 83.83, mode: 90, median: 87.5

B. Mean: 86.5, mode: 83, 90, median: 83.72

C. Mean: 1507, mode: 90, median 83

D. Mean 90, mode 83.72, median 90

(Easy) (Skill 5.1)

56. **A number line can be used to introduce which two operations?**

    A. Addition and multiplication

    B. Subtraction and division

    C. Addition and subtraction

    D. Multiplication and division

(Average) (Skill 5.1)

57. **Children use mathematical skills and concepts daily, usually without even realizing it. Which answer does not describe an activity students can do to incorporate math into their daily lives?**

    A. Writing their name 100 times on a piece of paper

    B. Redesigning the layout of their bedroom

    C. Playing the card game cribbage

    D. Making a batch of green slime

(Easy) (Skill 5.1)

58. **Emma did a presentation to the class of the data she collected. She organized her data in the following chart.**

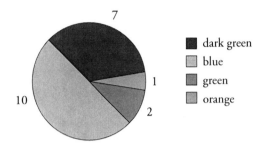

    Which display type did she use to organize her data?

    A. Line graph

    B. Pictograph

    C. Circle graph

    D. Bar graph

(Average) (Skill 5.1)

59. **You are introducing your students to measurement using the metric system. What is a good way to begin the lesson?**

    A. Have students measure items using the metric system

    B. Have students discuss items they have seen that have metric system labels such as measuring cups, thermometers, bottles of juice, mile signs

    C. Have students convert measurements between customary and metric systems

    D. Use metric measurement terms in problem solving

(Rigorous) (Skill 5.1)

60. You give your students this problem. What information would you tell them to help them understand and solve the problem?

Mr. Smith owns 560 acres of farm land. He leases out 430 acres to Mr. Gray for $125 per acre. The property tax is $15 per acre. What is the profit Mr. Smith earns on his property?

A. The problem can be done in one step

B. The profit is the difference between how much Mr. Smith earns in rent and how much he pays in taxes

C. You will need to use addition and division to solve the problem

D. The problem is too difficult to do

(Average) (Skill 5.1)

61. According to this graph, what group of people made up the largest percentage of the unemployed in 2004?

Unemployment rates of persons 25 years old and over, by highest level of education: 2004

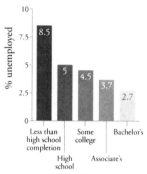

Highest level of education

U.S. Department of Labor, Bureau of Labor Statistics, Office of Employment and Unemployment Statistics, Current Population Survey (CPS), 2004.

A. Those who did not complete high school

B. Those who completed high school

C. Those who have taken some college credit

D. Those who possess a Bachelor's degree

(Easy) (Skill 5.2)

62. When students are checking for reasonableness of an answer, which problem solving strategy can be used?

A. Draw a diagram

B. Work backward

C. Guess and check

D. Estimation and approximation

(Easy) (Skill 5.2)

63. You are teaching your students how to solve problems using measurement. Items measured in fluid ounces, cups, pints, quarts, and gallons are all units for what type of measurement?

    A. Length

    B. Capacity

    C. Weight

    D. Mass

(Average) (Skill 5.3)

64. You are given a set of algebra tiles with your test book. How can you use these tiles to help teach your students equality?

    A. Place them on a scale or balance

    B. Divide the tiles into equal groups

    C. Factoring

    D. Model equations

(Rigorous) (Skill 5.3)

65. You are teaching a class in probability. You toss a coin and record the number of times heads and tails appear on each toss. How can the use of technology help you arrive at the probability of heads?

    A. You can toss the coin more times by hand

    B. You can run more simulations on the computer than you can in class

    C. You forget to record some of the tosses

    D. The coin used in class may be biased

(Easy) (Skill 6.1)

66. You are teaching your students a lesson on adding fractions with and without common denominators. To make sure that students understand the lesson, what types of formal assessment can you add to your lesson?

    A. Quizzes after each concept is presented

    B. Essay questions

    C. Gauge students' reactions

    D. Take a vote

(Average) (Skill 6.1)

67. You are teaching students a new concept that is related to a previously taught lesson. What is the best way to assess student's readiness for the new lesson?

    A. Jump right into the lesson without any connection to prior material

    B. Begin with a review and assessment of the previous skill

    C. Discuss how the new topic is related to a future topic

    D. Have students read the lesson and answer the exercises at the end of the lesson

(Easy) (Skill 6.1)

68. Your students are having a difficult time understanding how to subtract with borrowing. Some students "just don't get it." Your teaching style tends to be the teacher-directed approach. Which one of the answers is not something you can do to help the students?

    A. Have the students who understand the material help the others

    B. Bring in manipulatives to help the students see the concept

    C. Keep teaching the way you are and hope the students catch up

    D. Switch to a cooperative group activity

(Rigorous) (Skill 6.1)

69. Why is planning some formal assessment during a lesson important?

    A. It gives the teacher a break from teaching

    B. It allows students a chance to catch up on the material if they are behind

    C. It allows the teacher to make sure all students understand the material. If they do not, it allows the teacher an opportunity to adjust the instruction

    D. It's not a good idea to use formal assessment during a lesson

(Average) (Skill 6.2)

70. What is the most effective method to assess problem solving skills?

    A. Informal assessment

    B. Formal assessment

    C. Student portfolios

    D. Direct observation

(Easy) (Skill 7.1)

71. Which of the following describes the interaction between community members when one species feeds of another species but does not kill it immediately?

    A. Parasitism

    B. Predation

    C. Commensalism

    D. Mutualism

(Easy) (Skill 7.1)

72. An ecosystem can be described as:

    A. The connection between plants, plant eaters, and animal eaters

    B. Relationships between a community and its physical environment

    C. The specific environment or place where an animal or plant lives

    D. Organisms that live and reproduce there

(Easy) (Skill 7.1)

73. Which is not a characteristic of living organisms?

    A. Sexual reproduction

    B. Ingestion

    C. Synthesis

    D. Respiration

(Average) (Skill 7.1)

74. Which of the following is not a property that eukaryotes have and prokaryotes do not have?

    A. Nucleus

    B. Ribosomes

    C. Chromosomes

    D. Mitochondria

(Average) (Skill 7.2)

75. **Tornados often happen over the Midwest United States because:**

   A. Warm, dry air is forced to rise over the Rocky Mountains

   B. The maritime polar air mass and continental tropical air mass meet over the Midwest

   C. Cold air from the Rockies sinks rapidly and forces a funnel cloud to the surface

   D. The maritime tropical and continental polar air mass meet over the Midwest

(Average) (Skill 7.2)

76. **Why is the winter in the Southern Hemisphere colder than winter in the Northern Hemisphere?**

   A. Earth's axis of 24-hour rotation tilts at an angle of 23°

   B. The elliptical orbit of Earth around the Sun changes the distance of the Sun from Earth

   C. The Southern Hemisphere has more water than the Northern Hemisphere

   D. The green house effect is greater for the Northern Hemisphere

(Easy) (Skill 7.2)

77. **Earth's atmosphere contains mostly:**

   A. Carbon dioxide

   B. Oxygen

   C. Helium

   D. Hydrogen

(Average) (Skill 7.2)

78. **Which word will complete the sentence?**

   It will be ____ cold for us to camp outside this weekend.

   A. too

   B. to

   C. two

   D. tow

(Easy) (Skill 7.3)

79. **Which statement is true about temperature?**

   A. Temperature is a measurement of heat

   B. Temperature is how hot or cold an object is

   C. The coldest temperature ever measured is zero degrees Kelvin

   D. The temperature of a molecule is its kinetic energy

(Rigorous) (Skill 7.3)

80. **Which statement best explains why a balance scale is used to measure both weight and mass?**

   A. The weight and mass of an object are identical concepts

   B. The force of gravity between two objects depends on the mass of the two objects

   C. Inertial mass and gravitational mass are identical

   D. A balance scale compares the weight of two objects

(Easy) (Skill 8.2)

81. Which of the following is placed on the y-axis when plotting a graph?

    A. The control

    B. The independent variable

    C. The dependent variable

    D. The inference

(Rigorous) (Skill 8.2)

82. Stars near Earth can be seen to move relative to fixed stars. In observing the motion of a nearby star over a period of decades, an astronomer notices that the path is not a straight line, but wobbles about a straight line. The astronomer reports in a peer-reviewed journal that a planet is rotating around the star, causing it to wobble. Which of the following statements best describes the proposition that the star has a planet?

    A. Observation

    B. Hypothesis

    C. Theory

    D. Inference

(Average) (Skill 10.1)

83. Which of the following is not one of the six major themes in geography?

    A. Regions

    B. Religion

    C. Place

    D. Movement

(Average) (Skill 10.1)

84. The Northern Hemisphere contains all of which of the following?

    A. Europe

    B. South America

    C. Africa

    D. Asia

(Easy) (Skill 10.1)

85. Which of the following mountain ranges is located in Asia?

    A. Appalachian

    B. Atlas

    C. Himalayas

    D. Great Dividing Range

(Average) (Skill 10.2)

86. Which of the following is a weakness of "periodization"?

    A. It is arbitrary

    B. Facilitates understanding

    C. Identifies similarities

    D. Categorizes knowledge

(Easy) (Skill 10.2)

87. Archaeology is the study of which of the following?

    A. Norms, values, standards

    B. Material remains of humans

    C. Genetic characteristics

    D. The historical development of language

(Easy) (Skill 10.3)

88. **Which of the following are U.S. citizens guaranteed?**

    A. Employment

    B. Post-secondary education

    C. Driver's license

    D. Free speech

(Easy) (Skill 10.3)

89. **Voting is the most basic form of participation in the United States. Which of the following is not a prerequisite to vote in the United States?**

    A. Reached the age of 18

    B. No felony convictions

    C. Registered to vote

    D. Valid driver's license

(Average) (Skill 10.3)

90. **Freedom of religion means all of the following EXCEPT:**

    A. Government may not impose an official religion

    B. Citizens are free to practice their religion

    C. Citizens can obstruct those of other religions

    D. Government supports each religion

(Average) (Skill 10.3)

91. **Which of the following is NOT protected by the U.S. Constitution?**

    A. The right to speak out in public

    B. The right to hate speech

    C. The right to pursue any religion

    D. The right to avoid unreasonable search and seizure

(Rigorous) (Skill 10.5)

92. **In order to fully understand an era which of the following is not recommended?**

    A. Analyze an event from multiple perspectives

    B. Gather basic factual information from the era

    C. Comprehend an issue beyond a basic level

    D. Evaluate the era based on current social mores

(Average) (Skill 10.5)

93. **Teachers of social studies want to create what in order maximize student learning?**

    A. Reliance on primary sources

    B. Independent thought

    C. A focus on the textbook

    D. Ignore cultural competency

(Average) (Skill 14.1)

94. **Some areas that should be mastered by students and can be modeled by teachers include all of the following EXCEPT:**

    A. Create and evaluate art works

    B. Mixing paints in different shades and tints

    C. Producing a portfolio

    D. Selling created works of art

(Average) (Skill 14.1)

95. Skills necessary for character development include all of the following EXCEPT:

    A. Expression of feelings both verbally and nonverbally

    B. Assuming roles of the leader

    C. Recognition of appropriate dialogue

    D. Use of movement and voice to represent a feeling or action

(Average) (Skill 14.4)

96. Calisthenics develops all of the following health and skill-related components of fitness except:

    A. Muscle strength

    B. Body composition

    C. Power

    D. Agility

(Average) (Skill 14.4)

97. Adding more reps to a weightlifting set applies which exercise principle?

    A. Anaerobic

    B. Progression

    C. Overload

    D. Specificity

(Rigorous) (Skill 14.4)

98. Which is not a benefit of cooling down?

    A. Preventing dizziness

    B. Redistributing circulation

    C. Removing lactic acid

    D. Removing myoglobin

(Average) (Skill 14.4)

99. What is the proper sequential order of development for the acquisition of nonlocomotor skills?

    A. Stretch, sit, bend, turn, swing, twist, shake, rock & sway, dodge; fall

    B. Bend, stretch, turn, twist, swing, sit, rock & sway, shake, dodge; fall

    C. Stretch, bend, sit, shake, turn, rock & sway, swing, twist, dodge; fall

    D. Bend, stretch, sit, turn, twist, swing, sway, rock & sway, dodge; fall

(Average) (Skill 14.4)

100. Playing "Simon Says" and having students touch different body parts applies which movement concept?

    A. Spatial awareness

    B. Effort awareness

    C. Body awareness

    D. Motion awareness

ANSWER KEY								
1. B	13. C	25. C	37. C	49. B	61. A	73. A	85. C	97. B
2. A	14. D	26. D	38. D	50. D	62. D	74. B	86. A	98. D
3. C	15. D	27. C	39. D	51. C	63. B	75. D	87. B	99. C
4. B	16. C	28. D	40. A	52. A	64. D	76. B	88. D	100. C
5. A	17. B	29. D	41. A	53. B	65. B	77. B	89. D	
6. D	18. A	30. D	42. C	54. C	66. A	78. A	90. C	
7. A	19. C	31. B	43. C	55. A	67. B	79. B	91. B	
8. A	20. A	32. A	44. C	56. C	68. C	80. C	92. D	
9. C	21. C	33. D	45. B	57. A	69. C	81. C	93. B	
10. D	22. A	34. A	46. D	58. C	70. D	82. D	94. D	
11. B	23. B	35. B	47. B	59. B	71. A	83. B	95. B	
12. C	24. A	36. D	48. A	60. B	72. B	84. A	96. C	

RIGOR TABLE	
Rigor level	**Questions**
Easy 25%	6, 10, 11, 16, 20, 21, 25, 49, 53, 57, 59, 62, 63, 66, 68, 71, 72, 73, 77, 79, 81, 85, 87, 88, 89
Average Rigor 50%	1, 3, 7, 12, 14, 15, 27, 29, 30, 31, 32, 38, 40, 41, 42, 44, 45, 46, 50, 51, 52, 56, 58, 60, 64, 67, 70, 74, 75, 76, 78, 83, 84, 86, 90, 91, 93, 94, 95, 96, 97, 99, 100
Rigorous 50%	2, 4, 5, 8, 9, 13, 17, 18, 19, 22, 23, 24, 26, 28, 33, 34, 35, 36, 37, 39, 43, 47, 48, 54, 55, 61, 65, 69, 80, 82, 92, 98

CONSTRUCTED RESPONSE SAMPLE QUESTIONS

Reading Essay

Megan is a third grade student in your classroom. Megan is very quiet and shy particularly when she is asked to read aloud or speak in front of the whole class. When you listen to Megan read out loud alone, you notice that she often mumbles her way through words she does not automatically recognize. To get a better understanding of Megan's skills, you pulled Megan aside to read a portion of the current story out loud to you. Before asking Megan to read, you asked her to make a prediction about the story. Megan's prediction was very accurate and showed a deep schema from which to draw and a solid ability to make predictions. You completed a running record on Megan and found the following errors in Megan's reading of one paragraph:

Words in the Story	How Megan Read These Words
can't	cannot
reasoned	rasined
the	*skipped by Megan*
reach	retch
aboard	abode
preserve	pressure

At the end of the portion you had Megan read aloud, Megan's accuracy was eighty-eight percent. Then you asked Megan to finish reading the story silently. When you called her back to retell the story, she had several misunderstandings of the information in the story. She also had difficulty with answering literal questions correctly. Megan's parents have approached you and have requested a conference with you to discuss Megan's progress in reading so far this year.

1. Examine the information presented and make a list of Megan's strengths and weaknesses in the area of reading.

2. Develop an instructional plan of action that you could share with Megan's parents at the conference to address areas of weakness Megan is displaying in reading. Be sure to include specific objectives, goals, and activities that you and her parents can implement to ensure Megan makes the necessary progress in reading to end the year on grade level.

Reading Response

Megan demonstrates areas of strength and weakness. They are:

- Strengths:
    - Shows a strong knowledge of beginning and ending sounds
    - Applies concepts of consonant blends and digraphs
    - Consistently applies rules of syllabication
    - Excellent background knowledge
    - Good comprehension skills
- Areas to consider for improvement:
    - Medial vowel sounds (particularly vowel pairs)
    - Reading through the whole word
    - Applying meaning to sentence level reading

Plan for Action

Rationale

Megan appears to have a lot of background knowledge that she can utilize to make meaning of the passages she is reading. However, she is making many errors in her reading which is causing her to misunderstand what she has read. If her reading accuracy increases, her comprehension skills should be appropriate.

Focus area

In particular, Megan seems to be struggling with the specific phonics skill of vowel sounds. This can be seen in the errors she made in the words *reach, reasoned, aboard,* and *pressure.* At this point, the fact that Megan skipped the word *the* or read the contraction as its compound word equivalent is not affecting her comprehension. Therefore, I would leave these errors for a later time period.

Megan's goal

When presented with third grade level materials, Megan will increase her accuracy from her current level of eighty-eight percent to an independent level of ninety-five percent by the end of third grade.

Instructional Strategies

1. Megan will participate in a making words activity to address her phonics difficulties. In this activity, Megan will use letters and letter patterns to build words that become larger and larger. This strategy will allow Megan to use the phonics skills she has mastered in shorter words and see how adding new letters, or even syllables, changes the rules and what sounds the letters make. Daily practice of this sequential phonics activity will provide Megan with the foundational skills to read through the entire word and identify the correct vowel sounds in words.

2. When Megan is reading and miscalls a word, the teacher will use two prompts to help Megan begin to apply her new skills. The first prompt will be: *Does that make sense?* The use of this prompt will allow Megan to realize that the purpose of reading is to understand and that reading needs to make sense. The use of this prompt can be followed with the following prompt: *What sounds do the letters make?* While these prompts will not correct all of the errors Megan may make, they are a starting point to help Megan begin to address her areas which are in need of improvement. Megan's parents can utilize these same prompts at home when she is reading to them, thus providing Megan with continuity and additional practice with reading daily.

Math Essay

A school uses fraction tiles to introduce students to the concept of fractions. Students learn, for example, how to line up five $\frac{1}{5}$ tiles to get one. They also learn to use different tiles (e.g., $\frac{1}{3}, \frac{1}{6}, \frac{1}{4}, \frac{1}{2}$) to match the length of the 1 tile. Most children love this activity and learn very soon to line up the tiles correctly. Surprisingly, when the children move to higher grades they find it very difficult to do problems with equivalent fractions and addition and subtraction of fractions.

1. Why do you think students are unable to retain the learning they are supposed to have gained through the use of fraction tiles?

2. Suggest three strategies teachers can use with the manipulatives activity to improve student performance in higher grades.

Math Response

1. Learning theories based on Piaget's stages of development from concrete to abstract suggest the use of manipulatives and other relatively concrete representations to introduce a concept before moving on to more symbolic and abstract forms. The use of fraction tiles for introducing fractions, therefore, is a strategy solidly based in accepted educational practice. One important point that teachers sometimes overlook, however, is the need to build bridges from the concrete to the abstract. If the fraction tiles and the relationships between them are not linked to the higher level symbolic concepts they are supposed to represent, the activity will end up being all about tiles and students will be unable to apply their learning elsewhere. This is very likely the reason students in this example are not able to retain their learning. Even though they are able to line

up the tiles perfectly, they do not realize that this represents an operation (addition) performed on the fractions and a relationship (equality) between them and the whole.

2. The following strategies will be useful in bridging the concrete tile activity with symbolic fraction relationships:

   – Make it clear that when students place fraction tiles side by side they are adding the fractions that the tiles represent. Also, when they match up the tiles in two rows, they are setting up a relationship of equivalence between the two.

   – When students are comfortable with the use of tiles, introduce the actual symbols (e.g., +, −, =) that they will use later to represent relationships between fractions. Let them use both in parallel for a while so that they see the connection.

   – In addition to tiles, introduce other manipulatives and visual representations (e.g., a circle divided into fractions) so that they are comfortable moving between representations and do not associate fraction concepts rigidly with just the tiles.

Teachers can also consider the use of virtual manipulatives that are often very flexible in their use, can be modified, and allow one to superpose symbols on top of concrete representations.

Science Essay

Science is based on knowledge gained from the five senses. Examples of observations are: *the sky is blue* (sight), *sandpaper is rough* (touch), *sugar is sweet* (taste), *bananas smell like bananas* (smell), and *clapping hands makes a loud noise* (hearing). Other kinds of knowledge are inferences and predictions. What would be the instructional objective, lesson motivation, and student activities in a lesson about observations?

Science Response

The instructional objective is that students will be able to make observations and identify the sense with which the observation is associated. A motivation should give students an incentive or reason to be interested in the lesson. Relating the lesson to their personal lives is an effective method. Students know they are learning different subjects: reading, science, math. Ask the class what it means to learn and if there are different kinds of knowledge.

The lesson can be developed by eliciting from the class the observations that can be made of a candle:

1. The candle is white (sight)

2. It feels waxy (touch)

3. It has no odor (smell)

4. It is shaped like a tube (sight)

Possible activities would be to have the students write down a certain number of observations about a plant and for each observation state the sense that was used. Also, observations could be made about a stick of gum: before chewing, during chewing, and after chewing.

Social Science Essay

You are a fifth grade teacher. The reading/language arts curriculum used in your classroom dominates more than half of the school day. The math curriculum encompasses almost the other half of the school day. Because of the extreme importance placed on standardized tests, the resulting AIP and AYP scores, and how they affect the school's funding, the district has labeled items in the curriculums as "nonnegotiable." These nonnegotiable items leave very little room in the school day for science and social studies curriculum.

The sixth grade teachers at the local middle school have voiced numerous concerns regarding how unprepared the incoming sixth graders are for social studies and science and how they have to spend at least the first month of the school year teaching the students social studies and science skills to be able to start the sixth grade curriculum. These teachers are frustrated and angry that required state standards are being overlooked at the elementary school level, which leaves students unprepared for the middle school curriculum.

After meeting as a grade level, you have volunteered to create a plan for teaching social studies to the students. Knowing that you cannot eliminate any of the nonnegotiable language arts and math items, you can only find thirty minutes of time one day a week to teach social studies to your fifth graders.

Develop an instructional plan to teach social studies within the thirty minute time slot one day a week. Be sure to include specific objectives, goals, and activities for one unit of study.

Social Science Response

Initial steps

To begin, I will research the fifth grade and sixth grade social studies state standards and create a list of common themes between the two grade levels. Given my time constraints in the classroom, I will then list these common themes in order of importance per subject to ensure that the most important standards are taught to my fifth grade students. After creating this list and sharing it with my fellow fifth grade teachers, I will meet with at least one sixth grade teacher at the local middle school to discuss the list and share my plan of action. I will stay in contact with the sixth grade teachers throughout the year regarding our progress with the fifth grade social studies curriculum.

Instructional plan

One common theme stated in the state standards between the two grade levels is for students to analyze the geographic, political, economic, religious, and social structures of a settlement or civilization. Being that the fifth grade teachers will only have thirty minutes once a week for social studies, we will give each month a theme using the above commonality in the standards (i.e., in August we will teach geography of a settlement; in September we will teach politics of a settlement; in October we will teach economy of a settlement; in November we will teach religion of a settlement; and in December we will teach society of a settlement). The remainder of the year's lessons (January through May) will focus on at least two of the components (e.g., geography and politics) until, by the end of the year, the fifth graders will have analyzed all five components and so will be prepared for that standard in sixth grade. The idea is to increase the higher learning/thinking skills by building upon prior knowledge and background information. Each month as a new theme is introduced, teachers will connect it to the prior month's theme until, by the end of the year, students are able to make connections among all five components of the standard.

Here is a detailed plan for August:

Geography of a settlement

- **Week 1:** Introduce important vocabulary to frontload the lesson. Divide the class into teams of three to four students (smaller teams if there are more vocabulary words) and assign each team one vocabulary word. Using a piece of cardstock, each team will be responsible for defining the word, using the word in a sentence, creating an illustration for the word, and giving examples of the word. After all teams have completed this activity, they will share their word with the class. All of the pieces of cardstock containing the vocabulary information will be stapled together to create an Illustrated Dictionary and left on display in the classroom for reference.

- **Week 2:** This week's activity will revolve around reading material from the textbook about the geography of a settlement. An instructional strategy that can be used during the reading is "Talk to the Text." As students read a copy of the text, they complete the following steps:

  1. Box, circle, underline, or star difficult words

  2. Draw arrows from nouns to pronouns (or between ideas) as the relationship becomes clear

  3. Write brief notes in the margins near hard to understand sentences and paragraphs

  This strategy is followed by a class discussion driven by teacher- and student-driven questions.

- **Week 3:** This week can be similar to the previous week if there is more text that needs to be read and/or discussion that needs to be completed. If this is not the case, students will complete journal writing about what they've learned about this theme. The journal writing will include a description of the theme and how it relates to the specific settlement of study, predictions of how varying geographical features would affect other areas of settlement, and an explanation of what they would consider to be the ideal area in which to settle.

- **Week 4:** This week's activity will serve as an assessment. This could be an assessment take from the textbook. Another idea for an assessment could be to have the students work in teams of four to create a settlement and outline how the geography and climate influences the way they adjust to the environment. This could include explanations or drawings to explain the location of the settlement, the structures that exist, or how food and clothing are obtained.

PRAXIS

XAMonline publishes study guides for the PRAXIS I & II teacher certification examinations.

Titles Include:
- PRAXIS Art Sample Test
- PRAXIS Biology
- PRAXIS Chemistry
- PRAXIS Earth and Space Sciences
- PRAXIS Special Education Knowledge-Based Core Principles
- PRAXIS Special Education Teaching Students with Behavioral Disorders/Emotional Disturbance
- PRAXIS Early Childhood/Education of Young Children
- PRAXIS Educational Leadership
- PRAXIS Elementary Education
- PRAXIS English Language, Literature and Composition
- PRAXIS Sample Tests
- PRAXIS School Guidance and Counseling
- PRAXIS General Science
- PRAXIS Library Media Specialist
- PRAXIS Mathematics
- PRAXIS Middle School English Language Arts
- PRAXIS Middle School Mathematics
- PRAXIS Middle School Social Studies
- PRAXIS Physical Education
- PRAXIS Physics
- PRAXIS Para-Professional Assessment
- PRAXIS PPST-1 Basic Skills
- PRAXIS Principles of Learning and Teaching
- PRAXIS Reading
- PRAXIS Social Studies
- PRAXIS Spanish

PASS the FIRST TIME with an XAMonline study guide!

Call or visit us online!
1.800.301.4647
www.XAMonline.com